Conference Skills

put your knowledge into practice

- Written specifically for students on the Bar Professional Training Course

- Expert author teams include barristers and BPTC tutors

- Clear, authoritative guides to legal practice and procedure

Advocacy

Company Law in Practice

Conference Skills

Criminal Litigation and Sentencing

Drafting

Employment Law in Practice

Evidence

Family Law in Practice

Opinion Writing and Case Preparation

Professional Ethics

Remedies

 Online Resource Centre

www.oxfordtextbooks.co.uk/orc/barmanuals/

The Bar Manuals are also supported by an Online Resource Centre with further materials and updates to selected manuals.

The Bar Manuals are published by Oxford University Press in conjunction with The City Law School

 The City Law School
CITY UNIVERSITY LONDON

Conference Skills

The City Law School
CITY UNIVERSITY LONDON

Authors

Rosemary Samwell-Smith, Barrister, former Principal Lecturer, The City Law School
Marcus Soanes, Barrister, Principal Lecturer, The City Law School

Contributors

Susan Blake, Barrister, Professor of Legal Education, The City Law School
Lord Justice Brooke CMG, Lord Justice of Appeal
Ann Halpern, Barrister, former Reader, ICSL
Susannah Leahy, Barrister, former Senior Lecturer, ICSL
Debbie Lithman, Barrister, former Principal Lecturer, ICSL
Bartholomew O'Toole, Barrister, Middle Temple
Margot Taylor, Solicitor, former Principal Lecturer, The City Law School
Carl Teper, Barrister, Middle Temple

Editor

Marcus Soanes, Barrister, Principal Lecturer, The City Law School

Series Editor

Julie Browne, Barrister, Senior Lecturer, The City Law School

OXFORD
UNIVERSITY PRESS

OXFORD

UNIVERSITY PRESS

Great Clarendon Street, Oxford, OX2 6DP,
United Kingdom

Oxford University Press is a department of the University of Oxford.
It furthers the University's objective of excellence in research, scholarship,
and education by publishing worldwide. Oxford is a registered trade mark of
Oxford University Press in the UK and in certain other countries

Fifteenth edition 2010
Sixteenth edition 2012
Seventeenth edition 2014

Impression: 1

Published in the United States of America by Oxford University Press
198 Madison Avenue, New York, NY 10016, United States of America

British Library Cataloguing in Publication Data
Data available

ISBN 978–0–19–876603–2

Printed in Great Britain by
Bell & Bain Ltd., Glasgow

FOREWORD

These manuals have been written by a combination of practitioners and members of staff of The City Law School (formerly the Inns of Court School of Law), and are designed primarily to support training on the Bar Professional Training Course (BPTC), wherever it is taught. They provide an extremely useful resource to assist in acquiring the skills and knowledge that practising barristers need. They are updated regularly and are supported by an Online Resource Centre, which can be used by readers to keep up-to-date throughout the academic year.

This series of manuals exemplifies the practical and professional approach that is central to the BPTC. I congratulate the authors on the excellent standard of the manuals and I am grateful to Oxford University Press for their ongoing and enthusiastic support.

Peter Hungerford-Welch
Professor of Legal Education
The City Law School
City University London
2016

PREFACE

This manual is about what lawyers do on a daily basis. It is not an abstract study of the lawyer's skills, but a guide for those who wish to exercise those skills in a client conference with a member of the public. It is designed for use by those who are training to be lawyers and those who have recently qualified—specifically barristers. Our paramount concern is to help individual lawyers develop their skills to enable them to conduct a client conference competently and professionally. We recognise that conferences are live events held with real people who are facing genuine legal problems. We also acknowledge that the lawyer is an individual and that no two barristers think alike or will use identical methods to run the conference. Included therefore are plenty of how-to-do-it guides which isolate the essentials of each stage of the barrister's involvement with the client without setting a blueprint that ought to be followed rigidly. Although we have not been prescriptive, we have attempted to identify some general principles and basic rules which are applicable to every client conference and which should provide a framework for good practice. While there cannot be any one right way to conduct a client conference, there is usually a better way. In an attempt to keep the manual as practical as possible, we have used numerous examples from practice, including three full-length briefs. These are not only illustrations of the points which we hope to convey to the reader, but can also be used as study tools in their own right.

If there is a central philosophy running through this manual, it is that you cannot learn how to conduct a conference merely from reading a book. You must practise. Hopefully the reader will be able to use this manual as part of a programme of education that includes plenty of opportunities to have a go. We are firmly of the view that it is only by applying the lessons which you have learnt that you will be able to make real improvements to the skills that a barrister in conference with a client needs to have at his or her fingertips.

The manual takes the reader through the whole conference process, from receiving the brief to following up the client's case after the conference. There is also a practical and down-to-earth chapter, written by Lord Justice Brooke CMG, on the importance of avoiding racial and cultural intolerance and ignorance when dealing with members of the public. The authors would like to express their warmest gratitude for this invaluable contribution. We also thank Carl Teper and Bartholomew O'Toole who generously contributed overviews on the use of conference skills in criminal and civil practices and acted as practitioner consultants for this manual.

Our credentials for writing this manual stem from both our practice at the Bar and many combined years of experience gained at The City Law School in the field of teaching and assessing conference skills. In this respect, we have worked closely with a number of valued colleagues at the School, upon whose experience, expertise, and opinions we have drawn in writing this manual, and to whom we are enormously indebted. The responsibility for any errors and omissions remains ours alone.

Rosemary Samwell-Smith, LLB, LLM
Barrister, former Principal Lecturer in Law,
The City Law School, City University London
Marcus Soanes, BA, MA
Barrister, Principal Lecturer in Law, The City Law School,
City University London

GUIDE TO USING THIS BOOK

The Bar Manuals series includes a range of tools and features to aid your learning. This guide outlines the approach to using this book, and helps you to get the most out of it.

A practical-based approach

The authors have a practical approach to teaching conference skills. This will help you to enhance the skills that you will need to display on the Bar Professional Training Course and in its assessments. Their guidance will also help prepare you for the early years of practice when you will have to apply your legal knowledge and skills to clients' real-life problems.

Exercises

Conference Skills includes a sample exercise in the form of a brief to counsel. This will enable you to test your knowledge and understanding of the skills needed to conduct an effective client conference based on a real-life scenario.

Examples and 'How to do it' boxes

The worked examples show you how to apply the skills and techniques that are introduced to you in the manual. There are examples of case preparation and effective questioning techniques as well as plans for use in a client conference. The 'How to do it' boxes feature throughout the manual to offer hints and tips on how to approach a variety of issues commonly encountered in client conferences. All of this assistance is presented in ways that will enable you swiftly to put the theory into practice.

Online Resource Centre updates

For further material and updates to selected manuals in this series, please visit the Online Resource Centre at <http://www.oxfordtextbooks.co.uk/orc/barmanuals/>.

OUTLINE CONTENTS

DETAILED CONTENTS

Introduction and overview

1.1 Introduction

This manual seeks to identify and analyse the skills that need to be acquired in order to conduct an effective client conference. It considers in detail the sub-skills, elements, and component parts which, taken together, form the basis of conducting a sound and professional legal conference with the lay client. It is intended to give students a realistic and practical insight into methodology and to provide guidance on a variety of issues that can arise when meeting clients in conference, either in chambers or at court.

What this manual does not attempt to do is to prescribe any fixed or rigid set of rules that must be adhered to. However, there are some definite 'dos and don'ts' and some classic errors to be avoided when conducting a conference with a client. In addition, there are a number of preconceptions and misconceptions about clients and the client conference that need to be dispelled. There are also many less-than-obvious issues that, in order to ensure the conference is approached and carried out in a skilled and competent manner, need to be carefully and fully considered.

At the outset, it is important to remember that every barrister has a different personality; every client is an individual; both are human beings; and each and every conference will have its own specific requirement. Consequently, any attempt to set out a blueprint—a specific formula—that can be applied to every conference would be as unrealistic as it is impossible. What is clear, however, is that while there cannot be any one 'right way' to conduct a client conference, there is usually a better way. It is only by recognising and being aware of the sort of issue which can arise when meeting and representing clients that proper consideration can be given as to how best to prepare for and subsequently conduct the conference with the appropriate degree of professional skills.

The contents of this manual are intended to:

(a) assist students to recognise the potential difficulties and problems that can arise when preparing for and conducting a client conference, and to offer some solutions for dealing appropriately with these; and

(b) put forward some practical suggestions of ways and means of ensuring that every conference, with every client, is carried out in the most effective way.

The most important purpose of the text is to facilitate the development of each student's own individual skills. Those seeking to become barristers come from a wide variety of backgrounds. Most will already have a great deal of experience of interacting with others and many will already have well-developed social skills. However much experience one may have in mixing with a variety of different people and however socially adept one has become, conducting an effective client conference, and representing clients generally, needs a great deal more than this. The aim of this manual is to ensure that all students who are learning to acquire this skill are able to:

- build on the skills they already possess;
- develop and adapt those skills to a professional level;
- acquire the ability to conduct a professional and efficient client conference;
- be aware of the client's needs at all stages of the legal proceedings;
- be alert to potential difficulties that may arise in the course of the client–lawyer relationship; and
- be aware of professional conduct and ethical issues that can arise in a conference with a client.

1.2 Overview

In almost every case in which a barrister is instructed to represent a client, the first and extremely important step is the client conference. It can be very easy to underestimate the importance of learning and acquiring sound conference skills. An effective client conference is not merely meeting the client for a chat. The conference is vital to enable counsel to get full information, get a real feel for the case, and ensure that he or she is in the best position to advise the client properly as to the most appropriate course of action to take in the particular circumstances. The conference provides the foundation for the future conduct of the case. For example, it is necessary to decide such questions as:

- What are the client's objectives?
- What is the legal framework of the case?
- What is the strength of the case?
- What evidence is there for or against the client?
- Is this an appropriate case to contest in court?
- What procedural rules need to be considered?
- What sort of witness will the client make?
- Could this be an appropriate case for a negotiated settlement?
- What alternative (legal and non-legal) solutions may there be?

All these matters, and more, will be decided at the client conference.

Most importantly, the conference forms the basis of the relationship between the barrister and his or her lay client, which will continue throughout his or her professional involvement with the case.

The effectiveness of the conference is obviously dependent on many things apart from legal skill. In addition to the legal research and legal analysis, which form a major part of the preparation and planning for the conference, it is also necessary to learn how to:

- communicate effectively with the client;
- gain the client's confidence;
- identify the relevant issues;
- analyse the factual issues;
- identify what information is ambiguous;
- identify what information is missing;

- ask relevant questions;
- ask questions in an appropriate way to elicit the necessary information;
- accurately interpret what the client says;
- use time in a structured and efficient way;
- give advice that is clear and unambiguous and that the client can easily understand; and
- give proper consideration to the impact and realities of the advice offered to the client.

1.2.1   A practical example

For a barrister new to practice, the conference with the client will often be the first occasion on which legal skills, previously studied in the abstract, will have to be applied in a real and practical context. It often comes as something of a surprise that there are a whole range of issues, apart from the law, which must be considered. Take, for example, a straightforward Application for Bail—a seemingly simple task, and one that many pupils will undertake in the second half of their pupillage. The legal principles and relevant procedural rules can be discovered with relative ease. However, making a successful Bail Application on behalf of the client will depend to a large extent on counsel's ability efficiently to identify the issues involved and to elicit the relevant information from the client. More often than not, there will only be a few minutes in which to conduct the conference prior to appearing before the magistrates. The following is a typical example, which should assist to illustrate the point. Counsel's instructions are minimal and he or she will have ten minutes in which to interview the client and take instructions before appearing before the magistrates on his behalf.

EXAMPLE

INSTRUCTIONS TO COUNSEL

The defendant, Sammy Ellis, was arrested last night and kept in custody at Wood Grange police station. He is charged with (a) assaulting a police officer; and (b) having a bladed article in a public place. Unfortunately, instructing solicitors have not had an opportunity to interview Mr Ellis in person, but they understand (from the duty solicitor) that he was on his way to visit his sick mother when a van carrying four police officers pulled up beside him. He tried to run away, and a struggle ensued. He was then arrested and taken to the police station, where he was charged with the offences set out above. Mr Ellis denies assaulting the officer and denies that he was carrying a bladed article in a public place. He intends to plead Not Guilty to both these charges. Apparently Mr Ellis, who is 23 years old, has three previous convictions, two for theft and the other to do with missing a court appearance.

The police are objecting to bail on the grounds that they believe Mr Ellis will (a) fail to surrender to custody and/or (b) commit an offence while on bail.

Counsel is instructed to attend Wood Grange Magistrates' Court and secure bail for Mr Ellis.

There are many factors to which consideration has to be given (see **1.2.2**) but a good starting point, in these circumstances, would be the law.

Legal framework (relevant to these instructions)

- There is a presumption in favour of bail (s 4(1) of the Bail Act 1976).
- The prosecution (police) are entitled to raise objections to the grant of bail.
- The onus is on the court to justify any refusal of bail in accordance with Sch 1, Pt I to the Act.
- The magistrates are entitled to refuse bail if they are satisfied that there are reasonable grounds to believe that one or both of the police objections will occur.

In deciding whether to grant bail the magistrates will take into account all the circumstances of the case, especially:

- the nature and seriousness of the offence;
- the character, antecedents, associations, and community ties of the accused;
- his 'record' for answering bail in the past;
- the strength of the evidence against him.

What is it necessary to discover from Mr Ellis in order to be in a position to make a successful Bail Application on his behalf?

It is always important to identify precisely what the purpose of the conference is. This is not a conference to advise on a plea. This is not a conference to evaluate in any detail the evidence against Mr Ellis. This is not a conference to gather information for a Plea in Mitigation. Counsel is instructed to make a Bail Application and therefore it is necessary to work out precisely what information is needed and to ask questions that are specifically relevant to this issue. Table 1.1 shows examples of the sorts of questions that need to be asked and the sorts of answers that will enable counsel to make an appropriate and relevant Bail Application on behalf of Mr Ellis.

Table 1.1 **Bail Application for Sammy Ellis: Questions & Answers**

Questions	Answers
(a) The nature of the offences	
Assault	
Time?	10.00 pm
Where/scene?	Dark/side road/rather quiet
Why there at that time?	On way to visit sick mother
Why run away?	Unmarked van/inspired by fear/panic
Police in uniform?	Yes, but only saw after running away
Any assault on the police?	No, struggle as tackled to the ground
Any injuries?	Bruising to face and left hand
Any witnesses?	No, road deserted
Weapon	
What?	Folding penknife—3½-inch blade
Why carry it?	Used for work—temporarily employed as fishmonger's assistant—used for gutting fish
Why in pocket then?	Worked late that evening—his own knife; sometimes takes it home after work—in rush to visit mother that evening
(b) Personal circumstances: character and antecedents	
Address?	95 Hartley Road, Wood Grange
Permanent?	Recognised squat—has lived there for two years
Propose to remain there?	No, moving back to live with mother, who is crippled with osteoarthritis
Girlfriend?	Yes, six months pregnant—proposes to move to mother's as well to await birth of baby
Qualifications?	Biology graduate, University of Westminster
Job?	Fishmonger's assistant—temporary while seeking permanent job
Income?	£200.00 per week, about £40.00 per week in hand after living expenses
Prospects?	Interview next week for post as laboratory assistant at University of Westminster
Anyone willing to stand surety?	Yes, mother
Previous convictions	
Two for theft?	Both shoplifting—items stolen: food

Questions	Answers
Motive?	Student at time of both offences—grant inadequate to buy food
Plea at court?	Guilty to both—conditional discharge for the first; and fine of £50.00 for the second
Failure to surrender	
Why?	Went to wrong court—barrister had left by the time arrived at correct court; fine £50.00
Effect of loss of liberty	
Consequences of being refused bail?	Would lose: current employment; job interview next week; mother and girlfriend left unsupported

1.2.2 Conclusion

It will be apparent that by identifying the relevant issues and asking the right questions, and from the answers given by Mr Ellis, it is possible to elicit sufficient information to construct a Bail Application that addresses the prosecution's objections. Mr Ellis denies both the offences and intends to plead Not Guilty. He can justify his reactions at the time of his arrest. He has an explanation for why he was carrying the knife. He has strong community ties (accommodation, mother, pregnant girlfriend, job prospect). The reason for not turning up at court on the previous occasion was a genuine mistake. Although he does have two previous convictions for theft, these were hardly of the most serious nature and he did admit his guilt by pleading guilty on both occasions. There is nothing to suggest he will reoffend.

But, it will be equally apparent that this part of the exercise is only one part of the conference. As well as being able to elicit the necessary and relevant information that satisfies the objectives of any particular conference (here a Bail Application), detailed thought must also be given to the many other factors involved in this and every sort of conference. For example:

- Where is the conference being held?
- In the court cells?
- In a crowded court corridor?
- How is the client likely to be feeling?
- How to begin?
- Where to begin?
- How best to communicate with the client?
- How to gain his or her confidence?
- What sort of questioning technique will be most appropriate?
- In what order should questions be asked?
- How to manage time constraints?
- How to evaluate the answers received?
- What are the realistic prospects of success?
- How to ensure that the client clearly understands the advice given?
- What are the implications of the advice for the client?
- What, if any, further action needs to be taken?

It is these areas that the manual goes on to consider in detail. At the outset, however, it is clearly essential to remember that the skills needed to conduct any client conference effectively—even the most seemingly straightforward—are complex and require thorough, in-depth consideration and evaluation. There are obviously several different aspects to conducting a client conference. It is these separate issues that the following chapters will address in detail.

1.3   Why there is a need to learn conference skills

The Bar itself recognised the need for its trainees to learn the practical skills necessary in order to become competent barristers. One of the major recommendations of the Marre Committee (*A Time for Change—Report of the Committee on the Future of the Legal Profession*, July 1988) was that the vocational stage of training should 'concentrate on utilising modern teaching and examining methods and instilling practical skills' (para 14.55). The Lord Chancellor's Department (*Work and Organisation of the Legal Profession*, HMSO, 1988) said:

> The efficient and proper provision of legal services relies upon legal practitioners who have a good grounding in the areas of work they will be using and are well capable of applying it . . . practical skills will be honed by observation and practice in pupillage, but their foundations need to be laid during the vocational course.

In acknowledging the realities of modern-day practice, training for intending barristers was to include, in addition to legal knowledge (Evidence, Criminal and Civil Procedure), learning how to acquire practical lawyer skills. Thus, for the first time, in 1989, with the introduction of the Bar Vocational Course, three of the oral skills which most barristers commonly use every day of their working lives—ie, conference skills, dispute resolution skills, and advocacy skills—were not only taught, but also assessed prior to students being certified as competent to enter pupillage and practice. The major review of the vocational training stage that led to the formation of the Bar Professional Training Course (BPTC) confirmed the centrality of such interpersonal skills. (See further the *Advocacy* manual.)

It is interesting to note that, according to the research carried out by Joanna Shapland *et al* (Shapland, Johnson, and Wild, *Studying for the Bar*, Institute for the Study of the Legal Profession, University of Sheffield, 1993), since the Bar Vocational Course (BVC) was introduced, students 'universally acclaimed the overall philosophy and aims of the course. Its practicality, relevance to work at the Bar, and skills basis were constantly praised.' The research undertaken by the Wood Committee, which reviewed the BVC and led to the introduction of the BPTC in 2010–11, confirmed the usefulness of practice-based exercises as an effective method for engendering interpersonal skills and a client-centred approach to legal work.

Thus, both the profession and trainees entering the profession recognised the need for training to be practically based and the emphasis to be placed squarely on acquiring all the necessary skills, including the expertise needed to conduct an effective client conference.

By far the most important consideration, however, in the rationale of why there is a need to learn how to conduct a client conference is *the client*. For far too long the Bar has suffered from the reputation of being remote and out of touch with the realities of life. For many members of the public, forced for whatever reason to consult lawyers to resolve their legal problems, dealing with barristers often turned out to be a disappointing and disillusioning experience. The Marre Committee (see earlier in this section) identified several reasons for dissatisfaction with lawyers. These included, inter alia, a fear of lawyers and the law, and inefficiency or incompetence on the part of lawyers. Most pertinently, however, the report identified that 'the biggest single reason for dissatisfaction was, taken together, unhelpfulness, inconsideration and lack of communication'. The report went on to say:

> At an early stage of our work we identified the failure of [both solicitors and] barristers to communicate effectively with their clients . . . we are firmly of the view that there is a need for a fundamental change in attitude towards communications with clients. The advent of greater competition from other professions, and the increasing complexity of the law and the legal system, mean that lawyers will have to change to meet the needs of clients for better information.

This concern was underlined by Latham J (as he then was) (*Advocacy, Negotiation and Conference Skills Manual*, Bar Vocational Course, 1989–95), who said:

> One of the most frequently voiced criticisms of the Bar, and of solicitors, and of doctors, and indeed all people who operate in professional disciplines, is that we do not communicate well with our clients. We live in our little jargon world and we fail to recognise, as often as we should, that we are in fact trying to get a message across to somebody in a way which conveys the relevant information to them, and gives them comfort in so far as they can get true comfort and reassurance.

More recently, in 2015 the Bar Standards Board published its *Professional Statement for Barristers*, which describes the knowledge, skills, and attributes that all barristers should have on 'day one' of practice. It is the standard to be achieved by a barrister upon the issue of a full qualification certificate, on which basis they may apply for a full practising certificate. However, it is also explicitly designed to be used to inform consumers' understanding of the barrister's role and the service they can expect to receive. Included in its list of the barrister's personal values and standards is, '2.1 – Act with the utmost integrity and independence at all times, in the interests of justice, representing clients with courage, perseverance and fearlessness.' Thus, when acting in a professional capacity, a barrister representing paying clients (either privately or publicly funded) has a duty to ensure that the service provided to the public is professional, efficient, and at all times, in each and every case, of an appropriate standard that meets the needs of the individual client.

1.4 How to learn conference skills

Making the transition from studying traditional subjects at college or university to learning legal skills is something which students often find difficult. It is essential to recognise that acquiring practical skills involves a learning process that is entirely different from that with which most students are familiar. It is equally important to understand that the assessment of these skills also has very different dimensions from the traditional examinations that most students are used to. With skills, there can be no fudging of issues, no sitting on the fence, no 'topic spotting' for examination purposes, and, probably the most unpalatable for many students, no 'right answer'. And, of course, rather than theorising about the subject matter, learning to conduct an effective client conference means actually *doing it*—that is, performing the skill, interviewing live clients, taking instructions, and giving them advice on their case.

The experience gained by programme providers since the introduction of the BVC, and carried forward to the BPTC, indicates that there are three main strands to learning and developing sound conference-skills techniques:

- practice;
- observation; and
- receiving objective criteria-based feedback (from tutors and peers).

Practising the performance of conference skills is essentially a case of trial and error. Practising is a critical part of the learning process. Only when students are aware of, and are able to identify, some of the problems and difficulties encountered in a performance of a conference, can they determine how to improve and what sort of adjustments need to be made in order to make the performance better. Practice enables students to experiment with different techniques, to see and understand how various approaches might or might not work for them. As well as practice in the classroom, it is invaluable to use recordings to assist in developing effective skills. It is well known that many people, on hearing their voice on a recording, find it difficult to recognise it as their own and are convinced that they cannot possibly sound like that. By the same token, it can be a very salutary experience to watch your own performance on video clips and see at first hand the effect of what you are doing and how you come across. But it can also be enormously rewarding (and fun) to see how making improvements and adjustments can, and does, greatly enhance the quality of a performance (see **Chapter 12**).

Observing others conducting a conference is an equally useful learning process and can give valuable insight into different approaches and techniques. This process continues into pupillage, of course, in which pupils have the opportunity to observe the conference-skills techniques of their pupil master/mistress. Evaluating the effect of another's performance and analysing what works, what doesn't work, and, importantly, *why it does or doesn't*, is an excellent method of learning how to acquire and improve skills. As has already been said, everyone is different and everyone seeking to develop good conference-skills will come with their own particular style. Some pupils find that certain methods work well for them; others may consider that they prefer to take a different approach. By observing others it is possible to gain valuable information relative to your own performance.

Feedback on the performance is also a vital part of the learning process. Constructive criticism and feedback, from both tutors and fellow-students, can be of great assistance in the development of conference skills. However, to be of any value, the feedback has to be objective and based on stated criteria with which both the performer and the commentator must be fully familiar. It is of no use whatever to say, for example, of a performance or part of a performance, 'that was good', or 'that was bad', without analysing, against the criteria, why. **Chapter 12** sets out in detail the performance and assessment criteria that have been devised for conference skills. It is recommended that students become familiar with these and attempt to:

- relate them to the feedback received on their own performance; and
- use them as the basis for giving constructive criticism to colleagues.

In summary, the best and most effective way for individual students to develop and improve their conference skills is to understand the value of the learning techniques recommended above. Although, as already stated, there is no right way to conduct a client conference, there is usually a better way. Practice and observation, used in tandem with the performance and assessment criteria, will provide a solid framework for learning the skills that it is necessary to acquire in order to be able to conduct a client conference efficiently, effectively, and to the professional standard required.

1.5 How a conference with a barrister differs from an interview with a solicitor

A solicitor's perspective, when conducting interviews with clients, is quite different from that of a barrister, and the two roles are clearly distinct. A solicitor is retained by a client to conduct the case from beginning to end and he or she will have interviews with the client at various stages during the proceedings. For example, in a civil case, a solicitor will start the case with the initial interview at which the client first seeks assistance and continue through to enforcement of any judgment of the court. A barrister's involvement will be confined to undertaking specific tasks as instructed by the solicitor—for example, a written advice on merits/quantum, or the drafting of particular documents. The barrister may not meet the client until shortly before the full hearing of the case. Thus, a barrister's involvement is more limited and sporadic, which often means he or she has less opportunity to get to know the client as well as the solicitor knows him or her. When the barrister does meet the client for the first time in conference, it is clearly important for him or her to be able to communicate with the client in a manner that will immediately put the client at ease and gain the client's confidence.

The solicitor has a duty to discuss the costs that will be incurred by the client and to ascertain how they will be paid. The barrister will rarely, if ever, be involved in such a discussion with the client. In the first interview with the client and prior to any steps being taken, the solicitor should ensure that the client understands the costs elements of litigation. The solicitor should also obtain all the necessary financial details from the client and ascertain whether the costs will be paid by the client privately, by the Legal Aid Agency, or by some other means, for example funding by a sponsoring body. Where the client is eligible for public funding, the solicitor must ensure that a Representation Order is obtained and ensure that the work done, including any work undertaken by the barrister, is covered by the Order.

A solicitor's initial interview with the client also differs from the barrister's conference with the client in that, at an initial interview, the solicitor will usually have little or no information about either the client or the problem. It is for the solicitor to gather the basic information—address, telephone number, etc—and the detail of the client's problem. The solicitor will often have to question the client in a fairly open-ended way to explore fully the whole story, range of problems, and solutions being sought. When instructing or briefing counsel to represent the client, the solicitor should provide counsel with a distilled version of what the client has said, any advice he or she has already given to the client, and any information about any steps that have been taken to date. The subsequent conference with the barrister will usually be much more focused on the specific problem about which the client needs advice. However, you must be aware, especially in the early years of practice, that frequently the solicitor will not have had the opportunity, for a variety of reasons, to take full instructions from the client, and it will fall to counsel to gather the basic information from the client himself or herself at the conference. (See **Chapters 3** and **6**.)

1.6 Conclusion

It will be readily apparent that there are a variety of issues, some obvious and others less so, that need in-depth consideration prior to conducting any conference with a client. The following chapters address the specific areas to which detailed thought must be given when deciding how best to prepare and plan for, and to conduct, a client conference.

Chapter 2 sets out some general principles that are applicable to the conduct of every client conference.

Chapter 3 looks at a range of different types of clients (lay and professional) that a barrister is likely to encounter at some stage in his or her career.

Chapter 4 deals with the first meeting with the client and considers ways of ensuring a conducive atmosphere within the many different scenarios in which a conference might take place.

Chapter 5 addresses case preparation, the methods of analysing the contents of any brief/instructions, and planning efficiently for the conference.

Chapter 6 considers the need to think about the questioning techniques used in the conference and looks at difficulties that can arise in this area.

Chapter 7 deals with giving the client adequate, relevant, and professional advice.

Chapter 8 addresses the need to ensure that the conference is concluded appropriately, that the client is reassured, and that any further action to be taken by any of the parties to the proceedings is precise and clear.

Chapter 9 considers a range of ethical problems relating to clients which a barrister might encounter in practice.

Chapter 10 looks at some specific problems that can occur in any interaction between a barrister and his or her client.

Chapter 11, written by Lord Justice Brooke CMG, contains information and advice on the important issues relating to cross-cultural communication.

Chapter 12 sets out the performance and assessment criteria by which an effective client conference can be judged.

Chapter 13 considers the 'practitioners' perspective' on conducting a client conference and contains pieces written by two practitioners (one civil and one criminal) which reflect their experience in practice.

There is a selection of recommended reading at the end of this manual.

General principles

2

2.1 Introduction

The Bar Standards Board's (BSB's) *Professional Statement for Barristers*, at 1.6, requires entrants to the profession 'to be able to provide clear, concise and accurate advice in writing and orally and take responsibility for it'. Oral advice includes conducting face-to-face conferences and advising by telephone. For example, you will need to be able to advise on the need and preparation for trial and to convey unpalatable advice where necessary. Before addressing, in detail, the specific component parts that contribute to an effective, efficient, and professional conference, there are some general principles that are relevant to the conduct of every conference. Careful consideration should be paid to the points set out in the following sections as they should form the basis of your own, and every barrister's, approach to every client. These points should influence the attitude you adopt towards the client from the very first conference that you are instructed to undertake. As stated in the Marre Report in 1988, the public perception of the legal profession was less than complimentary. Any involvement with legal advisers often appeared to fall far short of the legitimate expectations of clients. It is vital for you, as a barrister new to the profession, to ensure that you embark on your career with a realisation and awareness that your own attitude towards the client, and the client conference, is a critical part of the equation. Not only is your attitude towards the client central to your ability to conduct the client's case successfully, but it is also important because it is this that will establish your reputation as an individual barrister, and reflect on the reputation of the profession as a whole. It is this basic principle that you should try to keep uppermost in your mind when you are considering how best to develop your own client conference skills.

2.2 The individual barrister

As has already been said, there is not a blueprint, nor special formula, that can be universally applied in the conduct of a client conference. By the same token it would be impossible, and indeed highly undesirable, to set out a rigid set of rules about the way in which any individual barrister performs and presents himself or herself in conference with a client. It is important to remember that every person is different and every person has a manner and style that is not only distinct to them, but borne of their own history, culture, background, and experience. Any attempt to try radically to alter your style in order to transform yourself into a figure resembling what may be commonly perceived as the stereotypical barrister is artificial and should be avoided at all cost.

For example, some people are naturally outgoing and witty, others more reserved and shy. The former will probably be able to crack an off-the-cuff joke which may amuse the client and help put him or her at ease, but the latter could run the risk of sounding false and patronising if attempting the same, merely for effect. The client will not care whether counsel is witty or not: what the client wants, and is paying for, is a skilled, competent barrister.

Students intending to practise at the Bar come from a wide variety of diverse backgrounds. It is not unknown for some to express concern over the quality of their voice and accent. Thankfully, the days are long-gone when a BBC 'Home Service' accent was considered essential for a barrister. Today it is irrelevant what accent counsel has. The central issue is clarity of expression and ensuring that the client can readily understand what is being said. The client would much rather counsel spoke sense in, for example, a Northern Irish, Yorkshire, or West Indian accent than spoke nonsense, albeit in 'pukka' English.

It is therefore important for all students to maintain their integrity and individuality and to build on their own attributes when learning how to develop effective conference skills. That is not to say, however, that some personal qualities will not bear examination when looking at the standard of interpersonal skills that are required when conducting a professional client conference. There are usually ways to improve your presentation—for example:

- ensuring that you use language that the client easily understands;
- making sure you think about methods of putting the client at ease;
- ensuring you give the client the confidence to be open and frank with you;
- taking stock of what messages you might inadvertently be conveying to the client;
- understanding what difficulties the client might be undergoing.

In considering these issues, careful attention should be paid to the performance and assessment criteria relating to client communication set out in **Chapter 12**. It is entirely possible that, in relation to performance, a student will need to learn how to be less patronising, austere, or aggressive; or possibly more robust, emphatic, or clear.

2.3 Ethical considerations—professional conduct

At all times, and on every occasion, it is vital to remember that any interaction with the lay client and any other persons involved in the proceedings must be conducted in accordance with the Code of Conduct for the Bar of England and Wales.[1] It is often the case, in the early years of practice, that there may be ethical questions raised which a newly qualified barrister finds difficult to answer. For example, in a criminal case, representing a defendant on a charge of theft, you may be informed in conference by the client that all the stolen property has not, in fact, been discovered by the police, and that although he or she intends to plead guilty to the offence(s) charged, he or she does not want you to men-

---

[1]   The BSB's Code of Conduct is in the *Bar Standards Board Handbook*, 2nd edn, April 2015 (with updates). Following the developments brought about by the Legal Services Act 2007, the BSB has undertaken to regulate advocacy-focused Alternative Business Structures (ABS), Legal Disciplinary Practices, and Barrister Only Entities (collectively known as 'entities') in addition to barristers in independent and employed practice. The BSB intends to commence its ABS application process from October 2016, but this cannot happen until the Lord Chancellor has approved the designation and the necessary secondary legislation is in place. However, it has resolved not to regulate Multi-Disciplinary Practices. You can find the draft rules and regulations in the Handbook, but note that these appear as scored-through text as they remain subject to approval by the Legal Services Board (LSB).

tion the undiscovered property. The issues raised here are twofold: client confidentiality (CD6 You must keep the affairs of each client confidential, Code of Conduct: see **4.3.3 Confidentiality**) and the duty every barrister has not to mislead the court (rC6, Code of Conduct). In such circumstances, you will have to explain the position to the client very carefully and clearly. First, the client must be reassured that in the absence of his or her permission, you will not divulge this information to anyone else. However, you will also need to explain that whilst you completely respect the confidentiality of the conference, as a barrister you additionally have a duty not to mislead, or to give inaccurate information to the court (gC4, Code of Conduct). Thus, in these circumstances, you would be unable to address the court on the client's behalf in a way that suggests that all the stolen goods have been recovered. It is important that the client is absolutely clear about the limiting effect this might have on, for example, a Plea in Mitigation on his or her behalf. Accordingly, it would also be your duty to advise the client what, in your professional opinion, you consider would be the right course of action for him or her to take with regard to the unrecovered property. Whatever answer the client gives, you are clearly bound by his or her instructions. You will have to act in accordance with those, but also within the parameters of the two principles set out above. This is just one example of the sort of ethical problem you might encounter in practice. There are further examples in **Chapter 9** and you should also refer to the *Professional Ethics* manual.

There may be circumstances where you are unsure of the ethical constraints upon you and are uncertain as to the correct way to proceed. If you find yourself in this situation, you must not proceed until you have taken further advice. A more senior member of chambers can usually be approached in this respect. In a matter of urgency, especially when the conference is held at court (as is often the case in the early years of practice), if there is no one available in chambers, the Bar Council is prepared and available to advise on ethical matters. (Note that barristers giving advice on the Bar Council ethics helpline have exemptions from the self-reporting and reporting of serious misconduct rule.) There is nothing wrong in seeking a short adjournment for the purpose of checking that the conduct of the case is proceeding in accordance with the rules relating to professional conduct. The golden rule is that, if you are not sure, you should not proceed until you have thoroughly investigated the matter. As well as being familiar with the Code of Conduct, it is also necessary to be aware of the rules of evidence in relation to Legal Professional Privilege that attach to communications with clients in legal proceedings. (See the *Evidence* manual.)

2.4 Dangers of preconceptions

The BSB's *Professional Statement for Barristers*, at 1.9, requires all barristers to 'Exercise good communication skills, through any appropriate medium and with any audience as required in their work'. Therefore, as a practising barrister, you should be alert to the inherent dangers of preconceptions. It is necessary to recognise that everyone is influenced to some extent by their own preconceptions, and how these can affect the conduct of your case and the relationship with the client and indeed with anyone you encounter in your professional life.

Preconceptions affect us all in many ways, either consciously or subconsciously. They affect the way we label, assess, or judge people, and the manner in which we communicate with them. They influence our expectations, how we behave towards others, our tolerance levels, and the relationships we make. For example, have you ever sat in a public place (on the tube, for instance) and found yourself assessing people on the basis of their physical appearance? Do you make assumptions about another's intellectual capacity on the basis of what book or newspaper they are reading? Have you ever assumed that an attractive-looking person must be pleasant on the basis of their looks? Do you assume that manual workers are less intellectually able than white-collar workers? Do you assume that most men who beat their wives belong to the lower socio-economic groups? Do you assume that most football supporters are thugs? Do you assume that someone who gives the appearance of being a dropout is usually high on drugs? Without a good deal of further knowledge, it is obviously impossible to tell and, therefore, any such assumptions are initially founded on preconceptions and prejudice.

Preconceptions can be both positive and negative and are triggered by many factors: upbringing and conditioning; previous experience (good or bad); what we see and hear; what we read; what we watch on television; what we learn from others. We are conditioned to classify people in our minds according to their looks, ethnic origin, colour, sex, religion, dress, speech, sexual orientation, education, intellectual ability, material wealth, employment, socio-economic background. When categorising people in this way we, in effect, label them and, therefore, potentially discriminate against them. For intending practitioners this must be avoided. At all times you must be aware of, and sensitive to, the fact that your clients (and others whom you will encounter in your practice at the Bar) will come from a variety of different backgrounds, which more than likely will be dissimilar to your own. In many cases, your clients will have lifestyles that are entirely different from yours. You must respect those differences at all times, and at all costs avoid forming preconceptions about individuals that could adversely affect your judgement of them and their case. For further information see **Chapter 11**, where Lord Justice Brooke CMG addresses important issues relating to cross-cultural communication and the Equality and Diversity Rules of the BSB Handbook.

As we have already seen, the dangers of preconceptions are readily apparent and this is specifically true in relation to your work as a barrister.

- Is the client more likely to be guilty because he or she fits your image of what a guilty person would be like?
- Is a man charged with indecent assault more likely to be guilty because he wears a dirty raincoat?
- Do you believe what your client tells you on the basis that he or she is articulate, well dressed, and well educated?
- Do you disregard what your client has to say because he or she is poorly educated and inarticulate?
- Does the fact that your client is a foreigner mean he or she is less likely to tell the truth?
- Does the fact that your client has a conviction for dishonesty mean he or she is more likely to have committed a crime of violence?
- Do you assume your opponent is trustworthy because he or she is approachable and initially friendly?
- Do you assume your opponent is less competent than you because he or she is younger than you?
- Do you assume your opponent is more competent than you because he or she is older than you?
- Do you assume your opponent is more competent than you because he or she boasts about his or her experience in this field of practice?

Common sense dictates that the answers to all these questions should, of course, be *'No'*. However, it is easy in practice to forget the potential influence of preconceptions, to fail to recognise the dangers that could adversely affect the manner in which you conduct the case. From the first meeting with the client in conference, it is vital to ensure that the proceedings are conducted on the basis of actual knowledge rather than on any assumptions or preconceptions.

In undertaking the preparation for any case, it is also useful to consider what, if any, preconceptions might exist for other parties to the proceedings as well as yourself. It is only by being alert to these possibilities that you can determine how to deal most effectively with them. A useful checklist is to ask yourself:

- Have any assumptions/preconceptions affected my judgement or approach to the case in any way?
- To what extent?
- Are they more/less/equally likely to affect my opponent or the court's approach/judgement?
- Will my opponent proceed on the basis of any preconceptions I have not made?
- Are these likely to support/undermine my client's case?
- Is the court likely to proceed on the basis of any preconceptions?
- Are they likely to influence a jury?
- Can I use them to my advantage?
- Do I need to dispel them?

2.5 The 'cab-rank' principle

It is important to remember, as a qualified barrister, that you are bound to observe the 'cab-rank' principle (rC29 and rC30 (as revised), Code of Conduct). As a barrister, you cannot pick and choose your clients so that you only act for those whom you choose to believe in or those you like. Nor can you refuse to represent a client because, say, you find the charge offensive, or he or she is of a different political or religious persuasion from you or has a lifestyle of which you disapprove. It is your duty to represent any client, in any case in which you are instructed. You may find that you are instructed to act for a client who is a member of a nationalist party; you may find that you are required to act for a client who, for religious reasons, is refusing to allow his or her child to have a blood transfusion; you may be asked to appear for a client who is a company director charged with a major tax fraud. No matter what personal views you hold, if you are instructed to represent a client in a particular case, it is your professional obligation to conduct that client's case objectively and to the best of your professional ability. In very limited circumstances, you are permitted to withdraw from a case. (See the *Professional Ethics* manual and **Chapter 9**.)

2.6 Effective communication

Throughout your working life as a barrister you will come into contact with a wide variety of people from all walks of life with whom you will need to communicate—and with whom you will need to communicate effectively. The most obvious is, of course, the client. But, in order to represent the client properly at all stages of the proceedings, there is a range of others with whom you will come into regular contact and to whom consideration ought to be given:

- professional clients;
- other barristers;
- other professionals;
- witnesses;
- expert witnesses;
- judges;
- juries;
- magistrates;
- court clerks and officials;
- police;
- colleagues in chambers;
- clerks in chambers.

While a good barrister will have knowledge and expertise in the law, the better barrister will recognise the need not only to acquire sound communication skills, but also to learn how to adapt these skills in order to communicate effectively with all the people— professional and non-professional—with whom he or she will become professionally involved during the conduct of a client's case.

The ability to communicate is a skill. It is a skill that can be learned, as with all other disciplines, by analysing the factors that make any interaction between people effective. It is also necessary to recognise how easily communications between people can break down if careful attention is not paid to what obviously creates barriers between people, as well as what behaviour can contribute to, or cause, lack of effective communication. Thus, it is necessary to be aware, at the outset of your career, that developing good communication skills is an integral part of becoming a professional barrister. Effective communication with clients is dealt with in more detail in **Chapters 3** and **4**. The acquisition of these skills is important for conducting an effective client conference, and is also relevant to other areas of your practice. For example, as an advocate, you will be addressing a wide range of audiences (magistrates, judges, juries) whom you will be seeking to persuade to adopt your arguments. You will also need to give careful consideration to how to communicate, in court, with a range of witnesses, for example in examination-in-chief and cross-examination. With each audience and each witness, you will need to have worked out, in advance, what you think will be the most effective way of dealing with that person in order to succeed in obtaining the desired result. (See the *Advocacy* manual.)

Negotiation forms a central part of a barrister's practice, as a large majority of cases settle before reaching court. With the implementation of the Woolf and Jackson reforms, and the increase of alternative dispute resolution (ADR) and mediation, out-of-court settlement is presently the norm for civil cases. As a negotiator, the ability to communicate appropriately with your opponent is an essential quality. As with advocacy, it is vital that you have given consideration, in advance, to the most effective methods of successfully achieving your objectives from the negotiation, and a major part of those considerations will be how best to communicate with your opponent.

As with all skills, the most effective way to develop your communication skills is . . . practice.

2.7 **Understanding what you hear**

One of the major purposes of the client conference is to gather the necessary information from the client in order to be in the best position to advise him or her on the most appropriate way forward with the case. (See **Chapter 7**.) Before the conference it will be necessary to:

- analyse your instructions and the contents of the brief;
- form a preliminary view as to what you consider the client's needs are;
- undertake any necessary legal research; and
- decide precisely what you need to discover from the conference with your client. (See **Chapter 5**.)

In addition, you should have given detailed consideration to the best method of questioning the client in order to elicit the necessary information, in the most effective way. Obviously there will be other relevant factors to consider here, for example how long you will have in conference with the client and where the conference is scheduled to take place. (See **Chapters 4** and **6**.)

More generally, however, it is important to remind yourself that in the conference you need to give adequate consideration to:

- listening to the answers that the client gives in response to questions; and
- seeking to understand what those answers actually mean.

The client will expect you to listen carefully to the information he or she is giving you. It is an all-too-common fault in barristers, having planned the conference from the papers, to push on too quickly and to give the impression that what the client says is not important. What is being said may not be crucial to the case, in your opinion, but it is often of vital importance to the client to be able to air matters that are uppermost in his or her mind. For example, a client may come to see you ostensibly for advice about gaining contact with his children. In fact, all he wants to talk about is the fact that his wife's lover has moved into the former matrimonial home—and how he is not only devastated by this but also furious that he is obliged to continue making the mortgage repayments on the house—rather than talk about the lack of contact he is having with his children. Part of your job will be to deal adequately and sensitively with the client's emotional concerns about the wife's lover and the money. But you will also need to ensure that you are in sufficient control of the conference to address the specific matter on which you are instructed, ie the client's contact with his children. Without being able to handle appropriately the issues that you may well regard as peripheral to your instructions, you will probably have difficulty in dealing satisfactorily with the main part of the case. Thus, you should expect to encounter clients who have their own agenda for the conference, which often does not accord with yours. You must be aware that you will have to listen carefully to what your client says to ensure that you are not dismissive of any problem that you consider to be irrelevant, but also have sufficient control of the conference to elicit the relevant information that you need for the conduct of the particular application.

It is important to be aware that all you will have had to go on before the first meeting in conference with your client is the information contained in your solicitor's instructions and the brief. There may be a variety of reasons why this information may be inadequate—for example, lack of time for the solicitor to interview/proof the client before the conference; a delay since the solicitor's interview with the client and the conference taking place, during which time further relevant information has come to light; or the client being reluctant to 'spill the beans' until the conference with counsel. And, importantly, especially in the early years of practice, you will often have to conduct the conference with little more than a back sheet for your instructions. It is not uncommon to be briefed thus:

> Mrs Jones was beaten by her husband last night and was forced to leave her home and spend the night in a women's refuge. Counsel is instructed to meet Mrs Jones at Oxbridge County Court and apply without notice for a non-molestation order, and an occupation order.

In such circumstances, it is clearly essential that the extent to which you will be able to represent Mrs Jones adequately will depend to a great extent on the answers that she will give you at the conference before the hearing. You must, therefore, be clear as to what your client is telling you. It will give your client no confidence if you fail to listen carefully and understand the information that you are being given. If you are in any doubt as to what is being said, ask for clarification. It is much better, and more productive in the long run, to stop the conference and ask the client to go back over certain points about which you are uncertain, rather than continue when you are unclear as to what your client is actually trying to tell you. You should, therefore, ensure that you:

- remain sufficiently flexible to deal with any unexpected information you may receive; and

- deal sympathetically with points which the client raises even if they are not, in your opinion, critical to the conduct of the case.

It is your duty to ensure that you then evaluate the importance of the information received as it relates to your client's case. While efficient use of time is important, you will certainly fail to be efficient overall if you do not develop the skill of listening properly. (See **Chapter 6**.)

2.8 Interpreting what you have heard

'Whenever anybody says to me "It's not the money, it's the principle of the thing"—it's the money' (Martin and War, quoted in Shaffer and Elkins, *Legal Interviewing and Counselling*, 2004, p 224).

It is also vital to be able to interpret what you hear accurately as the information could have a radical effect on the conduct of the case, or substantially change the initial perception you may have already formed of the case from reading the papers. There are many examples from ordinary, everyday experience that show that when a person says one thing, they may well mean another. For example, 'Do you want anything from the shops, Mum?' interpreted another way could mean 'I want to borrow the car, Mum.' 'I thought it would be nice if I went to visit Great Aunt Flo as she doesn't see many people' could well be interpreted as 'Isn't it time *you* went to visit Great Aunt Flo?'

Being alert to the client saying one thing but really meaning something else can be a difficulty in the conference. Try to remember that you cannot always accept the information given at face value and you may well need to explore a particular area with a client in more depth to discover which interpretation is the correct one. It would be simplistic to suggest that there are any hard-and-fast rules to enable you to detect whether the client is saying one thing but really meaning something else. However, there are some clues that may assist in determining whether a client could be avoiding the issue that is really uppermost in his or her mind. For example, the client may:

- find it difficult to answer a direct question in a particular area;
- become defensive and shift the conversation;
- keep on introducing a matter which, on the face of it, seems irrelevant to the proceedings;
- keep going round in circles;
- be inconsistent.

Although you have to be extremely sensitive, if you do suspect that the client is having some real difficulty in telling you what is really at the heart of his or her problem, you will have to probe and investigate the matter more fully. (See **Chapters 6** and **10**.)

2.9 Non-verbal indicators

Accurately interpreting another person's intentions/feelings/emotions from the way they behave physically is a complex area and beyond the scope of this manual. To attempt to set out any hard-and-fast rules on how to do so is impossible. As trained lawyers you are not expected to develop overnight into psychologists or anthropologists. But it is important that you are aware of non-verbal indicators from which you might gain some clues about your client, and equally important for you to be aware of the dangers of jumping to any conclusions about your client (or, indeed, anyone else involved in the proceedings) on the basis of his or her 'body language'. Living in a multicultural and multi-ethnic society, you should be aware that whilst a certain type of behaviour might be regarded as an indicator of something to one group in society, to another group the same behaviour might indicate the exact opposite. For example, white, middle-class children are told they look 'shifty' if they fail to look the person to whom they are talking in the eye. On the other hand, in some communities it is considered downright rude for a young person to look someone in authority in the eye when they are speaking to them. (For further information, see **Chapter 11**.)

The following are some simple illustrations of the inherent dangers of jumping to any speedy conclusions from a client's non-verbal behaviour. What messages do you receive when your client is looking distinctly uncomfortable? Is this an indication of guilt? Almost certainly not. Looking uncomfortable may well be a sign of guilt, but it can and does indicate a whole range of many other things: fear; nervousness; uncertainty; shyness; confusion. By the same token, what messages do you receive when your client appears calm and unruffled? Is this an indication of innocence? Again, almost certainly not. It may well reflect honesty, but equally the client could be extremely self-confident; putting up a smoke screen; a skilled liar; a practised con artist.

Beware of placing too much emphasis on tears. Crying is the most readily visible sign of distress and often does indicate exactly that. However, there are some people who are indeed in great distress but never cry—this does not mean that their distress is any the less. We are all familiar with the expressions 'She's a cold fish' or 'He's as hard as nails'. Just because a client does not react emotionally as you might expect, it does not necessarily mean that he or she is not deeply affected by the circumstances in which he or she finds himself or herself. And, of course, remember that there are those who can 'turn on the tap' at the drop of a hat—beware of placing too much weight on, or drawing inaccurate inferences from, what may be 'crocodile tears'.

Perhaps the safest way to draw any helpful clues from your client's non-verbal behaviour is to (a) observe his or her particular pattern of behaviour, and (b) be alerted if this changes in any material way during the conference. In this way, you may pick up some helpful indicators, which will assist you to pursue a line of questioning that you otherwise would not.

2.10 Be flexible—think laterally

'The best laid schemes o' mice an' men . . .'

No matter how diligently you have planned the conference, always be prepared to expect the unexpected. In an ideal world, every client would match up to your expectations, giving you answers much along the lines you had anticipated, and the conference would proceed neatly along your pre-planned path. The reality is often very different. Your client will not give the answers you expect, will depart radically from his or her proof of evidence that has been prepared by your instructing solicitor, and, further, will reveal in conference some information which you could not possibly have anticipated. In such circumstances, you obviously need to be flexible. It may be that the new information is something that you can deal adequately with there and then. But if you receive information that radically alters your opinion on the case in question, make sure that you have sufficient time to reflect on the consequences before committing yourself to a rushed opinion. There is nothing wrong in telling the client (and your instructing solicitor) that in the light of the new information you have received, you need some further time to deliberate on your final advice.

In addition, clients often bombard you with questions which were not obvious, or relevant, from the face of the papers. For example, a client whom you are representing in an action for unfair dismissal may want to know what his or her entitlement is under the lease of the premises he or she is renting with two friends; or a client who is seeking your advice on his or her forthcoming divorce may press you to give a detailed breakdown of his or her State benefit entitlements should he or she give up work.

It is easy to be taken by surprise and thrown off course when matters that you had not considered are raised by the client. Clearly you cannot avoid giving answers and have to deal with the situation. A golden rule is not to guess. If you do not know the answer or are not in a position to give accurate information, tell the client exactly that. It is much better to say, for example, that you do not know, but (if appropriate) that you will find out; or that you do not know but you will alert his or her solicitor that this is a matter with which the client needs assistance. It is easy to see the dangers in offering advice on a matter with which you are unfamiliar, and in which you are not instructed.

There may be occasions on which you consider that the best solution for the client's problem will be found in seeking a non-legal alternative. For example, you are instructed by a client who is contemplating commencing divorce proceedings and is seeking your advice. In conference you discover that the client and his or her spouse really do not want a divorce but cannot, at this point in time, live together. In such circumstances, it may be appropriate to recommend that the client seeks some other form of assistance, say from a relationship support service, before finally deciding that divorce is the only step to take. Another example could be that your client is seeking your advice on a remedy for a breach of an employment contract that contains an express restraint-of-trade clause. In conference you discover that the problem would be much better resolved by the client seeking the services of a mediator rather than pursuing a legal remedy, and you accordingly recommend to the client that mediation would be his or her best alternative at this stage. From the above examples, it can readily be seen that you must be prepared to think laterally about what the best solution for your client is and, in this respect, be aware of outside agencies and organisations who can, in addition to you, most properly assist your client. (See **Chapter 7**.)

2.11   Be non-judgemental and objective

As a barrister, meeting and representing clients can be a rewarding and fulfilling experience. It is your chosen career and you have spent several years studying to achieve your ambition. The realities of practice, however, are that in many cases in which you are instructed you are probably going to encounter a range of human behaviour that you may find distressing, disgusting, abhorrent, sad, inexplicable, incomprehensible. Clients usually need to be legally represented because they are in trouble and need a solution to the difficulties in which they find themselves.

It is absolutely crucial that at all times, when you are acting in your professional capacity, you remain:

- non-judgemental; and
- objective.

These two rules are, above all, fundamental and critical to your ability to be a successful and professional practitioner.

It is not part of your role to judge the client's case, to judge whether you think the client is guilty (or liable) or not, or to impose any personal view on the client's conduct. It *is* your role to take your client's instructions and evaluate for him or her the strengths and weaknesses of the case, within the particular legal context, and to advise accordingly. In order to do this effectively, it is essential to know the rules relating to the law of evidence and understand how they affect any particular case. For example:

- What are the facts in issue?
- What has to be proved?
- To what standard?
- By whom?
- Is a piece of evidence admissible?
- Can you attempt to exclude any damaging evidence?
- Can you render admissible any supporting evidence?
- What weight will be attached to any evidence?

(See generally the *Evidence* manual.)

It is equally important to be familiar with the rules relating to procedure. For example:

- What are the elements of the offence/alleged civil wrong?
- Can the offence/wrongdoing be made out?
- Have any formal procedural requirements been satisfied?
- Are there any procedural irregularities?
- What are the sanctions/remedies?

(See further *Criminal Litigation and Sentencing* manual and *Remedies* manual.)

In short, the evaluation of your client's case depends on your ability to identify the issues involved, and to analyse accurately the facts and the legal framework in which the case is placed. It is on these grounds that you advise your client as to the most appropriate solution to the case and *not* your personal opinion on the matter. (See **Chapter 5**.)

It is fatal to your professional judgement to be less than objective at all times. You cannot afford to be influenced by personal feelings about the case or the client. Any degree of personal involvement will invariably weaken your ability to act in the best interests of your client and will be more than likely to render your performance on his or her behalf inadequate.

From the time when you are first instructed to represent a client, and from the first meeting in conference, you need to adopt a non-judgemental attitude to the behaviour of your client and be completely objective. This will enable you to evaluate the merits of the case and ensure that you represent the client to the best of your ability—and to the standard that is expected of a professional barrister.

2.12 Conclusion

In considering the skills that it is necessary to acquire in order to conduct an effective conference with a client, you need to give careful consideration to the general principles as outlined in this chapter. It should hopefully be obvious that every interaction with every lay client needs a great deal of thought and care. It is only by being aware of the wide range of issues that are involved that you can begin to understand the complexities of conducting a conference with a client. The following chapters build on the general principles and look in more detail at the specific areas that are relevant to developing sound conference skills.

The client

3.1 Introduction

'I had no idea how difficult clients could be and how important it is to establish a working relationship with them . . . I think I would have found the task much less daunting if someone had explained in detail the basic techniques and pitfalls.' (The views of a junior tenant who qualified before compulsory vocational training: see Johnson and Shapland, *Developing Legal Training for the Bar*, University of Sheffield, 1990.)

- What type of client am I likely to get?
- Am I competent to deal appropriately with any client?
- What range of clients am I likely to be instructed to represent?
- How will I recognise their individual requirements?
- Will I be able to meet my professional obligations to the client?
- Will I be able to keep the conference within my control?
- What happens if I feel out of my depth?
- Will anyone else be involved?
- What ethical matters should I consider?
- What rules of professional conduct must I adhere to?

These are the sorts of questions that every barrister new to practice will ask themselves before meeting any client in conference. Sensibly, it is necessary to address these issues before you meet the client for the first time in order to ensure that you are confident in your ability to communicate professionally and sensitively with any individual whom you are instructed to represent. (See **Chapter 5**.)

This chapter considers the range of different clients, both lay and professional, that every barrister might expect to encounter during the course of his or her career at the Bar. At first blush it would be easy to assume that what is meant by the use of the word 'client' refers only to the lay client whom counsel has been instructed to meet in conference and, depending, of course, on the outcome of the conference, represent in the course of resolving that client's particular legal problems.

The reality is far removed from this. When conducting a case for a particular client, you should remember that (a) there is an enormous variety of potential clients whom you are likely to be instructed to represent; and (b) there is also a whole range of other individuals who can become involved in the case, especially if the conference is held at court immediately prior to the hearing. Consideration should be given to all those potentially involved when representing and advising the lay client at all stages of the proceedings.

The perception of who 'the client' is, or may be, must properly be addressed in every case in which you are instructed. It should also be considered in a much wider framework if you are to ensure that you are in a position to offer the best possible service to that client. What follows is divided into two main strands.

3.1.1   The client

This chapter will emphasise, in the following sections, the necessity to give thorough consideration to the individual needs of a range of clients whom you are likely to be instructed to represent. It also aims to raise your awareness of the importance of thinking about how to deal professionally and sensitively with each client. What follows should alert you to some of the problems that you might encounter with clients in practice and offer some suggestions as to how best to deal most effectively with any difficulties that might arise.

3.1.2   Other potential participants

You should recognise the importance of being aware of the other individuals who will, or may, be involved with the client's case, and the potential impact on the case and/or the client of such involvement. It will also help you to learn how to recognise and deal most effectively with any problems that may arise in these circumstances.

Thus, the following are considered separately:

- lay client;
- professional client;
- professional non-client;
- non-professional non-client;
- expert witness;
- potential witness.

3.2   The lay client

3.2.1   Client's perception

- What does the client feel about the prospective conference with his or her barrister?
- What emotions might be going through the client's mind prior to the conference?
- What experience is the client anticipating at the conference?
- What does the client expect from the conference?
- What does the client want from the conference?

These questions address the sorts of things which will probably be going through your client's mind before any conference. It is sensible to give consideration to what the client himself or herself is going through prior to the meeting with you. There is a whole gamut of emotions that a client may be experiencing before the conference and you must give adequate thought to what those might be in every case. You are the barrister. You are the legal adviser, the person to whom this client has come to seek advice as to the most appropriate way forward to resolve the difficulties in which he or she finds himself or herself. In addition to your legal expertise, however, the client will need much more if you are to provide a full, competent, and professional service.

The need to consult a legal adviser can arise in many different ways and from a variety of different circumstances. Sometimes the matter can be very straightforward; for example, it may be a question of drafting a particular document such as a will or a specialist contract. There may be a specific right to enforce, or terms and conditions of an employment contract to consider. Very often, however, the need for legal advice arises because the client is in trouble. It may be that the circumstances are not of the client's own making and the client's difficulties have arisen from an incident which was beyond his or her control; or it may be that the legal dilemma has arisen as a direct consequence of the client's own actions. Whatever the root cause of the problem, however, being in trouble and in legal difficulties can place enormous strain on individuals and create great anxiety. Anxiety and emotional strain can manifest themselves in many different forms. People react to stress in many different ways. It is well known that stress often causes people to behave in a manner that is totally out of character. Stress can make people become frightened, timid, angry, hostile, dogmatic, hypersensitive, tense, or unforthcoming. It can make people close up, refuse to confront reality, become evasive, or become obsessive. Indeed, it is not unusual for a client to be, literally, in a 'state of shock' because of the circumstances in which they find themselves. Every individual reacts in a different way and there is no magic formula to enable you to identify which of these, or any other, emotional responses any one client will have to the stress that is being caused by the predicament he or she is in. What is important, however, is that you recognise and are aware of any possible strain and anxiety that the client may be suffering and the potential effect of this on the client, particularly at the first conference.

3.2.2 Some common themes

Although, as has already been said, it is impossible to predict with any accuracy precisely how any individual client might react emotionally to the legal dilemma in which he or she finds himself or herself, there are some emotions/responses that clients can have which may generally be regarded as common themes. Set out in the following sections are some examples of what clients may well be thinking and, although far from a fully comprehensive list, these illustrations should give you some insight into the sorts of things which may be going through a client's mind when meeting you in conference.

3.2.2.1 'What will counsel think of *me*?'

Most people tend to want only a positive response from others and thus seek favourable evaluations from others. Most people want to be liked; most people do not want to look foolish; most people find negative criticism unpalatable and difficult to handle. It can therefore be a great blow to the ego to have to disclose negative conduct on their own part, and there may be a reluctance to give honest answers. For example, in divorce proceedings, it may be difficult for the client to admit to an extra-marital affair for fear of being judged negatively. Or perhaps the client may be reluctant to confess to an act such as entering a wholly inappropriate partnership agreement or failing to prevent something that was blatantly illegal, which he or she thinks will reveal his or her own stupidity and make the barrister think less of him or her. You must attempt at all times to assist the client in overcoming these fears. If the client is reassured that you are completely non-judgemental, and reminded that you are there to assist him or her to resolve his or her legal problem and not to judge his or her behaviour, this will help dispel some of these anxieties and encourage the client to have the confidence to be frank with you. It is vital for your client to be fully aware that:

(a) what is discussed with you in the conference is confidential (CD6, Code of Conduct) and, in the absence of his or her consent, you will not reveal to anyone any information which is given to you (although you should be aware that there are also professional conduct issues that may arise, some of which may compete with this duty of confidentiality: see *Professional Ethics* manual and see **2.3**);

(b) if, as counsel, you are not fully in the picture about all the relevant circumstances surrounding the case, you will not be in the best position to give him or her comprehensive and sound advice.

3.2.2.2 'I *don't* want to talk about it'

Many people try to avoid speaking about events that, if recalled too clearly, cause them to relive an experience that was painful or unpleasant. The reluctance to answer questions accurately in this regard is not fear of a negative response from the questioner, but rather a desire to avoid the bad memory with which the event has left them—for example, the moment of arrest by a store detective for suspected shoplifting, or the events directly before an accident in which injury was received. Recalling these incidents may indeed be difficult for some clients, who would much rather forget about them altogether. A parent being interviewed about an alleged sexual assault on her child by his or her partner might have considerable difficulty in discussing the matter because of the distress it causes. In these sorts of situations, the manner in which the client is questioned is of the utmost importance and you will need to give special attention to the questioning techniques you use. But, by skilful, thoughtful, and sensitive questioning, the client will be reassured and can often be prompted to give a more forthcoming response. (See **Chapter 6**.)

3.2.2.3 'Counsel's much cleverer and more important than me'

There is frequently an anxiety on the part of the client that the barrister he or she is about to meet in conference is on some superior level to him or her. After all, you are the specialist and the consultation with you is for the client to receive specialist advice. In most cases, the client will not have any knowledge of the law or procedure and, consequently, will often tend to regard the legal adviser with a certain amount of awe. It is important that you remember this and ensure that the conversation is pitched at a level that the client can comfortably understand. It is often useful to reassure the client that you are on his or her side and that you and he or she are 'in this together'. Making assumptions about the client's knowledge, or slipping into some sort of legal jargon or shorthand, will only succeed in making the client feel more at a disadvantage. Being patronising must be avoided at all costs. At all times during the conference, it is important to use plain English and to be absolutely sure that what you have said has been clearly understood.

3.2.2.4 'All I want to know is . . . '

In some circumstances there may be a very real fear, or dominant question, which is uppermost in the client's mind and which will need to be confronted early on. If this is the case, failure to recognise and deal with this will inhibit the effectiveness of the conference and render the client less than able to assist you. For example, questions may include: 'Will I go to prison?'; 'How long will I get?'; 'Will my child be taken into care?'; 'When will I get my money?'; 'How much will I get?'; 'What's all this going to cost me?'.

In such circumstances, an instantaneous answer is usually impossible. The whole point of the conference is to elicit the necessary information to discover what the answer is. But clearly, if the client cannot be deflected, you have got to address the matter satisfactorily before you can proceed with the conference. If you reassure the client that you too are fully aware that the question is critical, that *you* too understand the importance of the issue, and explain clearly that you will give an answer once you have obtained a bit more information, the client will usually permit the conference to proceed with the reassurance that you will, of course, address his or her main concern.

3.2.2.5 'I *don't* want to hear that'

You should be aware that it is not uncommon for some clients to refuse to listen to what you have to say, especially if you are giving them 'bad news'. Accepting advice that is contrary to the client's hopes or aspirations is sometimes extremely difficult. It may be a conscious or subconscious denial of reality, but nevertheless there will be occasions when your client will have genuine difficulty in facing the bare facts that you present to him or her. Unfortunately, delivering disagreeable advice is a task that will fall to you on many occasions. It is useful here to remind yourself that, in our adversarial system, for every person who 'wins' his or her case there is usually another who will regard himself or herself as 'the loser'. For example: 'I'm afraid the chance of you gaining a Child Arrangements Order for your child to live with you is virtually out of the question'; 'Regrettably, I must tell you that you are in breach of contract and, therefore, almost certainly liable'; 'Unfortunately, in my opinion, the prosecution evidence against you is extremely strong and I think there will be a real difficulty in persuading a jury that you did not believe that you were acting dishonestly.' In these circumstances, it can sometimes happen that your client simply refuses to believe your advice, or does not appear to accept what you are saying. The solutions to this are not easy. It is obviously your duty to give your client a clear view of what your professional judgement is and to advise him or her accordingly. If he or she has difficulty in accepting your opinion, it may be that he or she has not clearly understood your evaluation of his or her position. It is a good idea to check whether he or she would like you to go over your explanation again. If your client is still reluctant to accept what you are saying, invite him or her to go away and discuss the matter with the solicitor and/or a friend/relation before coming to any decision about what instructions he or she wishes to give you. Very often a bit of time will give a client the necessary 'breather' he or she wishes and enable them to come to terms with the unpalatable news you have given. If, however, you are at court and there is no time for your client to reflect on the matter, you will have to take a firm approach and remind him or her that as his or her legal adviser, although you will, of course, act upon any instructions he or she gives you, you nevertheless owe a professional duty to him or her to advise in accordance with your judgement on the matter. At this stage, whether your judgement is accepted or not, has to be a matter for the client. (See **Chapter 7**.)

3.2.3 **Range of clients**

Inevitably you can expect to encounter a whole range of clients in your practice. We live in a multicultural society, a diverse society, a society that comprises people from a variety of socio-economic backgrounds. Therefore, it is important to be aware of this fact and to understand the need to give consideration to the sorts of problems that can—and do—arise when representing clients in practice. Many of your clients will, of course, be forthcoming and cooperative. Others will not be so easy. The potential difficulties are well illustrated by the comments of a newly qualified barrister:

Problems in relations with clients are varied and included difficulties in dealing with juveniles and mentally disordered offenders, clients that were simply awkward, clients that said they were innocent but wanted to plead guilty, and difficulties with clients and relations when clients thought they had not got a good result.

(Shapland and Sorsby, *Starting Practice: Work and Training at the Junior Bar*, University of Sheffield, 1995)

As we have seen, clients who come to you for advice will come from a whole range of backgrounds and with a whole variety of legal problems. Not only are they likely to have their own preconceptions and anxieties about what the conference itself and you, the barrister, will be like, but they often come with their own agenda, hidden or articulated, and their perception of what could or should be the result of the meeting. This can often give rise to difficulties for counsel in conducting the client conference, especially in the early years of practice, and you should seek to identify potential problems that can arise in this respect. Although they do not form an exhaustive list, the following examples of possible difficulties when dealing with the client's own perceptions of their problem and the conference may usefully illustrate the point. What is important is that you are aware, at all times, that not only do clients come from all walks of life, but they also may have their own fixed notions, which will need to be handled with a great deal of sensitivity and care.

3.2.3.1 'I'll do whatever you tell me'

Many clients are indecisive and not prepared to make any decisions for themselves. Effectively they want, and are happy for, the responsibility of the decision-making process to be removed from them. They want you to tell them what to do. Giving clear and comprehensive advice to the client is, of course, your duty. However, it is also your duty to ensure that in the final analysis it is the client who makes the decision: it is the client who gives you instructions and it is the client who makes his or her own choice. The process of giving advice takes on a significant role in these circumstances and this process is addressed in detail in **Chapter 7**. As a general rule, however, if you have gained the client's confidence, recognised his or her fears and difficulties, set out simply and clearly the legal position and the range of options open, considered the consequences of pursuing any of these options, and explored any possible non-legal alternatives, you should be able to encourage the client to make the decision for himself or herself.

3.2.3.2 'I want my day in court'

You must be wary of the client who comes in fighting and suggests, for example, 'I want to proceed with this as a matter of principle'; 'I'm not going to let him get away with this no matter how much it costs'; 'I want to make sure I get a chance to get my side of the story across.' In such circumstances, it is likely that the client has decided what outcome he or she wants long before the conference. The only question left will be whether the end sought can be achieved by invoking the legal process. What you must ensure is that, following an analysis of the legal and factual position, the client is fully aware of the consequences that will necessarily follow if he or she insists on pursuing that course of action. It may be the right thing to do, but equally it may be inadvisable, especially if the motivation is unsound. As we have already seen, it is not your role to tell the client what to do. The ultimate decision on what course of action to take is exclusively for the client to make. However, it is your role to ensure that you have drawn the client's attention to the likely outcome and possible consequences of any course of action to be taken, and it is your duty to convey this clearly. You may be able to bring your client's attention to some matter that he or she had not considered—for example, the question of costs, win or lose; the question of potential delays and the consequential effect of these in getting the matter heard; the question of necessary continuing relations with any of the other parties directly or indirectly involved (business or personal). Ensuring that the client is fully informed, and in a manner which he or she clearly understands, will often encourage the client to make a more realistic decision.

3.2.3.3 'I just don't care'

For a variety of reasons, some clients will already have reached a decision about what they want to do, which may be potentially damaging to their own interests—for example, 'I want to plead guilty and get it over with' or 'I don't care if I am entitled to remain in the house, all I want to do is to get him out of my hair and never see him again.' Again, you cannot take over the decision-making process for the client, but it is your duty to ensure that he or she is fully aware of the consequences that could flow from any such decision that is adverse to his or her best interests. In such circumstances, it is important to set out clearly for the client precisely what his or her legal rights and entitlements are and what strengths his or her case has, and to remind the client that, although it is perfectly understandable, making a wrong decision in haste may be something that he or she will live to regret later.

3.2.3.4 'I know a little bit about this'

It is said that a little learning is a dangerous thing. This can be true of some clients who think they have an understanding of the law—the client who believes that he or she is a bit of a contract buff or who has a great friend who has explained the salient points of the provisions relating to unfair dismissal, or perhaps the client who has more than a fleeting experience of the criminal courts who tells you, 'You've got to make a submission of no case to answer—that's how I got off last time.' In such circumstances you will have to be reasonably robust and make it clear that, although you will act on the instructions of your client, it is your duty to conduct the case in accordance with the law as it actually is and your professional judgement of the client's position. A clear summary of your own opinion of the legal status of the proceedings should assist the client to make a realistic decision.

3.2.3.5 'I just can't cope'

In some situations a client will be so distressed by the circumstances of the case or the charge that he or she is facing that he or she becomes completely overwrought. Such a client may be in a highly charged emotional state and may not be able, for example, to stop weeping or control outbursts of extreme anger. First, it is never advisable for a client to make any decisions under these conditions. You must work out ways to help the client recover his or her composure; a short break, a cup of tea, or a cigarette can be obvious solutions. It is also important to ensure that you demonstrate to the client that you empathise with the stress that the client is experiencing and reassure him or her that such a reaction, under the circumstances, is perfectly normal. Often the client will recover sufficiently to be able to continue when he or she is permitted an opportunity to release pent-up emotions and realises that you are aware and uncritical of his or her feelings. However, it must always be remembered that a client under stress may have difficulty in making any rational decisions, and in some circumstances, where possible, it may be advisable to delay coming to a conclusion until a further occasion. In circumstances where such a delay is not possible—for example, a conference at the door of the court or when the client is in custody and the hearing is imminent—you will have to use your best endeavours to calm the client down there and then. (See **Chapter 10**.)

3.2.3.6   'I want my friend to be at the conference too'

It is often the case that a client, thrown into unfamiliar and unnerving circumstances, will feel the need to be supported by a friend or a relation. The client may well turn up for the conference in chambers or arrive at court with someone else and expect them to be able to participate in the conference. For example, in matrimonial proceedings the new partner may wish to accompany your client and seek to add his or her views on the matter, or a relative or friend may wish to accompany your client when you are advising on quantum or damages in a personal injury claim. Although it is up to you, the strong recommendation is that you resist the request for the presence of the friend or relation. It may be that the client has a valid reason for wanting this third party to be present, but in most situations such involvement is undesirable, as it can hinder both the interview process and the decision-making process. (See **Chapter 10** in respect of juveniles and mentally ill clients.) In every case, however, it is crucial to remember that:

- you take instructions from your client;
- it is your client who will give evidence;
- the presence of such a third party is unethical if he or she is likely to be a witness (see **3.5**).

If the friend or relative is likely to be a potential witness, you will properly be able to request him or her to leave by explaining that, as a potential witness in the proceedings, his or her presence at the conference is not permitted.

If the third party does not fall into this category the situation needs careful handling, given that it is almost always preferable to exclude him or her from the conference with your client. You will have to give consideration to the reasons why the friend/relative is there. How reliant is the client on this person for emotional support? Is the third party imposing their presence on the client? Might the client himself or herself be relieved if the friend/relative is asked to leave for the duration of the conference? Does the client merely wish to consult with the friend/relation before coming to a final decision on the matter in hand? Having ascertained the role of the friend/relation, you can properly, if you think fit, suggest that it is inappropriate for him or her to remain for the duration of the conference. The impact of this request can be softened by:

- reassuring the client that there will be an opportunity to talk to the friend/relative before reaching any decision if that is desirable;
- reassuring the friend/relative that you will inform him or her after the conference (providing your client agrees) of any conclusions which have been reached in the conference.

If you think it appropriate, for whatever reason, that the friend/relative does attend the conference and such attendance is not breaching any ethical rules, you should be alert to the difficulties that may arise. If the friend/relative keeps on interrupting, or attempts to give answers for the client, this will seriously hamper the conference process. In such circumstances you will have to take a firm stand and ensure that he or she understands that he or she either refrains from interrupting or leaves the conference.

3.2.4   Conclusion

In summary, you can expect to encounter a wide range of clients from diverse backgrounds and with very varied problems for you to solve. To set out a fully comprehensive list of every sort of client you could meet is, of course, impossible. However, as long as you remember, at the outset of every meeting in conference with your lay client, that they will inevitably come to you with a range of fears and anxieties, and very often with their own preconceptions and expectations about you and their case, you will be in a much better position to ensure that you adapt your conference-skills techniques in a manner which will best suit that particular client. At all times, it is important to remember that:

- every client is different;
- every client is an individual;
- every client will have particular needs to which different considerations must be given.

In addition to the detailed analysis of the factual and legal framework in which any particular case may fall, it is equally vital to ask yourself these questions before you meet the client for the first time in conference:

- What is *this* client's perception of his or her case and the conference likely to be?
- What do I know about him or her that might influence the way I conduct the conference?
- Are there any clues in my instructions that could give me any insight or signpost any potential hidden agenda?

3.3 The professional client

3.3.1 Your instructing solicitor

Your instructing solicitor is the link between you and the client.[1] The relationship between you and your solicitor is of paramount importance in all aspects of the conduct of the lay client's case. It is essential that good lines of communication between you and your instructing solicitor are always open (see **1.5**).

It is the solicitor who:

- meets the client first;
- makes the first assessment of the client's position;
- first gains the client's confidence;
- writes the instructions to counsel based on his or her own perception of the client and the client's needs;
- will usually accompany the client to the conference;
- will be the intermediary between you and the client for the duration of the proceedings.

It should be remembered, however, particularly in the early years of practice, that there will be occasions when you will meet the client in conference without an instructing solicitor present—for example, in the magistrates' court or County Court—or you will

---

[1] This section in particular—and the manual in general—is written from the perspective of barristers working in independent practice acting on instructions from a solicitor. Barristers taking advantage of direct access arrangements and those who are employed operate in significantly different settings; see the BSB website: <http://www.barstandardsboard.org.uk>.

meet the client in conference with a representative from the solicitor's firm, such as an articled clerk or outdoor clerk.

If you find yourself in the former situation, where it is permissible to conduct a conference with a client without a representative present from the instructing solicitors, you must be careful, at all times, to ensure that you keep an accurate record, which the lay client both understands and has agreed to, of any decision taken during the conference. (See **Chapters 8** and **9**.) If you find that you are conducting the conference and the client is accompanied by an outdoor clerk from the solicitor's office, be aware that in these situations most outdoor clerks will not be legally qualified and therefore will not be in a position to give you the sort of back-up service that an articled clerk or the solicitor would.

When you are in conference with the client and the solicitor is present there are several points that are important to bear in mind. Do not appear to be having some private dialogue with the solicitor to the exclusion of the client. It is the client's case. It is the client who has come to you for advice. You will probably know the solicitor and it can be very easy to slip into a conversation that could exclude the client. Try to ensure that you address the client rather than the instructing solicitor during the conference.

In some circumstances there may be a matter that you regard as technical, or a matter that your client could or would not understand, which needs to be discussed in the absence of the client. If this is the case, ensure that you explain to the client what you are doing and why there is no need for him or her to be present for this particular discussion.

As has already been said, it is the solicitor who first meets the client, who drafts counsel's instructions, and who very often will have formed his or her own view of the case and given the client preliminary advice on the matter. You may find that you disagree with some or all of the conclusions that the solicitor has reached. It is obviously your professional duty to convey to the client what your own particular judgement is on the matter. If your opinion differs from that of the solicitor, this can create difficulties, particularly if the solicitor has already expressed his or her view to the client. The client may prefer the solicitor's view. The client may lose confidence in both advisers if they cannot agree. The solicitor may feel undermined. You may feel constrained in some way. In short, it is likely that the conference will proceed on an uncomfortable footing for all parties involved. You must make every attempt to defuse this type of situation. For example, telephone the solicitor before the conference and let him or her know of your preliminary conclusions. If this is not possible, make sure you have an opportunity to speak to him or her in the absence of the client before the conference begins. (See **Chapter 7**.)

A client may often feel confused, and sometimes aggrieved, by the fact that he or she is obliged to have two legal representatives. If the solicitor has gained the client's confidence, taken their instructions, and drafted, for example, a witness statement, an affidavit, or proof of evidence, the idea that the client has to go through it all again with a complete stranger can sometimes cause resentment and/or anxiety. The client may feel comfortable with the relationship that he or she has developed with his or her solicitor and simply be unable to understand why there is a need for your involvement at all. It is important that you ensure that the client fully understands what your role is and why there is a need for your involvement. (See **Chapter 4**.)

In all circumstances, however, it is obviously important to ensure that both the client and the solicitor have had the opportunity to state their views and ask you any questions during the conference. It is equally important to ensure that at the end of the conference both the client and the solicitor are confident that they clearly understand the outcome. (See **Chapter 8**.)

3.4 The professional non-client

In the course of representing a client, in addition to the client himself or herself and your instructing solicitor, there will usually be a range of other professionals who will be involved, to some extent at least, with the client's case and to whom you should give consideration at certain stages in the proceedings. Therefore, as well as thinking about the needs of your client, you need to be aware that the involvement of others can also affect the conduct of the case. You should consider what, if any, impact they might have on the effectiveness of conducting your case. At every stage of the proceedings it is important to ensure that your client knows what you are doing; therefore, if, for example, you do feel it necessary to have a private interchange with your opponent or, perhaps, the court clerk, tell the client what you are doing and why. It can be very off-putting for a client if you suddenly disappear to talk to someone else and they are unaware of what your purpose for doing this is.

3.4.1 Your opponent

Apart from your client, the person with whom you are likely to have most involvement during the case is your opponent. Your ability to respond effectively to your opponent during the course of representing your client is of the utmost importance. Establishing a professional and amicable relationship with your opponent usually ensures that you are best able to represent your client and enable the case to proceed in the most appropriate way. The concept of the stereotypical barrister engaging in 'robing room tactics' to bluff or bully an opponent into taking a certain course of action is something better left to the movies. You should remember that the Bar is a small world and reputations (good or bad) are easily acquired but not so easily lost. The reality is that getting the best result for your client is almost always achieved by tact and diplomacy and good communication skills. The reputation you should strive to acquire, from your first case, is that you are approachable, reasonable, realistic, straightforward, and, at all times, ethical.

A good illustration of the sort of dealing that you will have with an opponent is, of course, negotiation, a skill which you use frequently throughout your professional life. Many cases settle, some at the eleventh hour and often at the door of the court. In others you may be specifically instructed to negotiate a settlement on behalf of your client. For example, an illustration of the type of circumstance that may require a negotiation at the door of the court could be a case in which you are instructed to represent a client who is seeking an injunction against a neighbour on the basis of the tort of nuisance. On the face of it, there is clearly a legal right to enforce but, as is often the case with neighbour disputes, rather than invoke the full legal process, you advise your client that it may be possible to settle the dispute another way that may, in the event, be much more appropriate. If your client agrees, it will be your duty to attempt to negotiate a compromise, such as an agreement in the form of undertakings given by either or both parties that can then be placed before the court.

You may be specifically instructed to negotiate a settlement on behalf of your client. For example, your instructions may be to negotiate a financial settlement between divorcing parties in an attempt to settle, out of court, the ancillary relief and property adjustment claims for your client and thereby obviate the need for a full-blown hearing. In such circumstances, a successful negotiation may not only save your client costs, but will also remove a great deal of the stress that such a court hearing would probably mean. Importantly, if there are children involved, a solution that saves a 'fight' in court will have enormous benefits.

You must always be aware, however, that the rules of professional conduct apply equally to every negotiation that you are instructed to conduct on behalf of your client. When advising your client about the prospects of a negotiated settlement you must ensure that the client is fully aware of, and agrees to, this course of action (see **Chapter 8**) and that you conduct the negotiation professionally and ethically.

In addition to negotiation, you should be aware that, during a contested case in court, many procedural or evidential issues that arise can properly be agreed between counsel prior to and during the hearing itself. Therefore, good relations between counsel are essential if you are going to represent your client effectively. For example, the following can be made between counsel: an agreement to admit a piece of evidence which is technically hearsay; an agreement not to challenge a procedural irregularity; an agreement about what evidence can be led; an agreement as to the order in which certain evidence is to be adduced. (See also *Evidence* manual and *Criminal Litigation and Sentencing* manual.) In effect, counsel are in the position to negotiate between themselves, within the rules of professional conduct, how the proceedings will be conducted. The absence of such agreement between the parties will usually mean that the case is protracted and more adversarial than necessary, and consequently may result in a disservice to your client.

One other area that needs to be considered in this context is the complicated subject of what is colloquially known as 'plea bargaining'. In certain cases it is not unheard of, for example, for the prosecution to indicate to defence counsel that he or she might be prepared to consider dropping the more serious charge on the indictment if the defendant pleads guilty to the lesser offence, or for defence counsel to seek an indication from the prosecution that if his or her client were to consider pleading guilty to the lesser offence, the more serious charge might be dropped. The professional conduct and ethical issues involved in this area are extremely complex, and it is not the function or within the scope of this manual to address them in any depth. However, when representing a client, you should be aware that this sort of situation can arise and you should equip yourself to deal appropriately with it should it occur in your practice. (For further information, see *Professional Ethics* manual, *Advocacy* manual, and *Criminal Litigation and Sentencing* manual.)

3.4.2   The court clerk

When appearing in front of lay magistrates, remember that the Bench will be directed on the law by the court clerk. It is always useful, therefore, to ensure that you establish good working relations with the court clerk and that you are in a position to have a constructive dialogue with him or her on matters pertinent to your client's case.

3.4.3   The court usher

Very often the court usher is the person who can most readily assist you and your client at the courtroom in the most practical of ways. If you have established a good rapport with the court usher, this can often make proceedings much more comfortable for your client, especially as at many magistrates' courts and County Courts you are likely to find the atmosphere less than favourable and the facilities rather limited. The court usher is the person who may be able to find you a quiet corner in which to conduct your conference (in some courts something of a luxury), who may be able to change the running order on the list of cases to be heard to give you a little more (and often much-needed) time with your client before the appearance. There will be occasions when you will need a photocopier, or want to make an urgent telephone call in private, and it is for these kinds of facilities that you will often be reliant upon the court usher. Therefore, it is easy to see that a very sound principle to adopt is to make sure that you and the court usher have established a good working relationship.

Your opponent, the clerk, and the usher are some of the other professionals you will encounter in your role as counsel for your client. It is important to remember that when acting for your client, if you are confident in your own communication skills and able to adapt these to meet the specific needs of other individuals who may be involved in some way with the proceedings, you will be in a much better position to ensure that you conduct your client's case in the most efficient and effective way possible. While it is not possible to set out a comprehensive list of all the people whom you are likely to have dealings with during the course of any case, the following list includes some of the most obvious:

- police;
- court welfare officer;
- probation officer;
- non-opponent barrister;
- gaoler.

3.5 The non-professional non-client

In some circumstances you will be required to deal with other people who are relevant to the conduct of your client's case, but who are not professionals and not your client. For example, you may have to take details from someone who is offering to be surety for bail for your client. In these circumstances, you must apply the same general principles as you would to every client conference and ensure that you communicate with him or her courteously and sensitively, question him or her appropriately, and make sure that he or she fully understands the implications and consequences of what he or she has agreed to do. (See also *Criminal Litigation and Sentencing* manual and *Advocacy* manual.)

A less easy situation, but one of which you should be aware, is dealing with friends or relations of the client who feel that they have some kind of interest in the case or right to voice their opinion on the matter. Often friends and relatives turn up at court (or in chambers) and expect to participate in the proceedings. Unlike the client conference in chambers where you can usually exclude the friend or relative (see **3.2.3.6**), at court it is sometimes difficult to remove those people whom you would wish to exclude. Unless the hearing is 'in private' (eg an application for a non-molestation injunction), the public is admitted to the proceedings and you will have no choice in the matter. In circumstances where a third party is disruptive, or sometimes even abusive to you about the way in which you are advising the client or conducting the case, you will have to take a firm but polite stance and ensure that you control the intervention of the third party if it is obviously counterproductive. (See **Chapter 7**.)

3.6 The expert witness

Counsel is permitted to interview and/or settle the report of an expert witness. Such interviews are frequently conducted at chambers, although a meeting 'on site' or discussions at court are commonplace. It should be noted that the rules relating to expert evidence and case management are to be found mainly in the rules of procedure and evidence. Reference should be made to the Civil Procedure Rules (CPR) 1998, Parts 32 and 35, and generally to Part 28.

The extent of any discussion with an expert witness is likely to vary, depending on such factors as the complexity of the case, whether the party has already prepared his or her report, and/or whether you are in possession of the other party's expert report. The following is therefore only a general guide to the matters that you may need to cover during a conference with an expert witness:

(a) his or her professional qualifications;

(b) the extent of his or her experience generally (eg surveyor for 20 years);

(c) the extent of his or her experience/expertise in the specific field or area which is relevant to your case (eg last 10 years spent as surveyor in Hampstead);

(d) the extent to which he or she has authority in that field/area (eg whether he or she has written any books/articles on the subject, or whether he or she is considered a 'maverick' by other members of the profession);

(e) details of the standard works in the area of his or her expertise;

(f) his or her knowledge and use of approved, up-to-date techniques, and an explanation of such techniques;

(g) a definition of any relevant technical terms;

(h) the information or facts which were: known to him or her at the time he or she carried out the relevant inspection/test/examination; or assumed by him or her at the time; or unknown to him or her at the time; and

 • the extent to which such assumed or absent facts (may have) affected his or her calculations or influenced his or her judgement;

 • the nature of the inspection/test/examination carried out by him or her;

(i) his or her opinion and the basis for that opinion;

(j) the consistency of his or her opinion with the facts and whether any other theory is equally consistent with the facts;

(k) any hypothesis based on another set of facts, such as what he or she would have expected to find if 'X' and 'Y' existed instead of 'A' and 'B' (eg if a seat belt had not been worn, the extent and type of injury which he or she would have expected to find);

(l) further detail or expansion of his or her opinion—for example, if an expert medical witness states that 'the claimant has a 20 per cent chance of developing arthritis within the next 10 years', you will probably want to know:

 • what the ordinary risks would have been were it not for this injury;

 • the risks of developing arthritis over a long period;

 • if the arthritis develops, in what manner is it likely to affect the claimant—pain, suffering, loss of amenity, earning capacity/handicap on the labour market;

 • treatment at that stage;

 • the long-term prognosis if arthritis does develop within 10 years;

(m) the strength of the expert's conviction or belief in his or her opinion;

(n) the weaknesses, if any, in your case and how you could/should deal with them;

(o) any further material facts in his or her possession which may assist or harm your case;

(p) in respect of the other party's expert report:

- whether he or she knows the other expert;

- details of the other expert's qualifications, experience, and authority within the profession;

- his or her view of the other expert's opinion—identify any areas of agreement between them and, where a divergence of opinion occurs, the reasons for this; the flaws in the other expert's evidence; the unreliability of any tests/examination carried out by the other expert; the falsity of any premise relied upon by the other expert; the strength of his or her disagreement with the other expert's opinion;

(q) illustrative aids such as diagrams or charts, which the expert ought to prepare for use in court;

(r) preparing the expert to give evidence—whether he or she has given evidence before; how he or she should give his or her evidence, for example by avoiding too much technicality. (See *Evidence* manual.)

3.7 A potential witness

The new Code of Conduct does not prescribe what permissible contact barristers may have with witnesses. The former guidance was set out in Section 3, Miscellaneous Guidance, Written Standards for the Conduct of Professional Work. It explicitly permitted counsel to introduce himself or herself to a witness, explain the court's procedure to that witness, and answer any questions that the witness might have in relation to the hearing. It is suggested that this remains the position under the new Code. In addition, counsel has a duty to ensure that those unfamiliar with court procedure, especially those who are nervous or vulnerable, are put as much at ease as possible. Barristers are advised that in conducting any interchange with witnesses they must always remember that the 'guiding principle must be the obligation of counsel to promote and protect his lay client's best interests so far as that is consistent with the law and with counsel's overriding duty to the court' (Written Standards for the Conduct of Professional Work, para 6.2.3).

Interviewing a potential witness presents more difficulties. There is no rule that prevents a barrister from taking a witness statement in civil cases. However, save in exceptional circumstances, a barrister who has taken witness statements (rather than settling statements prepared by others) should not act as counsel in the case. In contested criminal cases in the Crown Court, it was the case that, save in exceptional circumstances, it was 'wholly inappropriate for a barrister . . . to interview any potential witness' (Written Standards for the Conduct of Professional Work, para 6.3.1). If such an interview is exceptionally conducted, that fact was to be disclosed to all other parties in the case before the witness is called and 'a written record must also be made of the substance of the interview and the reason for it' (Written Standards for the Conduct of Professional Work, para 6.3.4). It is suggested that this will remain the expectation for self-employed barristers. In practice, the need to interview a potential witness arises most frequently when counsel is briefed to attend a magistrates' court or a County Court in the absence of his or her professional client or representative. Should you find yourself in this position, where practicable, it is courteous to inform your opponent of the necessity to interview a potential witness yourself. It may be necessary to inform the court of your difficulties, for example when you need more time to conduct the interview. Most courts are sympathetic to such requests and will usually grant a short adjournment.

There are several important points to remember if you find yourself in the position of conducting an interview with a potential witness (see rC9, Code of Conduct, see **9.6 Conferences with witnesses**, and also see *Professional Ethics* manual):

(a) Do not interview a potential witness in the presence of your lay client or any other (potential) witnesses.

(b) Do take a written note of the witness's account, or alternatively provide the witness with a series of written questions and ask him or her to provide the answers in writing. Avoid an attempt to elicit and retain oral information. If the witness changes his or her account in the witness box, you are risking the subsequent wrath of both your lay client and your instructing solicitor, who will want to know why on earth you called that witness. In these circumstances, therefore, a written proof of evidence provides you with (i) a measure of self-protection and (ii) a clear reminder of what the witness will say.

(c) Do not ask leading questions or put words into a potential witness's mouth. You should elicit the information as if you were conducting an examination-in-chief.

(d) Do invite the potential witness to sign his or her proof of evidence, whether you have taken a written note or provided him or her with a series of questions.

(e) Do use your judgement in deciding whether or not to call a potential witness to give evidence. Just because you have taken a proof of evidence, this does not mean that you have to call that person—unless you are satisfied that calling him or her will assist, not harm, your case.

(f) If you decide to call that person as a witness, do ensure that you are clear about the issues on which he or she can assist you.

3.8 Conclusion

You should recognise from this chapter the importance of giving consideration to the individual needs of the wide range of clients whom you can expect to encounter in your career. Also, there is a need to consider a range of others, professional or non-professional, who may, in some way, be participants in the proceedings. You need to be in a position to make a legal judgement, and also to understand the emotional and psychological needs of the client so that you can pursue his or her best interests. The information you obtain at the conference stage is vital to the conduct of your client's whole case. If you are successful in creating an atmosphere of mutual trust and respect, the client is likely to respond accordingly and participate fully in the conference. If you are successful in creating professional and amicable relationships with others who have a role in the proceedings, you will ensure that the proceedings are conducted in an efficient and productive atmosphere.

Meeting the client—conducting the conference

4.1 Introduction

The first meeting between you and the client is obviously of tremendous importance. This meeting will provide the basis of the working relationship that you and your client will develop throughout your professional involvement. It will also provide the necessary framework for the effective conduct of the case. It is often said that first impressions are important, and this is particularly true in relation to the client conference. As we have seen, clients will invariably be nervous. They will often be in a location that is completely unfamiliar to them; they will be frightened at the prospect of the unknown consequences of the predicament they are in; they will frequently be in awe of you, the barrister, and fearful of appearing foolish; and, for a variety of reasons, they may sometimes be reluctant to be interviewed at all.

In addition to thorough preparation and planning for the conference (see **Chapter 5**), which will ensure that the client's legal problem is adequately addressed, it is also necessary to give careful consideration to the most appropriate method of meeting the client and putting him or her at ease. There are a number of factors that can influence both the conduct of the conference itself and the manner that you decide to adopt with the client. At the outset, however, you should remember that the benefits of creating a positive first impression are immeasurable for both you and the client. It is the atmosphere that you create that will be a major factor in assisting the client to overcome some of his or her fears, dispelling any preconceived notions he or she might have of aloof barristers, and giving him or her confidence in your ability. If you succeed in gaining the client's confidence at the start, the conference will be much more effective and the objectives (yours and the client's) of the conference much more readily achieved.

4.2 Location of the conference

You will need to give consideration to where the conference is taking place. The location in which you conduct the interview with the client will, of course, influence both (a) your planning for the conference and (b) the way in which you conduct the conference. The most commonly perceived notion of the conference is the one conducted in your chambers: you will have received the papers in good time and you will have had ample opportunity to prepare for the first meeting with the client. This is not always so, however, and, in fact, is seldom the case for a newly qualified barrister, who will be required to meet, interview, and advise clients in conference in a variety of circumstances. As well as contending with difficult circumstances and adverse surroundings, you may have to conduct the conference with the client in the absence of any, or any adequate, instructions (see **Chapter 1**). In the early years of practice, it is not unusual to conduct a conference:

- in a crowded and noisy corridor of a magistrates' court;
- through the bars of a prison cell;
- on the steps of a courtroom;
- in an interview room beside the cells;
- in a room begged from a friendly court usher.

Therefore, you should recognise that in addition to solving the client's legal dilemma, you will often have to contend with less-than-favourable circumstances in which to conduct the conference. Whatever the circumstances surrounding the location of the conference, it is necessary to ensure that adequate consideration is given to making the most of the conditions, in a way that will best reassure your client and put him or her as much at ease as possible.

4.2.1 Conference in chambers

If you are conducting the conference in your chambers, you are usually in the best position to ensure the atmosphere you create on first meeting the client is one that is appropriate in all the circumstances. You will have control of the environment and it is up to you to decide in what manner you wish to proceed. Some of the things that can assist a productive meeting with the client may be obvious, others less so. It may appear to be somewhat simplistic to suggest that common courtesy should be observed at all times, but regrettably, in the light of the experience of many clients, it is a message which cannot be stressed strongly enough. Perhaps this is best summed up in the words of Latham J (as he then was):

> The rules are in a sense rules which can be boiled down to being considerate, being understanding, remembering that you are a professional trying to help somebody, not somebody trying to show off your own knowledge and ability.

(*Advocacy, Negotiation and Conference Skills Manual*, Bar Vocational Course, 1989–95)

In planning the best approach, the following are some points that you should try to remember.

(a) Inform your clerk of the time the conference is scheduled to take place. Tell the clerk the name of the client, the solicitor, and of any other person who may attend with the client. In this way, you can be sure that, when the client arrives, he or she is expected at the chambers and dealt with appropriately and courteously.

(b) Try to make sure you go and meet the client and show him or her into your room. If a client is shown into your room and you remain firmly seated behind your desk, even if you are diligently involved in the preparation of the case, this could come across as unfriendly, thoughtless, and even rude. Remember that the prospect of this meeting is likely to have created anxiety for the client in any event, and anything that can alleviate that anxiety will assist the client in settling down more easily.

(c) Introduce yourself clearly. Ensure that the client knows exactly who you are and what your role in the proceedings is (see **4.3.1**). You may well recall incidents that you yourself have experienced (eg, being referred to a medical specialist by your GP) when the professional whom you consulted failed even to tell you their name, let alone explain their involvement in your affairs in sufficient detail to make you feel comfortable. If the client is absolutely clear about who you are and the nature of your involvement in the case, you will usually gain his or her confidence early on in the proceedings.

(d) It is always appropriate to attempt to put the client at ease, and this can be done in a number of ways. It is up to you to think about what method best suits you and clearly what you actually do will, to a large extent, be influenced by the exact nature of the client and the circumstances of the case. You should have some information in your instructions that may give you some clues in this respect. However, try not to leap straight into talking about the case. Give the client a little time to settle down and recover his or her composure. For example, ask whether the client had a reasonable journey, found chambers easily, and so on. You may have some information in your instructions which can assist in this respect; for example, if you know the client has young children, ask who is taking care of them while the client is at the conference with you. As the client invariably will be nervous and may have travelled some distance for the conference with you, check whether he or she would like a cup of tea or a glass of water. It would also be helpful to check whether the client would like to use the lavatory. Embarrassment can often be caused if the client has to ask you for these facilities.

(e) Try to arrange your room in a way that will make the client feel most comfortable. Many clients leave the conference with the impression that they have been interrogated in a manner more akin to a cross-examination than an interview with their legal representative. Think about the seating arrangements. With a little forethought, for example in relation to arranging the furniture, you can ensure that the client does not feel they are being put through the 'third degree'. Do you need to sit behind your impressive desk? It may make you feel important, but it is more than likely that the client will feel disadvantaged by the barrier that is created between you.

(f) If possible, attempt to clear your desk. We are all familiar with the image of a successful barrister seated at a desk surrounded by masses of briefs piled high. It may be that this will indicate to your colleagues that you have plenty of work, but for the client it can be extremely off-putting. Remember that you deal with a variety of legal problems every day of your working life, but for the client the conference with you will often be their first encounter with the law and the resolution of their problem the most important thing to them. The client needs to be reassured that you too recognise how important their case is. Anything that you can do to underline the fact that this client, and his or her case, has your undivided attention will certainly assist in creating good relations between you.

(g) Ensure that you (or someone else) take the client's coat and anything else he or she may be carrying. Difficulty and embarrassment can be caused if the client is uncertain where to put his or her belongings. This may sound obvious, but it is surprising how many barristers leave the client feeling stranded and awkward with their coat, briefcase, and carrier bags piled on their lap or around their feet.

(h) Your instructing solicitor (or solicitor's representative) will need somewhere to sit in order to take a note of the conference. Make sure that there is a place for him or her to do this that is comfortable and spacious enough for the job which has to be done. You and the solicitor are part of a team and will be working together on behalf of the client. It may be that your solicitor does not attend the conference and that the client is accompanied by an articled clerk (or outdoor clerk) from the firm. Although, in these circumstances, the solicitor's representative may not have any direct input into the conference, he or she will need to take a note and report back to the solicitor on matters which have been discussed and on which further action needs to be taken. Whoever accompanies the client to the conference, it is important that consideration is given to their needs and that the client is reassured that you are all working together on his or her behalf.

(i) When the conference is under way, try to ensure that you are not unnecessarily interrupted. Inform your colleagues (especially if you share a room) that you have a conference. If it is possible, divert any telephone calls until the conference is finished and turn off your mobile telephone!

4.2.2 Conference outside chambers

As we have seen, the conference in chambers is generally within your control and you are able to ensure that attention is paid to the various aspects that assist in putting the client at ease at the start of the conference. The reality of practice, however, particularly in the early years, is that many conferences take place outside chambers and in locations that are not conducive to conducting an effective client conference. Not only is the location itself likely to create some difficulties for you, but it is usually the case that there will also be a restriction on the amount of time you have available for conducting the conference. It is easy to recognise that these factors, which are outside your control, can add to the stress and anxiety of the client. There is no magical panacea or instant solution to many of the problems that you may encounter when conducting a conference outside chambers, but there are some general suggestions that could assist you in resolving some of the difficulties.

Many of the points referred to previously in relation to conducting the conference in chambers are, of course, equally applicable to the effectiveness of the conference wherever it is being held. The important thing to remember is that, whatever the location and whatever the potential difficulties, you should endeavour to put the client at ease. At all times you should remember to:

- observe common courtesies;
- introduce yourself properly;
- ensure the client is as comfortable as possible;
- make the best of the location you are in.

4.2.3 Conference at court

It is common to be instructed to attend court and meet the client prior to representing him or her at the hearing, which has been fixed for that day. This means that you will meet the client for the first time at the court, hold a conference, and take instructions for the case on the spot. Even if you are familiar with the court, it is recommended that you should observe the following suggestions.

4.2.3.1 Time of arrival at court

Arrive at the court in good time and preferably be there before your client arrives. There is nothing more off-putting to the client than seeing his or her barrister come rushing in at the last moment. In order for you to give the client confidence, you must ensure that you give the appearance of being calm and in control of the situation. By arriving in advance of the client you can ensure that you have all the information that you require for the conference, some of which will need to be conveyed to the client, and much of which will assist in reassuring them (and you) that the situation is under control. For example:

(a) Make sure that you have all the relevant papers for the conference and the court appearance. It is always useful to have a little time to check that you are in possession of every document that you need. By the same token, you can remind yourself of any gaps or conflicts in your instructions which need to be cleared up with the client in the conference. Remember that the conference at court usually involves taking the client's instructions, advising them on the merits of the case, and then representing them in court.

(b) Decide if there are any other necessary documents or materials that you may need. For example, do you need to find or photocopy any relevant authorities? Are there any pro forma documents that you may need to fill in and which can be collected from the court before the client arrives?

(c) Check with the court list the time of the hearing and in which court you are scheduled to appear. This information is obviously important for two main reasons: first, the client will be reassured to know the precise details of what is about to happen and when; and, second, you need to know how much time there is available for the conference itself.

(d) Discover which judge you will be appearing before. It can be invaluable to the conduct of your case if you know in advance who will hear you and whether that particular judge has any 'foibles' of which you should be aware. Again, if you can give the client an insight into the particular tribunal, it can assist in putting him or her more at ease. It is useful to remind yourself that as well as meeting you for the first time in conference, the client will have the daunting prospect of probably having to give evidence, which will more than likely be uppermost in his or her mind and causing anxiety. For example, if you are appearing on behalf of a client who is seeking a non-molestation injunction and you are able to tell her that the judge who will hear the case is 'very sympathetic and likes to hear full evidence from the applicant, but a stickler for procedure', or 'this judge usually deals with matters in a very informal way and it may be that you will not have to give evidence at all', the client will at least have some idea of what to expect when going into court.

(e) If appropriate, make contact with your opponent. As we have seen, good relations with your opponent are helpful to the smooth conduct of the case. It may be that the matter is something that is appropriate for some kind of agreement before the case is heard, for example settling an injunction application by way of undertakings; or you might need to agree upon what evidence is admissible, or a point of procedure, and so on. If you can 'test the water' prior to meeting and taking instructions from your client, your conference will usually be more productive, although you must always remember that any contact with your opponent must be conducted in accordance with the Code of Conduct. It is your client who will instruct you after you have elicited the necessary information and given him or her your considered advice on the matter.

(f) You may have identified the need for further information from your solicitor, or you may need an update on your instructions before meeting the client. In some circumstances, you may need advice from someone in chambers on an ethical point about which you are unsure. Being at court well before the conference will give you the opportunity to make any last-minute checks that are necessary prior to conference. If you are confident that you are in control of all the detail, you will be best placed to create a good impression with the client when you meet him or her.

(g) Make contact with the court usher and inform him or her who you are, the name of the case, who you are representing, and who your opponent is. You may need to hand in any authorities on which you intend to rely, or inform the usher of the sort of timescale you anticipate the hearing will take. If you decide that you need more time before the court appearance either to take fuller instructions from your client or to make an attempt to settle the matter with the other side, tell the usher. In these circumstances, it is the usher who will often be most helpful to you and, therefore, the smooth running of the case.

4.2.3.2   Finding somewhere to sit and talk

Try to find a room where you can conduct the conference with your client, or at the very least somewhere where you and the client can sit down to talk. Again, it is often the case that it is the court usher who can most usefully assist in this respect. If you have established good relations with the usher your life can often be made much easier. In some courts, however, finding a room for the conference is something of a luxury, but if you can, the client will clearly feel much more comfortable, especially in circumstances where the matters involved are particularly sensitive. If a room is not available, then you should attempt to find a quiet corner where you can talk about the case with the minimum disruption. You should be aware, however, of the difficulties that can arise when you are obliged to discuss the case 'in public', as it were. A client who is already extremely anxious about the impending proceedings may feel much less able to be forthcoming if she or he feels there is a possibility of being overheard. Many clients tend to feel confused in circumstances where there is little privacy and they are surrounded by a lot of noise. It is also useful to remind yourself that, as frequently occurs, the 'other side' may be only yards away from you and your client. This is something that can be very intimidating, especially if the matter is of, say, a domestic nature. There are no easy solutions to the problems that can arise when conducting the conference in these circumstances, as the business in hand clearly has to proceed. However, if you are aware of the difficulties, make every effort to reassure the client that you recognise how awkward the situation is, show that you empathise with him or her, and underline that you are there to represent his or her interests, you should be able to instil confidence in the client. From your own point of view, you should also be aware of the dangers of discussing the case within the hearing of a potential witness.

4.2.3.3   Knowing the geography of the court

Check where the tea bar is located, or where the nearest cafe or restaurant to the court is. Your client will usually appreciate a cup of tea and, if the case is likely to last for the day, then the client will probably want some sort of meal. If the client is accompanied to court by friends or relations, it is useful to know where to send them to wait (as appropriate) for the conference to be completed, or the court appearance to take place. Knowing a little of the geography of the court or the locality in which the court is situated is invariably useful.

4.2.3.4   Other people involved in conducting the case

Make sure that you introduce the client to anyone else who is involved in the conduct of their case. In the hustle and bustle of a normal court, where there are usually a lot of other people involved in many different matters, it can sometimes be difficult for the client to know who precisely is doing what. Your client needs to be clearly informed about who is involved in the case and what role that person has. For example, the client may have dealt directly with only one partner at the firm of solicitors and if, for some reason, that person is unavailable to be present, explain the role of the representative who is in attendance.

4.2.3.5 What to take with you

Go equipped. This may sound obvious, but it is useful to remind yourself that you will need to take a note, the client may need to write out a statement, or draw a diagram for you, and so on. So take spare pens, highlighters, and paper—bringing their own will probably be the last thing on the client's mind. Think about any materials that you could usefully take with you to assist in the conference. Each case will have its own specific requirements, of course, but, for example, if the case involves an accident, a map of the location will usually be useful. If you recognise that the emotions may run high in any particular case, arm yourself with the sorts of things which may help the client: have a spare handkerchief, change for the telephone, and so on. Again, this may sound all too obvious, but many barristers do not give sufficient consideration to the sorts of things that can, and do, make the conference run more smoothly.

4.2.4 Conference with a client in custody

There will be occasions when your client is in custody when the conference takes place. The client may have been arrested the previous evening and kept overnight in police cells. If this is the case, he or she will usually be transported to the relevant magistrates' court and placed in the cells at court. In other circumstances, your client could already be on remand and to conduct the conference you will need to go to the prison where he or she is being held. In this type of situation, you obviously have no control whatsoever over the environment and will have to make do with whatever facilities the prison or court officials choose to provide for you. Whatever facilities are available, however, you should reasonably assume that conducting a conference with a client who is in custody brings with it additional constraints and tensions. You will need to be particularly aware of the impact that the surroundings are likely to have on your client and to do your best to compensate for the strains of the location.

The best scenario is that you will in fact be permitted to use an interview room that is quiet and where you are able to meet the client in a reasonable degree of privacy. While the atmosphere is likely to be less than pleasant and furnishings usually meagre, you should at least have somewhere to sit and take instructions.

The worst scenario arises when you have to conduct the conference with your client through the grille in the door of a cell. The most you can see of your client will be his or her head and shoulders, you will usually both be standing up, there may be another prisoner in the same cell as your client, there are usually several other prisoners in the same situation and in very close proximity, and there are gaolers patrolling the cells. With all this going on, you will also need to take a note of your client's instructions. More often than not the client's first and only concern is when you are going to get him or her out of there. In these circumstances, gaining the client's confidence, creating a favourable impression, and eliciting the necessary information is clearly far from easy. To assist you in this task, you obviously need to follow some of the basic rules that are applicable to every client conference: introduce yourself properly; explain your role clearly; reassure the client that you are on his or her side and want to resolve his or her dilemma as effectively as possible; and ensure that the client understands that you will only be able to assist him or her if you are fully informed of all the relevant circumstances. In addition, you must also be aware of the strain that is usually put on people by being in custody. You should recognise that it is perfectly normal for a person in this situation to display a range of emotions (especially anger, often even hostility, and sometimes depression); to have very strong feelings about a particular issue which may or may not be relevant to the actual case (concern, for example, about the well-being of a partner or children); and often to be reluctant to cooperate fully with the central issue of the case (being more concerned with being released than with talking about what plea he or she will enter, or making any relevant decisions about the next steps to be taken).

If you are alert to some of the difficulties that you may encounter when conducting a conference with a client who is in custody, you will be in a better position to equip yourself to deal with these. Again, there is no magic formula that can realistically be offered as to exactly what to do—this will be a matter for your own judgement in each and every case. But there are a few points that it may be helpful to remember:

- Do not be surprised at the client's reaction or overreaction to the circumstances.
- Expect the client to be angry.
- Expect the client to be set on pursuing matters which may seem irrelevant to you.
- Be flexible.
- Reassure the client at all times that you are on his or her side.
- Remain non-judgemental.

4.2.5   Conclusion

In summary, the location in which you find yourself will be an important factor in determining the most effective way of conducting any particular client conference. You will have to be flexible and adaptable to meet the individual needs of your client in whatever circumstances you find yourself. There are ways in which you can alleviate some of the difficulties that you will encounter in this respect. If you have given adequate consideration to where the conference will be held and what, if any, method can be adopted to ensure that the client is as comfortable as possible in those particular surroundings, you can be confident that you will have the best possible start to the meeting with your client.

4.3   Conducting the conference

This chapter is concerned with meeting the client in conference and how best to put the client at ease. In addition to giving consideration to the location of the conference, it is also necessary to determine what other factors may be relevant to ensuring that the conference is conducted in the most effective manner possible. There are a number of issues that can be identified as being important in this respect. It should be emphasised here that the elements that make up the main content of the conference—case preparation, questioning, giving advice, ethical considerations—are considered in detail separately in the chapters that follow. Thus, for the purposes of this chapter on the conduct of the conference, those elements are not specifically addressed. It would, however, be proper to remind you that, taking any conference as a whole, all the elements that contribute to a satisfactory conference will need to be drawn together.

Consideration has already been given to the general principles applicable to any client conference (**Chapter 2**); the individual client (**Chapter 3**); and the various locations in which a conference might take place (**4.2**). What follows is intended to assist you in devising methods that will help you conduct the conference in a structured and efficient way, and in a way which will ensure that the client is put at ease and feels confident in your ability to conduct his or her case to the expected professional standard.

4.3.1   Your introduction

As has already been said, common courtesy dictates that you should introduce yourself properly at the first meeting with any client in conference. To take this further, it means telling your client what your name is. Whether you use your first name and surname is a matter for you, but it can be a little off-putting to a client if you say 'My name is Mr Smith', rather than 'My name is John Smith.' The former can sound distant, formal, and potentially unfriendly; the latter tends to reassure the client that you are a human being. If you are attempting to create a relaxed atmosphere for a nervous client, it is usually preferable to tell the client your full name. It is also advisable to explain to the client what your role in the proceedings will be. Be aware that a simple announcement such as 'I am your barrister in this case' may also create difficulties for some clients. Many clients will be entirely unaware of precisely what a barrister does and why a barrister has to be involved in the case at all, and will not have a clear idea of the distinction between a barrister and a solicitor. You will have to judge each client individually when you are deciding how best to explain the purpose of your involvement. Obviously, a company director who is coming to you for specialist advice will be fully aware of the part you will play in their case. Similarly, a client with more than a fleeting acquaintance with the criminal justice system will be all too familiar with what 'my brief' is there to do. These are two obvious extremes, but try to remember that many clients will not know what your role is and, to be made to feel more comfortable, will desire an explanation. If you think the client is unclear, the best thing to do is to ask them whether they would like an explanation from you about that particular point.

By the same token, at the introduction stage, it is important to check that you have got your client's name right and that you pronounce it correctly. It can be more than discouraging for clients if their legal representative does not address them properly. In many circumstances it is appropriate (and courteous) to ask the client what he or she would prefer to be called. This is especially important when you are instructed to represent a client who is a member of an ethnic minority, or someone from abroad (see **Chapter 11**).

4.3.2   Getting started

After the formalities of the introduction you will have to consider how best to proceed with the conference itself. It is again important to stress that it is impossible to prescribe a 'right way' to start off the interview, but there are some points which it will be useful to bear in mind when deciding where to begin. Exactly how to start will depend on many different factors: the nature of the case; the time available; the particular client involved; the knowledge (or lack of it) that you have gleaned from the instructions; whether the solicitor is present; and so on. But there are some general principles that are applicable to almost every conference. Most clients will invariably want to know the following:

- Can I win?
- What are my chances?
- What if I lose?

- What, if any, are the alternatives?
- How much will it cost me?

However, some clients are unable to recognise (or articulate) what it is that they actually want. It will be up to you, at the outset, to ensure that you set up the conference in a framework that the client will readily understand and in a way that will enable him or her to be confident that you will address the issues that are his or her main concern.

Structuring the conference in a sensible way has two major advantages. First, you will invariably be limited to a great extent by the amount of time you have in which to conduct the whole conference. Thinking in advance of the best order in which to deal with all the matters that need to be addressed should enable you to manage your time more efficiently. The key to this is case preparation. In advance of any conference you should have already (inter alia): identified the relevant legal issues involved in the case; evaluated the facts in relation to the legal issues; given consideration (if you have sufficient information) to the personality of the client; and decided what further information you need to elicit from the client. (For further detail, see **Chapter 5**.) This analysis should provide you with a firm idea of what you need to know and in what order you can most usefully deal with all the issues involved. If you have a clear idea of the shape the conference is going to take, you can usually ensure that you have all relevant matters under your control and have a logical framework to follow to ensure the conference is kept on the right track.

Second, if the client can see that you have a clear agenda for your meeting, which in large measure concurs with his or her perception of the conference, he or she will be immediately reassured that you are, in fact, on top of the case. At the start of the conference, the client should be confident that you have:

- read the papers and are fully familiar with the case;
- clearly identified his or her areas of concern;
- recognised his or her needs and expectations of the conference; and
- decided on an appropriate order in which to deal with the issues.

If the client is informed of the manner in which you intend to conduct the conference, he or she is invariably going to be more relaxed and more amenable to providing you with the necessary information, and the conference is more likely to proceed in the most appropriate and efficient manner.

As we have seen (**3.2.1–3.2.2**), many clients come to the conference with their own preconceptions about you and the meeting, and often with fixed ideas about what they think are the most important issues. Explaining clearly to the client at the beginning of the conference precisely what you are going to deal with will often serve to reassure the client that you will indeed address the issues which are uppermost in his or her mind.

A golden rule that is applicable to every conference is always to tell the client what you are doing and explain clearly why. If, at the start of the conference, the client is provided with this sort of information and can readily see the rationale behind what you are proposing (or doing), it is more than likely that he or she will be willing to co-operate with you as much as possible. If his or her confidence is gained in this manner, the conference will usually be much more efficient and productive, for both you and the client.

So what form should this sort of beginning take? A useful way of looking at the task is to think about ensuring that you set some sort of agenda for the client. It is probably not appropriate to spell out to the client that you are 'setting an agenda' per se: it is generally advisable to refrain from putting 'labels' on what you are doing, as it can often come across as jargon and patronising. But for your own benefit as well as for the benefit of the client, setting an agenda is an effective way of ensuring that both you and your client are comfortable with the manner in which the conference will progress.

After the necessary introductions (4.3.1) it is important to start the conference by ensuring that you explain clearly and fully to the client precisely how you intend to proceed. It is not helpful merely to say, 'I need to ask you a few questions and then I'll be able to give you some advice.' The sorts of points you need to set out for the client are:

- a summary of the problem as you understand it;

- the exact areas of questioning that you intend to pursue, in what order, and why;

- the fact that you will be unable to advise the client adequately before you have gathered sufficient information from him or her;

- reassurance that, at an appropriate point, you will answer his or her questions;

- an acknowledgement that you recognise there are further or additional matters on which you will advise.

EXAMPLE

You are representing a client with a claim for damages suffered as a result of a road traffic accident. You are in possession of a fairly recent medical report, but need an update on the client's medical condition. Liability and quantum are both in issue. There is an allegation of contributory negligence. The defendant is planning to make a Part 36 offer (CPR, Part 36) of a sum far less than would be recovered should they be found wholly liable. You understand that the client wants advice on whether to accept the Part 36 offer. In addition, your instructions inform you that the client seeks advice on what the effect on the current claim would be if she accepts a recent job offer, with a higher income than she currently receives.

A suitable beginning could take a similar form to the following:

[After appropriate introductions] Miss Bloggs, I understand that you were involved in a car crash two years ago in which you received some serious injuries. I also understand that the defendants are claiming that you contributed in some measure to the accident and the injuries you received. You have come to see me today in order to get some advice on the strength of your claim and the sort of sum you could expect to receive if we can establish that the defendants were entirely liable for your injuries. I am aware as well that the defendants have offered to settle and you need my advice on exactly what this means and on how we should respond to that particular point. In addition there is the point of your new job offer, which we need to consider. Clearly there are several points here upon which you need advice. With your agreement, I thought it might be an idea if I tell you the sort of order in which I'd like to deal with all these issues. This way I think will best assist us to resolve your problems. I am fully aware that you want me to answer all the questions raised in your case, but I hope you understand that I will only be able to give you adequate advice once I have some more information from you. What I'd like to do is first ask you questions about the accident itself. I recognise that it is now a long time ago and that you have already told the story to your solicitor and the doctor who examined you, but I hope you accept that it is important for me that I get a clear picture as well so that I can consider the strength of your case and check through what the other side are saying happened. I'd then like to deal with the actual injuries you suffered. I do have a medical report from Dr Khan, but that is now six months out of date and I need an update on what has happened since then and how you are now. In the same sort of area I will need to ask you some questions on the effect of the accident and your injuries on you, your earning capacity, and social life. Again, I trust this will not be too distressing for you, but I need the information to assist me in coming to a conclusion about any possible sums of money you may be entitled to recover. Once I've got that information, I should be in a position to advise you on the likely outcome of the case, what sort of compensation you could recover, and whether you should consider accepting the defendant's offer to settle. At that stage we'll discuss your new job offer and anything else that you think I may have missed and which could be relevant to the proceedings. At the end, in the light of what we discuss, I'll also be in a position to explain what will happen next. Is there anything that you'd like to ask me before we start on the accident?

This form of words is only one possible beginning to a conference such as in the example given. It does not take long to do and generally assists in putting the client at ease by creating a sensible structure for the conduct of the conference. Essentially, an effective beginning to any conference, after the formal introductions have been completed and normal courtesies observed, should properly consist of a clear, unambiguous, and full explanation to the client of:

- your understanding of the issues raised by the case;
- in what order you intend to deal with these issues; and
- expressly why you need to take that particular route through the conference.

You will obviously find your own form of words that best suits you for any client you meet in conference. Each case will have its own specific requirements and the needs of every client will have to be considered individually.

4.3.3 Confidentiality

As we have seen, in many circumstances a client may be reluctant to answer questions that, for a variety of reasons, cause them to be nervous, anxious, and less than forthcoming at the conference. There are many factors, some of which have already been identified, that can usefully contribute to putting the client sufficiently at ease to enable him or her to be open with you (eg be non-judgemental, reassure the client you are on their side, introduce yourself properly, and so on). If faced by a reluctant client, you could reassure the client that what passes between you in the conference is generally confidential. (However, it is important that you remember the parameters to this set by the Code of Conduct, see below.) If the client is reminded of the confidential nature of the conference, it will often assist them to be more willing to answer your questions and give you the information that you need. Be careful not to assume knowledge on the part of the client. Some clients will understand what confidential actually means, but others may need a fuller explanation of the concept. If, in your judgement, it is appropriate, spell it out for the client. Tell them precisely, that in the absence of specific instructions from them, what is raised in the conference will not generally be passed on any further. Reassure them that your role is to act as their adviser, that you take instructions only from them. The nature of the relationship that has been created between you precludes you from revealing any information given to you without their express consent. Such reassurance is often very useful in assisting to establish a trusting and mutually cooperative environment. You should be aware, however, that although the duty of confidentiality is a high one and must be observed by you at all times, some information which you may receive in conference could professionally embarrass you, and (a) you could be limited in the extent to which you could effectively represent the client or (b) you may need to withdraw from the case. Should this arise, the Code of Conduct provides guidance on the proper steps to take. (See also **Chapter 8**.)

In tandem with the information about client confidentiality, it can also be useful to remind the client that your role (and duty) is to advise and assist him or her with his or her legal problem. To do this properly you need to be in full possession of all the relevant information about the client and his or her case. It is no use to you if the client ducks issues or avoids giving you the full picture. For example, you could be embarrassed in court if some evidence, about which you were unaware, arises for the first time during the course of the proceedings. Or, in ancillary relief proceedings, you could be unwittingly ambushed by the other side if your client fails to provide you with all the relevant financial details. Your client should be made fully aware of the possible consequences to his or her case if you are not in possession of all the relevant information. Your client needs to know that in order for you to act as effectively as possible, full and frank disclosure is of the utmost importance. If, therefore, you feel that the client is holding back some information, a gentle reminder to this effect will often assist. You must, of course, be extremely careful, if you decide to do this, not to give any indication to the client that you do not believe him or her, or consider him or her to be less than frank.

4.3.4   Taking a note

In most conferences, you will need to take a note of the instructions given by your client. For a barrister, consigning things to memory is a dangerous occupation. Keeping an accurate record is important for many reasons: the instructions you take from the client will form the basis of the advice you give; those instructions will often form the basis of the conduct of the case in court—making applications (eg a Bail Application), making submissions (eg a Plea in Mitigation), cross-examining witnesses, and so on. In addition, as many cases can span a considerable length of time, you will need a thoroughly prepared document from which you can readily refresh your own memory as to the exact circumstances of the particular case. You should be aware, however, that taking a note during the conference often appears intrusive to the client. To limit any difficulty that might be caused in this respect, tell clients that you may need to write a few things down, reassure them that it is for their benefit, and explain that an accurate record is important for the effective conduct of the case on their behalf. If the client knows what you are doing, and why, any potential damage caused can be substantially diminished. (See further reference to note-taking in **Chapter 6**.)

4.3.5   Using appropriate language

When first meeting the client, it is clearly important that your use of language should be appropriate to the client and the circumstances of the case in which you are instructed. As we have seen, if you are to succeed at putting the client at ease at your first meeting, there are many factors that need to be given careful attention. One way of alienating a client is to talk to him or her in language that is inappropriate. Thus, it is essential that you determine what manner and style of language you should adopt before meeting any client. The way you speak to a well educated and articulate client will obviously differ from the way you speak to a client who has not had the same advantages. Your client may be a company director, or a specialist in one particular field or other, and you may, quite properly, judge that he or she is perfectly capable of understanding technical terms and complicated legal concepts. But, more often than not (and no matter how articulate), a client will not readily understand legal jargon or legal terminology. At the start of every conference, you will have to make an instant judgement as to the level at which you pitch your conversation for that particular client. A good rule of thumb is to ensure that at all times you speak in plain, clear English that the client can easily understand. Check that your client really does understand what advice you have given. It is equally important that at all times you avoid being condescending or patronising to any client. Coming across as such will usually only succeed in alienating your client and making it much less likely that you will establish a good working relationship. If you fail to do this, the conference may turn out to be less than productive on many levels (see **Chapter 2**).

4.3.6   Controlling the conference

In addition to considering methods of putting the client at ease at the start of the conference, consideration should be given to ensuring that the conference is under your control at all stages. It can be seen that most conferences operate in the shadow of a variety of constraints that may hamper their effectiveness to some degree. With some forethought and consideration many of these difficulties can be overcome, in large measure at least. We have considered the location, thought about introductions, and looked at starting off the interview, setting a clear agenda for the conduct of the conference, and using appropriate language. During the conference, however, especially with the usual constraints on time, you will need to be confident that you can keep the proceedings under your own control. After the first minutes of the conference, particularly if you have done everything possible to put the client at ease, you may find that your valiant attempts to relax the client result in him or her wanting to take over the whole proceedings. On the other hand, the client may be the kind of person who never stops talking, or wants to wander off the relevant issues to discuss something else, or is generally preoccupied with matters other than the case in hand. In some circumstances, you will find it necessary to take a firm stance. In order to complete the job that you have been instructed to do, you may need to think about ways of keeping the client under control.

You should be aware that on many occasions you will have to give consideration to various methods of controlling the conference and, in some circumstances, controlling the client. However, you should also expect to encounter some clients who, for whatever reason, have genuine difficulty in participating in the conference with you, for example a client who is mentally ill, a client who is drunk or drugged, a juvenile client, and so on. In such circumstances, you will have to give different consideration to the client's needs and the methods of control that you use in the conference. **Chapter 10** considers some of these possibilities in more detail.

How to do it: controlling the conference

As with many of the tasks that you will perform as a barrister, controlling some clients is often not that easy. You will probably have some ideas of your own, but in order to control a client effectively you should give consideration to the following points:

(a) At all times remain polite. Being firm does not mean that you can depart from the usual courtesies.

(b) Explain exactly why you need to interrupt the client and bring the conversation back to the point that you need to discuss.

(c) If you are at the door of the court, it can be useful to remind the client that the case is due to be heard in a short time and without the relevant information your conduct of the case could be less than effective.

(d) If you are in chambers, you will probably still be operating under a time constraint. Remind the client of this. For privately funded clients, a gentle reminder that 'your time is their money' can often be salutary.

(e) Reassure the client that you are, of course, interested in what they have to tell you. However, the realistic fact is that in order to conduct the case to the best of your ability it is necessary for you to exercise your professional judgement on what is or is not relevant to the issues involved.

(f) Do not be afraid to be robust if the occasion demands. Your duty is to elicit the necessary information from the client, which will enable you to advise him or her clearly and to proceed with the case in the most effective way possible.

4.4 Conclusion

It will be apparent that there are many factors that will influence the way you meet the client and the manner in which you conduct the conference. Every client and each case, of course, will be different. By giving consideration to the sorts of issues that can arise and thinking about how best to deal with them, you will be in the best position to ensure that:

- your first meeting with the client is effective; and
- the conference is conducted efficiently.

If the meeting is effective and you gain the client's confidence early on and the course of the conference is as smooth and efficient as possible, your ability to perform your role as counsel during the conference will be greatly assisted—as, in fact, will any further function which you may have to undertake on behalf of your client, for example a court appearance or attempting a negotiated settlement.

Before meeting any client you should check that you have given consideration to:

- where the conference is taking place;
- what factors could inhibit the client from feeling comfortable;
- how to improve the location;
- how to introduce yourself effectively;
- methods of gaining the client's confidence;
- what language will be most appropriate;
- at what level to pitch the discussions;
- in what order to deal with the relevant matters;
- what materials you need at the conference.

In thinking about the sort of factors that can, and do, contribute to the success (or not) of the conference with your client, at all times you should ensure that you:

- are courteous;
- behave sensitively;
- remain flexible;
- are non-judgemental about the client and/or his or her behaviour; and
- act ethically and within the rules prescribed by the Code of Conduct.

5

Case preparation

5.1 Introduction

As we have seen, when deciding how best to conduct an effective client conference, there are many issues that arise and which need careful thought. Many of the factors to which you should give detailed consideration are set out in the previous chapters: some general principles (**Chapter 2**); the client (**Chapter 3**); and meeting the client and the conduct of the conference (**Chapter 4**). In addition to those matters, perhaps the most important key to the success of the conference lies in your ability to prepare and plan for it. Effective case preparation will enable you to ensure that both you and your client derive the maximum benefit from the conference.

The conference can too often be seen as only a minor stage in the context of the case as a whole. The reality is quite the contrary. The conference has a vital bearing on the success of the case itself and to shaping the final outcome of the whole proceedings. It therefore follows that thorough planning for the conference is essential if you are to succeed in obtaining the best outcome for your client, in whatever context his or her legal problem is placed.

Your ability to prepare adequately obviously depends on many factors, some of which will not always be under your control—for example, the time available before the conference, the quality of the information (or lack of it) in your instructions, the particular issues involved in the case, and the nature of the client. These sorts of factors will often influence what you can realistically do, and affect in some measure your ability to carry out the necessary preparation in as much detail as you would wish. However, it is possible to provide some general guidance as to what constitutes adequate and effective planning. This chapter will indicate a range of points to which you should give consideration when planning for the conference before you meet the client. Clearly, not all of these will be relevant, or even appropriate, to every conference that you will be instructed to undertake, but the issues raised are of general application and intended to provide a framework in which you can consider what preparation and planning is necessary in each case.

It should be noted here that good conference-skills practice suggests that in planning for a conference it is useful to divide your work into two distinct parts. The first stage is the preparation—the legal and factual analysis—for the conference with your client. Having completed this sometimes lengthy preparatory stage, which is essential for an effective conference, you should be in a position to draw up a working plan for the conference itself. The plan is the second stage. This is a short form of your preparation and will be the document that you actually use in the conference with your client. Your conference will be much more efficient if you are in a position to work from a plan which is manageable and clear. However, it is only possible to draft an adequate conference plan after all the preparatory stages have been completed. What follows addresses the first stage, ie the preparation. For an example of a conference plan, see **5.8**, which provides an illustration of a practical and realistic plan for conducting a conference in the context of a worked example of the preparatory stages for a full conference.

5.2   **Gutting your brief**

The first information about the case, and the client, that you will receive is usually contained in your instructions from the solicitor and the brief itself. This will be the initial source material from which you will need to work. As has been pointed out, the quality of these instructions is variable. At best you will receive clear, comprehensive paperwork addressing the relevant issues. At worst you will receive a back sheet with little more than the name of the client, the address of the court with the time of the hearing, and the nature of the case/charge. Somewhere in the middle you can expect a whole range of instructions, with a variety of documents and pieces of information that, through no fault of those instructing you, may be muddled and insufficient for your purposes. Whatever the quality of your instructions, it is your job to unravel the pieces and put the case into some semblance of order so that you can decide how to set about preparing for the conference.

When you receive your brief, what are the sorts of issues that you need to start off with and which will best assist in determining how to proceed with your preparation? What follows is not intended to prescribe any particular order in which you should deal with your instructions, but should give you some indication of the type of issues involved and influence the way you prepare for the conference.

5.2.1   **Who is the conference with?**

To place the conference in context, you will have to ascertain who the conference is with. This is not as obvious as it sounds. More often than not, particularly in the early years of practice, it will be with a lay client and that fact will be clear from your instructions. You should remember, however, that you will be instructed to conduct conferences with a range of people who will fall into other distinct categories. Therefore it is necessary, at the planning stage, to identify the participants with some accuracy in order to prepare efficiently for the conference. For example, the conference could be with:

- the Crown Prosecution Service;
- your professional client;
- an expert witness;
- a local authority;
- a court welfare officer;
- a children's guardian;
- the Official Solicitor;
- the Treasury Solicitor.

When the conference is with a lay client, there will be several questions about that client to which you should give consideration. If you can discover answers to these questions prior to preparing for the conference it will undoubtedly assist you at this stage of the proceedings. The following is not an exhaustive list, but should give some indication of the sorts of points you should be looking for. For example, can you ascertain from your instructions:

- the age/sex of the client;
- from what socio-economic background the client comes;
- whether it is a private or business matter;
- whether the client is a professional;

- whether the client has had any dealings with lawyers before;
- whether the client has any previous convictions—if so, what and when;
- whether the client is privately or publicly funded;
- whether the client is part of any business organisation?

The answers to these sorts of questions will assist you, at the planning stage, to decide in what way you should prepare to approach the client. Although you must, of course, guard against forming any preconceptions about your client, and always remember to remain open-minded, it is useful to have some idea of what you may expect at your first meeting. Indeed, it would be unrealistic, and probably counterproductive, if you did not give some forethought, when preparing for the conference, to the sort of person that your client is likely to be (see **Chapter 3**).

5.2.2   What does the client want or need?

As well as considering the nature of the client whom you are instructed to represent, it is also useful to attempt, where possible, to ascertain what the client's needs or expectations of the conference will be. Your instructions may give you some insight into the possibilities in this respect. In many cases, the purpose of the conference from the client's perspective will be plainly obvious, for example advice on plea or liability and quantum, or gathering information for a Plea in Mitigation or Bail Application. In other cases, the client's objectives may not be so obvious and you should give consideration to any clues in your brief that might alert you to a hidden agenda. It is useful to ask yourself:

- Can I identify from the papers the client's needs with sufficient accuracy?
- Are there any other less obvious interests of the client that might need to be protected?
- Might this client benefit from a solution or remedy outside the legal framework of the case?

5.2.3   What are the legal issues?

From the papers, you should be able to ascertain exactly what the client's particular problem is. Your brief should also contain specific instructions as to the job you will be expected to perform for the client. You could be instructed to do any number of things— for example, in criminal proceedings, to make a Bail Application; to prepare a Plea in Mitigation; to advise on plea and likely sentence; or to advise on the evidence. In civil proceedings, the instructions could also cover a whole range of different issues: to advise on quantum and liability in a personal injury case; to settle a witness statement or affidavit; to advise on the merits and likely outcome of the case; to settle an expert report; to appear at short notice in an application for a without notice injunction.

Whatever the specific instructions for the conference and whatever the context of the proceedings, it is only by identifying the legal issues involved that you can properly consider the nature of the problem and the legal framework in which the case is set.

If, for example, you are instructed to represent a client in criminal proceedings, the sort of information the brief will give you might include:

- the charge(s) which your client faces. What has he or she been charged with? Is there an indictment or a charge sheet?

- what stage the proceedings have reached. Is this the defendant's first appearance in the magistrates' court? Does there need to be a Bail Application? Is the client on bail? Has the client elected the mode of trial? Has a date been fixed for the next appearance? What is the purpose of the next appearance? Has a date for trial been fixed?
- what papers have additionally been served—witness statements, police reports, expert reports, custody records, police interviews.
- your client's proof of evidence.
- your client's defence statement—has it been drafted and/or served?
- any previous convictions—antecedents?
- court welfare officer's report.

In a civil case, the instructions you receive should enable you to discover:

- what legal issues this case involves. Is your client claimant? Defendant? Applicant? Respondent?
- what is contained in the statement of case.
- what stage the proceedings have reached. Is it pre-action? Is it at interim stage? Has a hearing date been fixed?
- what occurred at any previous hearings. What advice has the client already received and from whom?
- what additional papers there are—witness statements, expert reports, medical reports.

When you have identified the legal issues from the papers, you will be able to consider the legal implications and ensure that the planning for the conference is directed at addressing those. You will be in a position to decide what legal rules are likely to be applicable and on what legal areas you should concentrate in your case preparation. In addition to these matters, you should also be alert to any obvious omissions in the papers and the sorts of areas on which you need more, or fuller, information.

5.2.4   What are the factual issues?

In addition to the legal issues, it is equally important that you analyse any factual information that is contained in the brief. Factual analysis is central to your ability to prepare effectively for the conference. It is from the facts that are available that you can, for example:

- become fully familiar with the circumstances and events relevant to the case in hand;
- identify what information is missing;
- recognise areas of uncertainty or ambiguity;
- compile a list of information that will assist the conference—eg a chronology of the sequence of events, pinpointed dates, the names and roles of people involved;
- draw up a plan—eg where an accident occurred, the layout of any premises or relevant locations.

Effective management of the factual issues enables you to ensure that you can prepare for the conference in the most efficient way. A sound knowledge of the relevant facts contained in the brief will not only demonstrate to the client, in conference, that you are on top of his or her case, but it will also place you in the best position to determine what issues need to be raised during the interview with the client.

5.2.5   How do the legal and factual issues tie together?

It can be seen that the analysis of the legal issues and factual issues are both essential parts of thorough preparation for the conference. You should be aware, however, that a critical part of your planning is putting these two important elements together. An application of the relevant law to the factual issues enables you to determine the framework in which the conference should be conducted. By so doing you should be able to identify:

- what areas of research you will need to undertake. These will inevitably depend on the nature of the particular case, but will often include any (or all) of the following:
  - evidence
  - procedure
  - substantive law
  - case law/statute law specialist texts;
- what additional information you need to elicit from:
  - the client
  - instructing solicitors
  - any other parties involved;
- the areas of uncertainty that need to be clarified;
- your initial perception of the strengths and weaknesses of the case;
- the possible implications for your client;
- in what order to deal logically with the issues involved.

Taken together, it can be seen that the analysis of law and fact will form a major part of your preparation and planning for the conference. In addition, effective analysis will provide you with a clear idea of how any conference will be structured and what it should achieve. (See also *Opinion Writing and Case Preparation* manual.)

5.2.6   Conclusion

It will be apparent that the starting point of the preparation for, and planning of, any conference begins with the instructions you receive and the information contained in the papers that accompany those instructions. You will derive your initial perception of the case from the brief. This information will direct you towards any research into the relevant law or procedure that may be necessary. In addition, it will assist you in deciding what questions you should ask the client and what uncertainties need to be cleared up with the client, and form the basis for your preliminary advice on the matter.

There are, however, two important points which you should remember when you are setting about preparing any case for a conference from the information contained in your instructions.

5.2.6.1   Don't jump to conclusions

Beware of jumping to conclusions or forming fixed ideas about the client, what he or she is probably like, or likely to say. You must remain flexible and ensure that any preconceptions, at the planning stage, do not interfere with the conduct of the conference. The realities of the situation may turn out to be entirely different when you meet the client. A good rule of thumb is to ensure that you guard against taking anything as a 'given'. In any event, most of what is contained in your instructions will invariably need to be thoroughly checked, verified, and confirmed.

5.2.6.2   Use all the material fully

Despite the caveat in **5.2.6.1**, it is important to ensure that you do use all the material that is available to you, prior to the conference, to the best possible advantage. The information should enable you to undertake the necessary legal research and analysis that will, in turn, facilitate the conduct of an efficient and effective conference. Your instructions are your only source of information at the pre-conference stage and you should endeavour to use that material to the full. Learning how to gut your brief effectively is an important part of the process of conducting a professional client conference.

5.3   The purpose of the conference

When you are preparing a case for a conference with the client, it is proper that you should have a clear idea of what you perceive as the desired outcome of the conference. We have seen how it is possible to identify with reasonable accuracy what expectations the client may have. Equally, it is important when planning the conference, that you recognise what your goals are. Although the conference may have a primary objective—usually to advise the client—it can, and does, serve many other purposes in addition to providing advice. Indeed, it is usual for the conference to fulfil many different functions at the same time, and often these are not mutually exclusive. When planning for a conference, you must identify for yourself what needs you, as counsel, require to be satisfied. It is useful, therefore, at the preparation stage, to ask yourself: 'What is the purpose of this conference?' It could include any, or any combination, of the following:

- to discover and elicit information;
- to clarify facts and issues;
- to discuss available options;
- to advise;
- to identify individuals;
- to receive instructions;
- to provide reassurance;
- to negotiate a settlement;
- to assess the client as a potential witness;
- to prepare for a court hearing.

It is only when you have identified the purpose(s) of the conference as you see it that you will be able to plan the best approach to achieve those ends. If, at the outset, you have a clear view of what the objectives of the conference should be, you will be able to determine whether at the end of the conference you have succeeded in what you set out to do. It is clearly in the best interests of the client that you are certain and clear about the purpose of the conference and what outcome should be expected.

5.4 Legal and factual analysis

It will be apparent that effective preparation and planning for any conference involves many separate considerations. From your instructions you should be able to identify matters such as:

- who the client is and what their likely objectives are;
- the legal and procedural areas involved;
- the stage of the proceedings;
- your own objectives for the conference.

It is within this framework that you can begin to prepare for the conference. What is adequate preparation? What elements of case preparation should you be thinking about when deciding what form the conference should take? The ability to prepare for the conference is a skill that often, regrettably, has a tendency to be overlooked. The absence of thorough preparation and planning is all too often the reason for a conference being less than effective for the client and consequently failing to resolve his or her case in the most satisfactory way. A client does not want to see that you are uncertain about the legal position. A client does not want to suspect that you are unclear about the facts of the case. Any doubt that is cast on your ability in these areas will inevitably cause confusion and uncertainty and result in a lack of confidence that will permeate the whole process. It may sound simplistic, but no matter how well you communicate with your client, no matter how careful and sensitive you are about the language you use or the surroundings of the conference, and so on, if you are unable to analyse the case (both law and fact) in sufficient detail to enable you to elicit the necessary information, and provide sound legal advice, you will almost certainly be failing in your professional duty to the client.

You should always aim to begin each conference knowing that you have done everything possible to ensure that you have mastered both the facts and the law involved in the case. If you observe this golden rule, you can be confident that you will be in the best position to represent your client's interests. Remember that the client has retained you as his or her legal adviser. Your role as a professional in this context means that you should be able to display to the client a thorough knowledge of the individual facts of the case and demonstrate a clear understanding of the legal implications of the proceedings.

It will be useful at this stage to consider separately the different elements that comprise effective preparation and planning. However, before moving on to consider each of these in turn, it should be pointed out that the real skill of sound preparation and planning requires not only that you consider the component parts, but also that you are able to pull all the parts together to make a complete picture. When you have the complete picture, you will be able to determine with a great degree of accuracy what form the conference should take.

5.4.1 Legal analysis

Thorough legal analysis of your case is clearly of the utmost importance. Identifying the legal issues and detailed analysis of those issues form the first stage of effective preparation for the client conference. At first sight, identifying the legal issues involved may appear relatively straightforward: the client is being sued for negligence; the client has been charged with theft; the client wants to defend an application for summary judgment. So far, so good. But usually a whole range of other points emerges for consideration, about which much more detailed knowledge is required. Without this knowledge, you will be unable to (a) determine what further information you need to elicit from the client and (b) consider what solution may be most appropriate for the client. In addition to identifying the legal issues involved, it is necessary to decide the following:

- How do the rules of evidence affect the case?
- What rules of procedure are relevant?
- Is the case governed by statutory provisions?
- In what way have the courts interpreted the statute?
- What are the leading cases?
- In what way have the courts applied the law?

It can be seen, therefore, that in undertaking the necessary legal analysis of the client's particular case, a host of other legal considerations will come into the equation and potentially affect the outcome. It is important to ensure that every legal aspect of the case is addressed in order that you can be certain that your analysis of the client's overall position is complete. Thorough and detailed legal analysis will enable your preparation for the conference to be focused on the relevant and pertinent issues that you will need to raise with the client in conference. It will additionally ensure that you are best placed to give your client a full evaluation of their case and the likely outcome. Whether the matter settles or proceeds to trial, your preparation should enable you to provide, by the end of the conference, clear and comprehensive advice to your client as to the most appropriate way to deal with their case. (See **Chapter 7**.)

Some examples to illustrate this need for comprehensive legal analysis are provided below.

EXAMPLE 1

Your client is charged with causing grievous bodily harm [with intent] contrary to s 18 of the Offences Against the Person Act 1861. On the face of the papers, the case against your client is strong. The prosecution intend to rely upon identification evidence and a confession made by the accused after his arrest. However, there appears to have been a failure on the part of the police to comply with the procedures set out in Code D (issued under the Police and Criminal Evidence Act 1984 (PACE)) in respect of the identification of your client. In addition, the factors surrounding the confession of your client indicate that it could have been obtained in circumstances that might render it unreliable under PACE 1984, s 76(2)(b). In respect of the identification evidence, at the discretion of the judge, this could be excluded at trial (PACE 1984, s 78; see, for example, *R v Forbes* [2001] 1 AC 473). In so far as the prosecution seek to rely upon the confession, once the point on reliability is raised, as a matter of law, it will be for the prosecution to prove beyond all reasonable doubt that the confession was not obtained in circumstances that may render it unreliable. Obviously, if the evidence upon which the prosecution are seeking to rely can be rendered inadmissible in the proceedings, the case against your client will be substantially weakened. Such factors need to be thoroughly considered by you at an early stage and it can be readily seen that to analyse the legal issues of any case properly, you need to have a sound grasp of the rules of evidence. With this, the focus of your questions will be clear. In addition, your knowledge will enable you to evaluate effectively the answers given within the relevant legal framework. (For further detail see *Evidence* manual.)

EXAMPLE 2

Your client is pleading guilty to a charge of theft. The theft was committed by your client while he or she held a position of responsibility (eg while an employee of the Post Office) and is likely, therefore, to be considered as a breach of trust. You are instructed to prepare a Plea in Mitigation and advise your client on the likely sentence. The Sentencing Guidelines Council sentencing guidelines Part 14 Theft and SG-448 Theft, including Theft in Breach of Trust, suggest that in breach of some degree of trust cases valued between £500 and £10,000, save for very exceptional circumstances, a high-level community order sentence is inevitable, and that there is some risk of custody should the Bench consider the degree of trust to be a high one. In order for you to be in a position to advise your client realistically, you clearly need to be aware of both the sentencing guidelines and any cases relevant to this area of sentencing, and also to know, if possible, how the specific court has applied them. (See *Criminal Litigation and Sentencing* manual.)

EXAMPLE 3

Your client is seeking Child Arrangements Orders in respect of a child of the family. Section 1(3) of the Children Act 1989 provides a statutory checklist of all the factors to which consideration must be given when making such an application. Your preparation for this type of case requires that you are not only aware of the factors which the court will take into account when coming to a decision about the upbringing of a child, but also that you use the statutory checklist as the basis for the conference with your client to ensure that you elicit the necessary relevant information. Being fully aware of the criteria within which the case will be decided will also enable you to have the necessary legal framework to be in the best position to advise your client properly. (See *Family Law in Practice* manual.)

EXAMPLE 4

Your client is seeking to set aside a Judgment in Default that has been entered against him or her. To be able to advise the client on the prospects of success you will need to be clear about the procedure that is involved in making such an application (CPR, Part 13). You need to be aware of the requirement that the witness statement in support of the application must disclose a defence that has a real prospect of success, or that there is some other good reason. *ED&F Man Liquid Products Ltd v Patel* [2003] EWCA Civ 472 is useful on the exercise of the court's discretion on whether the defence has a real prospect of success. Without this sort of knowledge, you will be unable to ensure that the rules of procedure are complied with, and that your consequent advice to the client is full and comprehensive.

It can be readily seen from the examples set out above that the legal analysis necessary for effective case preparation usually includes a number of elements which may not at first sight be apparent. The nature of the case (or charge if the proceedings are criminal) will usually be clear from your instructions. The legal analysis, however, usually requires that you give detailed consideration to a range of other factors which will be relevant to the preparation for the conference, the decision about what further information you need to elicit from the client, the advice you give your client, and the eventual resolution of the problem in question. Therefore the sorts of questions you must ask in each case include:

- Who bears the burden of proof?
- Does this burden shift during the proceedings?
- What standard of proof is required?
- What rules of evidence need to be considered?

- What procedural rules come into play?
- What statutory provisions may be relevant?
- What are the leading authorities?
- What are the latest authorities?
- What guidance can be derived from case law?

5.4.2 Legal analysis in context

We have seen that thorough legal analysis, in the broader sense as described previously, is central to your ability to prepare in the most effective way for the conference with your client. It should be clearly emphasised, however, that while you can and should analyse, in advance of the conference, the legal issues that appear relevant from your instructions, what actually occurs in the conference itself may place an entirely different perspective on the case itself. (See **Chapters 6** and **7**.) It is suggested that you follow two golden rules in this respect:

(a) Undertake the necessary legal analysis that is apparent from your instructions to ensure that you are fully familiar with the legal implications and are able to answer any specific questions contained in your brief.

(b) Remember to remain flexible and open-minded about the answers you receive from your client and the instructions he or she gives you at the conference.

The following are two examples of legal analysis in the context of a particular legal problem. They are intended to illustrate good practice in legal research and legal analysis, and provide an indication of the sorts of points that you should be considering when planning the conference. It is important to remember that the core of every case lies within the legal, evidential, and procedural framework in which it is placed.

EXAMPLE 1

The charge your client faces is burglary, contrary to s 9(1)(a) of the Theft Act 1968. Your client was arrested leaving a private dwelling house at 2.00 am. He was carrying a number of domestic items (electrical goods and some jewellery) worth about £750, which were all recovered at the time of arrest. There was no violence, but the occupiers of the property were in residence and asleep at the time. There was no damage to the property. Your client, aged 22, was acting alone and on the spur of the moment and says he had no intention to steal anything unless there was something worth stealing inside. You are instructed to advise on plea, mode of trial, and likely sentence. Your client has two previous convictions for theft. On the last occasion (nine months ago) he was fined £150.

Plea

What the prosecution has to prove (beyond reasonable doubt) is that your client:

- entered
- a dwelling house
- as a trespasser
- with intent to steal therein.

On the face of the instructions the first three items above seem to be satisfied. But note, it is important to verify with the client in conference that this is accurate. The legal issue appears to be conditional intent. See *Attorney-General's References (Nos 1 and 2 of 1979)* [1980] QB 180. By entering a building as a trespasser with intent to steal therein (and there is no reference to the stealing of specific items), that person is guilty if he had an intention to steal anything in the building and the fact that there was nothing in the building worth stealing is immaterial.

Mode of trial

Most forms of burglary are triable either way (Magistrates' Courts Act 1980, s 17, and Sch 1, para 28). If the occupants of the dwelling house were subjected to violence (or threat of violence) the offence is triable only on indictment (Sch 1, para 28(c)). In the Sentencing Guidelines: Part 12 Magistrates' Court Sentencing Guidelines SG-246 and SG-247, separate guidelines are given for burglary at a dwelling house and burglary at a non-dwelling. For burglary from a dwelling house, magistrates can try the case summarily unless the court considers that one or more of the following features is present and that its sentencing powers are insufficient:

- entry when occupier is present, or after entry, victim returns;
- violence used or threatened against victim;
- theft of/damage to property causes significant loss;
- soiling, ransacking, or vandalism of property;
- trauma to victim beyond the normal inevitable consequences;
- context of general public disorder.

It seems that the only aggravating factor in this particular case is the first item above and the likelihood is that the magistrates will not decline jurisdiction in these circumstances. The choice will have to be made, by the client, about which forum—the magistrates' court or the Crown Court—will be the most appropriate in all the circumstances. Thus, you will need to advise the client on the advantages and disadvantages of the different modes of trial.

Likely sentence

Statutory provisions: the maximum penalty for burglary of a building or part of a building which is a dwelling is 14 years' imprisonment on indictment, six months, or a fine not exceeding the statutory maximum, or both, summarily (Theft Act 1968, s 9(4)).

However, this is likely to be categorised as a Category 3 offence, and the 'starting point' is a higher-level community order.

From January 2012, the Crown Court and magistrates' courts follow the Sentencing Council's definitive guideline for the sentencing of burglars. The guideline covers aggravated, domestic, and non-domestic burglary. Offenders burgling people's homes can usually expect a custodial sentence. The sentencing range for domestic burglary is set at up to six years for domestic burglary, a two-year increase on the four years proposed by the Sentencing Council's predecessor body, the Sentencing Advisory Panel.

The guideline aims to put the effect on victims at the centre of considerations about what sentence an offender should receive. Therefore judges and magistrates focus on the harm to the victim, as well as the culpability of the offender.

The court will determine culpability and harm caused by reference only to factors as set out in the guidance, ie the principal factual elements of the offence. For example:

Factors indicating greater harm:

- theft of/damage to property causing a significant degree of loss to the victim (whether economic, sentimental, or personal value);
- soiling, ransacking, or vandalism of property;
- occupier at home (or returns home) while offender present.

Factors indicating lesser harm:

- nothing stolen or only property of very low value to the victim;
- limited damage or disturbance to property.

Factors indicating higher culpability:

- victim or premises deliberately targeted;
- a significant degree of planning or organisation;
- equipped for burglary;
- member of a group or gang.

Factors indicating lower culpability:

- offence committed on impulse, with limited intrusion into property;
- mental disorder or learning disability, where linked to the commission of the offence.

The court will then go on to consider the seriousness of the offence and personal mitigation, using the non-exhaustive list of factors, for example:

Aggravating factors:

- previous convictions (a third domestic burglary results in at least three years in custody, see below);
- offence committed whilst on bail;
- offence committed at night;
- gratuitous degradation of the victim;
- commission of offence whilst under the influence of alcohol or drugs.

Factors reducing seriousness or reflecting personal mitigation:

- offender has made voluntary reparation to the victim;
- subordinate role in a group or gang;
- no previous convictions or no relevant/recent convictions;
- remorse;
- good character and/or exemplary conduct.

Where sentencing an offender for a qualifying third domestic burglary, the court must apply s 111 of the Powers of Criminal Courts (Sentencing) Act 2000 and impose a custodial term of at least three years, unless it is satisfied that there are particular circumstances which relate to any of the offences or to the offender which would make it unjust to do so.

There will then be a reduction for a guilty plea, if one has been entered. In all cases, courts will consider whether to make compensation and or other ancillary orders, and will take into consideration any remand time served.

Conclusion

Thus, it can be seen from a brief legal analysis of the charge and the likely sentence that you will be in a position to plan the structure of your conference. It is within this legal framework that you will be able to:

(a) decide what further information you need to elicit from the client about the offence itself and his own personal circumstances;

(b) provide specific advice required by the instructions received: that conditional intention is no defence to the charge of burglary; that it seems likely that the client is entitled to elect for trial in the magistrates' court or the Crown Court; that although the 'starting point' for most burglaries is custody, the guidelines suggest that low-level offending and personal mitigating factors can exceptionally save an offender from a custodial sentence.

(c) after taking the client's instructions, advise on what the likely sentence will be if he pleads guilty or is found guilty at trial.

(See **Criminal Litigation and Sentencing** manual.)

EXAMPLE 2

Your client, the claimant, is seeking an order for summary judgment under CPR, Part 24 (and PD 24). The defendant has served a witness statement in reply to the application, asserting that there is a defence to the claim with a real prospect of success. Your client instructs you that, in his opinion, the defendant has no arguable defence. In addition, he suggests that the witness statement in reply raises spurious matters, invented at the last minute, in an attempt to avoid paying the debt owed. Your client has also indicated that he is unclear as to the procedure that will be adopted and wants to know what the likely outcome will be. It appears that the defendant will attend the hearing. This is due to be heard before a Master in the High Court. To be in a position to elicit the relevant information and advise your client on the likely outcome, you must be aware of the procedures involved in making the application and the legal framework in which the court will make the decision.

The procedure

Check that:

(a) the claimant's application notice, witness statement, and exhibits were served on the defendant not less than 14 clear days before the hearing (CPR, Part 24);

(b) the witness statement sworn in support:
  (i) verifies the facts of the claim; and
  (ii) deposes to a belief that there is no real prospect of success (r 24.2(a)(i));
(c) the witness statement in reply to the application was served and filed seven days before the return day and any response by the applicant was served and filed three days before the hearing.

The hearing

If both parties attend, counsel for the claimant addresses the Master on the nature of the application and refers to the witness statement (and exhibits). The claimant argues why there is no defence and that summary judgment should be given. Counsel for the defendant refers the Master to his or her witness statement setting out the reasons against entering summary judgment and why the application should be dismissed. No oral evidence is taken at the hearing. The claimant does not have to attend, although in many circumstances it is advisable that he or she is at court. There is a range of possible orders that the court can make, depending upon the witness statement evidence and supporting arguments:

- judgment on the claim;
- a conditional order;
- dismissal of the application.

The legal framework

The legal issue involved here is whether the defendant's claim has any real prospect of success. How do the courts approach this? In *Swain v Hillman* [2001] 1 All ER 91, Lord Woolf said that the words 'no real prospect of succeeding' did not need any amplification as they spoke for themselves. The word 'real' directed the court to the need to see whether there was a realistic—as opposed to a fanciful—prospect of success.

Conclusion

When you have undertaken this legal analysis you should be in the position to ensure that at the conference you are able to:

(a) decide what further relevant information you need to elicit from the client in response to the case itself and the defendant's witness statement in reply in particular;
(b) inform the client of the procedural rules which are applicable to summary judgment hearings;
(c) advise on the merits of the case and the likely outcome.

5.4.3 Legal analysis—conclusion

Whether the case you are advising the client on is a criminal or civil matter, it can be seen that thorough legal analysis, prior to the conference, will enable you to determine what further information you need to elicit from the client and, in the shadow of the legal and procedural framework, provide a provisional view of the merits of the case. Thorough legal analysis includes: rules of evidence; rules of procedure; up-to-date case law; relevant statutory provisions.

5.4.4 Factual analysis

In order to prepare effectively for the conference and plan the best approach to adopt with the client and the particular legal problem, it is also important to analyse the facts of the case and determine what the facts (or lack of them) indicate. It is only by examining, in detail, the factual information available in your instructions, that you can decide in what way the conference should progress most effectively. No matter how thorough your legal analysis is, the absence of thorough factual analysis may render 'the law' virtually meaningless in the context of the case as a whole. Identifying the relevant factual issues is a critical part of your case preparation. For both the conduct of the conference itself and, indeed, to ensure the most satisfactory outcome to the case as a whole, your attention to the factual issues involved should form a central part of the case preparation. There are many reasons for adopting this approach, some of which may be obvious, others less so.

5.4.4.1 Importance of first impressions

It has already been stated that the first impression created by you at the beginning of a conference is important. It will undoubtedly influence the conduct (and effectiveness) of the whole conference. If, when you first meet the client, you can demonstrate that you are fully familiar with his or her case, this will almost certainly inspire confidence and get the meeting off to a productive beginning. If, on the other hand, you have to scrabble around in the papers to find relevant pieces of information, for example the exact nature of the case (charge), the date of the incident, the names of other parties involved, you run the risk of giving a poor impression to your client. It is useful to remind yourself that although you deal with a whole range of legal matters on a daily basis, for the client this case is probably the most important issue in his or her life. In this respect, the most reassuring thing for a client is to be able to see that you are clearly on top of the facts of his or her case and that you are fully familiar with it. A client who is so reassured is much more likely to be forthcoming from the start of the conference.

5.4.4.2 Identifying what information is still needed

It is often the case that some of the most vital information about your client or the case will not appear in the papers at all. By analysing the facts that are available, you are likely to identify several areas upon which you need to discover much more information from the client. Identifying the gaps in your instructions will enable you to determine what further information you need to elicit from the client (or anyone else involved in the proceedings). A major part of any conference is the fact-finding exercise on which you will embark with your client. To do this effectively it is necessary to identify clearly the areas on which you need to question your client and what relevant information is missing. If you are able to ask the right questions that fill the gaps in your instructions, you will be best placed to advise the client in the most appropriate way. It is easy to fall into the trap of taking your instructions at face value and, as a consequence, failing to probe, in sufficient detail, into matters which might not be readily apparent. When presented with a piece of information, try to ensure that you evaluate it carefully and decide what impact it could have on the proceedings in question. For example, you are instructed to advise on the merits of a case in which the client is a claimant in an action for damages for personal injuries suffered in a tripping-up accident on a public footpath. The defendant (a local authority) is denying liability and claiming that the claimant contributed to her own injuries. Your instructions contain her proof of evidence in which she gives a seemingly clear account of her version of the incident. What is missing, however, is any adequate information as to precisely what she was doing leading up to and immediately prior to the fall, and without which you cannot evaluate the strengths of her (or the defendant's) claims. You should therefore be immediately alerted to the need for further information in this respect in order to address the unanswered questions in your instructions. It should be clear that identifying the areas in which there is little or no information forms an important part of your preparation. When you recognise what factual matters are missing, you will be able to decide what further information is required. (See **Chapter 6**.)

5.4.4.3   Are the given facts unambiguous?

In addition to missing information, you will often discover that the facts you do have in your papers are: capable of being ambiguous; unclear or uncertain; in direct conflict with other facts in the instructions. It is therefore essential that you give detailed consideration to the sorts of issues that can arise in such circumstances. In each case you should evaluate the factual information, in the context of the case as a whole, to discover what further answers you require to clarify the facts in your papers. For example, your client, who has commenced divorce proceedings, is seeking advice on what would constitute an appropriate financial settlement. Your instructions reveal that your client has been away on holiday with a friend and that this particular friend has been a regular weekend visitor to the former matrimonial home. In these circumstances, you are obviously aware of the fact that there is a third party involved with your client. What is unclear, and may be ambiguous, is the nature of the friendship and the potential impact it might have on the proceedings. You will be fully aware that the other side will doubtless press this point. It will therefore be up to you to ask the client relevant questions in order to determine the extent to which the friendship might influence, or affect, any potential settlement. You will need to clarify the nature of the friendship, the future of the relationship, whether there are any plans to remarry, and whether the friend is making any financial contributions. The answers to these questions will have a direct relevance to the nature of the advice you end up giving to the client. (See **Chapter 7**.)

Another example of the sorts of conflicting facts that you should be alert to could be where your client, charged with a criminal offence, has given a somewhat different account of the events in his or her proof of evidence from the version that appears in the police interview. In these circumstances, by asking the client relevant questions, you should be in a position to unravel the conflicting versions of events. A failure to recognise a conflict of facts leads to obvious problems if the matter proceeds to trial. For the purposes of preparing for the conference, what is important is that you recognise, from your instructions, factual issues that may be unclear, or capable of different interpretations, or in direct conflict. In this way you are clear about which areas of the case need to be pursued in the conference and you can ensure that you prepare your line of questioning effectively.

5.4.4.4   Full familiarity with essential facts

A thorough analysis of the facts should also assist you in compiling the material in a form which best enables you to be in control of the conference and place the case in a logical context. If the case is one that involves several different parties—for example, a multiple car crash, or a multi-handed affray—draw up a list of all the people involved, what their (alleged) role is in the proceedings, and any other relevant information about that person which could affect your client. In family matters where there may be a whole range of interested parties such as parents, step-parents, grandparents, and so on, make sure you have a list which clearly identifies all these people and what their potential claim or interest is in the proceedings.

Dates are often crucial to the case. Try to ensure that you have identified all the relevant dates and have compiled a practical list of these that will assist you in being on top of the sequence of events. If there have been previous court appearances in the case, make sure you are clear about when they took place and what decision was taken at that time. By the same token, a list of relevant events, in chronological order, is usually extremely helpful. For example, the sequence of events leading up to a road traffic accident, or the events leading up to an incident of domestic violence, will assist you in getting a clear picture of what happened and in what order the events took place.

There are many different ways of drawing up chronologies and lists of information that will assist you in the preparation for the conference. You should decide what method is the most effective for you. However, it is important to remember that, whatever methodology you adopt in your preparation, it should place you in the position of being fully familiar with all the relevant facts and enable you to have all the relevant information at your fingertips during the conference. It should also be pointed out that effective preparation in this way for the conference will form a vital part of your preparation for any subsequent court appearance, should the matter either go to trial or result in a negotiated settlement.

5.4.4.5   Preparation of a sketch plan

In many cases, it can be useful to draw some sort of plan of any relevant locations: the position of cars in a road traffic accident; a plan of the premises where an alleged burglary took place; a plan of an area of a supermarket where the charge involves shoplifting, and so on. Preparing a plan of the *locus in quo* will usually assist you to get a clearer picture of the location and surroundings in which the incident occurred. In addition, a plan can be invaluable when questioning your client in conference, as it is likely to help your client to give you more accurate information about the incident itself. (See *Opinion Writing and Case Preparation* manual.)

5.4.5   Thoroughly analysing the brief

> **How to do it**
>
> Thorough factual analysis forms a necessary part of the preparation and planning for any conference, whatever the legal context. You can analyse the facts contained in your instructions before the conference commences with the aid of these suggestions:
>
> - identify the context of the relevant events and any litigation to date;
> - compile a list of useful information, eg a chronology, map, plan;
> - identify areas of conflict, uncertainty, or ambiguity;
> - identify what information is missing;
> - decide what factual gaps can be filled by questioning the client;
> - identify what information you need to elicit from the solicitor, CPS/other side in advance of the conference;
> - determine what order will best deal with the areas of questioning;
> - decide whether you need further information after the conference from persons other than your client, eg instructing solicitor.

5.4.6   The merits of the case—law and facts combined

It can be seen that effective preparation for any conference requires careful attention to detail—attention, that is, to both the legal framework in which the case is set and the factual circumstances of the case. It can also be seen that by undertaking these preparatory stages, you will be able to decide, in advance of meeting the client:

- what legal rules are relevant;
- what procedural requirements are involved;
- what further information you need to elicit from your client;
- what potentially relevant information is missing; and
- what ambiguities need to be resolved.

However, another vital part of your preparation for the conference is your evaluation of the merits of the case—that is, those elements of the case (law or fact) which tend to support your client's position; and those factors which tend to go against his or her case.

When preparing for the conference, it is equally important to remember that, in addition to undertaking the necessary legal and factual analysis, you should give consideration to the strengths and weaknesses of the case and any potential resolution. Your client will expect clear and comprehensive advice as to the likely outcome of the proceedings and the consequences for him or her of pursuing any of the options that you identify. Thus, your preparation should, inter alia, address:

- evaluation of the merits of the client's position; and

- a *preliminary* conclusion about what options are available to resolve the case most successfully.

Even at the preparation stage, you will to some extent be considering the available options and the likely solutions for your client. There are many issues to which you should be giving consideration when deciding what factors could influence the likely outcome of the case. The sorts of points which you should bear in mind are listed in the next section, **5.4.6.1**.

5.4.6.1   Legal alternatives

Consider the following points:

- how the tribunal of law is likely to resolve the issues in dispute;

- how the jury/tribunal of fact is likely to evaluate the disputed facts;

- how the jury/tribunal of fact is likely to respond to a particular witness/piece of evidence;

- how the tribunal of law is likely to rule on the issues of law;

- how the tribunal of law is likely to exercise its discretion on any issue;

- the financial consequences of the proceedings, or as a direct result of the proceedings (eg costs orders);

- any further litigation as a result of commencing (continuing) these proceedings, ie additional litigation, or prospect of going to a higher court;

- the effect of any potential delays in the resolution of the matter;

- whether a negotiated settlement or other form of alternative dispute resolution (ADR) is possible, or practicable;

- abandonment of claim;

- in criminal proceedings consideration will be given to all matters listed above, and these may be usefully categorised as:
    - proceed to trial;
    - plead guilty;
    - negotiate (ie plead to a lesser offence).

5.4.6.2   Non-legal alternatives

When planning for the conference and forming a preliminary view of available options/ solutions for your client, there are often additional non-legal factors that may need to be taken into account. The following examples, although far from a fully comprehensive list, provide some illustration of the sort of non-legal consequences of any decisions taken, which could properly be taken into account at the preparatory stage. Consider the following:

(a) Economic: eg the realistic effect of a divorce on the parties being able to rehouse themselves; employment prospects of a person convicted of an offence of dishonesty; costs of the proceedings being greater than any sum recovered.

(b) Social: eg the effect on any children who have to move school because of the sale of the matrimonial home; how neighbours will regard a conviction for shoplifting.

(c) Psychological: eg emotions of someone forced, because of an accident, to take employment which may be regarded as inferior to a position previously held; emotional damage to children after breakdown of family relationship.

(d) Involvement of any non-legal agency to resolve the dispute: eg enrolment in a voluntary programme of family therapy (some evidence of child abuse); agreement to seek counselling (some evidence of alcoholism or compulsive gambling).

5.4.7   The merits of the case—conclusion

In addition to the detailed analysis of the legal and factual circumstances of the case, effective preparation also means that attention is given to the merits of the case from every possible perspective. You should be alert to information contained in your instructions, both express and by inference, which could influence the manner in which you plan to advise your client. Efficient case preparation in this respect will assist in ensuring that you are in the best position to offer clear, comprehensive, and realistic advice. (For further detail see **Chapter 7**.)

5.4.8   Advice at preparation stage

Although this chapter is primarily concerned with the preparatory stages for a conference prior to meeting the client, it is obviously important to ensure that you give adequate consideration, at the planning phase, to the range of possible outcomes, or solutions, which may be available to your client. It is appropriate to remind yourself that a major part of your job, after meeting the client in conference and taking their instructions, is to advise him or her fully and comprehensively about the issues that their case raises and the difficulties in which they find themselves. This involves, inter alia, conveying to the client your considered opinion as to what is the most appropriate way forward to resolve the matter as favourably as possible in all the circumstances. You will be unable to perform this role effectively if you have not already given consideration to a range of likely consequences for your client, whatever instructions you actually receive during the conference.

It has been already pointed out that considering, in advance of the conference, any possible advice that you may offer to your client could be a double-edged sword. It is always useful to remind yourself of some of the dangers involved in prejudging the issues. Try to remember, at all times, to be on your guard against forming preconceptions (about the case or the client) before the conference takes place. (See **Chapters 2 and 3**.)

It would, however, be highly unusual (and certainly unwise), when undertaking the preparation for a conference, if you were to fail to give some detailed thought to any potential or likely outcome(s) of each case in question. In virtually every case in which you are instructed, there is certainly a need to ensure that your preparation and planning for the conference include consideration of the preliminary advice (and any consequences which flow from this) that might be appropriate in all the circumstances of the case.

The following provide some examples.

EXAMPLE 1

You are instructed to represent a defendant in an application for summary judgment under CPR, Part 24. The papers reveal that there is a real prospect of success and you will probably succeed in defeating the claim for summary judgment at this stage of the proceedings. However, you also recognise that, in all the circumstances, your client's case is not that strong, and leave to defend will almost certainly be conditional upon your client paying a substantial amount into court. Your client will clearly expect you to have worked this out in advance and to convey this information to him or her.

EXAMPLE 2

You may be instructed in a case which you consider, for a variety of reasons, would be resolved in a much better way for your client by attempting to negotiate a settlement rather than embarking on a protracted court battle. In such circumstances your client will obviously expect to be informed about why you take this view and what likely outcome will be achieved by following your advice.

EXAMPLE 3

In a case where the prosecution evidence against your client is very strong and a custodial sentence is virtually inevitable, it would be improper if you had failed to give some consideration as to the likely length of sentence that your client should expect. Your client will expect you to be in a position to realistically inform him or her in this respect. This analysis should additionally ensure that your preparation for the conference includes adequate planning of questions relating to the personal circumstances (mitigation) of your client.

5.4.9 Advice at preparation stage—conclusion

It can be seen that in the preparation and planning stages prior to any conference, it is necessary to give adequate consideration to any likely (or possible) outcomes/solutions for your client. You would be failing in your duty if you were unable to identify and evaluate, as a preliminary at least, the range of alternative options that may be available to your client.

At the preparation stage, when considering a range of possible outcomes/solutions which might be appropriate for your client, and which will form the basis of your preliminary advice, you should try to:

- identify any possible outcomes; and
- evaluate the viability of any potential solution.

But whatever solutions may appear to be viable on the face of your instructions, and following your legal and factual analysis, during the conference itself, always remember:

- to keep an open mind and remain flexible;
- not to be surprised if you receive contradictory and conflicting instructions, but to be prepared to deal with them.

5.5 Summary

In conclusion, it is readily apparent that effective case preparation is of considerable importance if you are to ensure that every conference is productive and efficient for both you and your client. As we have seen, there are many factors—some outside your control—that can affect your ability to carry out your instructions for the conference in the most professional manner possible. However, as a golden rule, and obviously where practicable, you should try to ensure that every conference you undertake has been thoroughly prepared and planned in advance of meeting the client.

The following is a checklist of the sorts of factors to which you should give consideration when preparing for a conference. Not all the issues set out will necessarily be relevant or appropriate to every conference you undertake. The points raised, however, are intended to provide general guidance and to assist you when preparing your papers for a conference.

5.5.1 Pre-conference planning

> **How to do it**
>
> At the start of your case preparation, you need to identify:
> - the location of the conference;
> - who will attend the conference;
> - the client's aims;
> - the client's needs;
> - whether the above two points are compatible;
> - the legal issues;
> - the factual issues;
> - how the facts and law combine;
> - the purpose of the conference from:
>   - your perspective;
>   - the client's perspective;
>   - the perspective of any other parties involved.

5.5.2 Preparing for the conference

> **How to do it**
>
> When you have identified the preliminaries in the previous section, you need to prepare for the conference by:
> - analysing the legal issues;
> - undertaking any necessary legal research;
> - analysing the factual issues;
> - identifying missing, ambiguous, or conflicting facts;
> - deciding what information should be elicited from the client;
> - forming a preliminary view of the merits of the case;
> - analysing the strengths and weaknesses;
> - reaching a provisional view on any likely/possible outcome;
> - considering what preliminary advice might be appropriate.

5.5.3   Planning to conduct the conference

> **How to do it**
>
> Once you have undertaken all the preparatory steps for the conference, you need to:
>
> - identify all relevant matters which need to be raised with the client;
> - decide in what order it is most appropriate to deal with the issues;
> - ensure you are fully in command of legal, evidential, factual, and procedural issues;
> - prepare a short working plan for the conduct of the conference;
> - carry out the conference in an efficient and professional manner.

5.6   A worked example

It can be seen that there are many elements that comprise sound case preparation and planning for any conference. It is also clear that the more efficient you are at putting all these elements together, the more effective the conference is likely to be.

The following is a worked example of the preparation and planning for the case of *R v Mary Brinda*, a criminal case involving an alleged theft from an employer. This example of case preparation is not intended to be a 'blueprint'; it is intended to provide an illustration of one way of setting about the preparation of a case for a client conference. There are, of course, other methods that are equally acceptable. It is recommended that you work out a method of preparation that is best suited to you and your own style.

The most important thing, however, is to ensure that whatever method of preparation you adopt, all the relevant issues (as outlined earlier) are fully addressed prior to meeting the client in conference.

At the end of the case preparation for *R v Mary Brinda* (**5.8**), you will find a conference plan for the same case, which is designed to be a short form of the case preparation, and an example of a workable document for use during the conference itself.

IN THE WEST LONDON CROWN COURT

THE QUEEN

v

MARY BRINDA

INSTRUCTIONS TO COUNSEL TO
ADVISE IN CONFERENCE

Horace Pink & Co
81 Kensington Park Road
London W11

1

IN THE WEST LONDON CROWN COURT

THE QUEEN

v

MARY BRINDA

INSTRUCTIONS TO COUNSEL TO
ADVISE IN CONFERENCE

Counsel has herewith:

1. COPY OF INDICTMENT
2. PROSECUTION WITNESS STATEMENTS
3. DEFENCE STATEMENT
4. DEFENDANT'S PROOF OF EVIDENCE

The defendant is charged with theft from her employer. She denied the charge in interviews and claims she was visiting her father in Bath.

Mrs Brinda works in the Central Blood Bank, and has done so for nearly 17 years. She is concerned about an internal dispute over her salary, and feels that this could in any event justify her taking goods from her employer. The defendant has applied to an Employment Tribunal for the £2,000 she claims she is owed.

Instructing Solicitors note the value of the blood is estimated at £2,000. If the defendant admitted this, could she argue a claim of right or some sort of set-off?

Instructing Solicitors are aware of one previous conviction. The CPS does not seem to be aware of this conviction. What is the position regarding this; do we have to disclose it?

Counsel is instructed to advise Mrs Brinda in conference in chambers on plea and likely sentence if she pleads guilty or is found guilty at trial.

It seems that Mrs Brinda has considerable mitigation in any event. The case is listed for a Plea and Trial Preparation Hearing (PTPH) on 20th October 2016.

2

IN THE WEST LONDON CROWN COURT

THE QUEEN v MARY BRINDA

MARY BRINDA IS CHARGED AS FOLLOWS:

STATEMENT OF OFFENCE

Theft, contrary to section 1(1) of the Theft Act 1968

PARTICULARS OF OFFENCE

Mary Brinda on 14th April 2016 stole one hundred pints of blood from the Central Blood Bank.

Officer of the Court

3

Statement of Witness

STATEMENT OF   PETER JOSEPHS

Age of Witness (date of birth)   Over 21

Occupation of Witness   Supervisor, Central Blood Bank

This statement, consisting of one page each signed by me, is true to the best of my knowledge and belief and I make it knowing that, if it is tendered in evidence, I shall be liable to prosecution if I have wilfully stated in it anything which I know to be false or do not believe to be true.

Dated the 25th day of April 2016

Signed Peter Josephs   Signature witnessed by Herbert Brown

I am a Supervisor at the Central Blood Bank in West London. I have worked there about nine months. On 14th April 2016 I was working as usual. About 10.00 am in the morning I saw a woman whom I recognised from the third floor—the Blood Testing Department. She is quite tall with long dark hair and high cheekbones. She was waiting for the lift on the basement floor, where the car park is. I had been taking some glass containers to a recycling container in the basement. She was accompanied by a very tall man with a pale complexion and black hair. I got in the lift with them. They got out at the third floor.

On either 14th or 15th April, 100 pints of blood were stolen from the testing department. If sold on the black market it would be worth around £20 per pint. The blood was in a large refrigerator and could be used until the end of 2016. Anyone who stole it would need to be aware of its storage requirements.

I have checked with personnel, and Mary Brinda was absent from work all that week. She had booked the time to spend with her father, who is apparently very ill. This was ordinary holiday leave and as such was not unusual. I definitely saw her at work that week.

I attended an ID parade at Notting Hill police station and positively identified the woman I had seen entering the building on 14th April. It was Mary Brinda.

No one had permission to take the blood.

I am willing to attend court and give evidence.

Signed Peter Josephs   Signature witnessed by Herbert Brown

4

Statement of Witness

STATEMENT OF   SALLY REID

Age of Witness (date of birth)   Over 21

Occupation of Witness   Blood tester

This statement, consisting of one page each signed by me, is true to the best of my knowledge and belief and I make it knowing that, if it is tendered in evidence, I shall be liable to prosecution if I have wilfully stated in it anything which I know to be false or do not believe to be true.

Dated the 25th day of April 2016

Signed Sally Reid   Signature witnessed by Herbert Brown

I have worked in the testing department of the Central Blood Bank for about a year. During this time I have worked with Mary Brinda on a couple of occasions, but do not know her at all well.

   I was working on 14th April 2016, when Mary came in about 10.00 am. I saw her move a large container next to the refrigerator. I asked her what she was doing and she replied she was doing some HIV testing. She appeared very irritable.

   I thought this might have something to do with a pay dispute I have heard Mary is having with the management. She discovered about nine months ago that they should have given her a pay rise for a certificate she gained. She was particularly incensed last week when we all heard the director had been given a massive pay increase.

   I then saw Mary's husband arrive. I had to go to another department. They had gone when I returned.

   I knew Mary was having financial difficulties, but I did not think she would ever steal.

   I am willing to attend court and give evidence.

Signed Sally Reid   Signature witnessed by Herbert Brown

5

Statement of Witness

STATEMENT OF   OSCAR MEADOWS

Age of Witness (date of birth)   Over 21

Occupation of Witness   Detective Sergeant

This statement, consisting of one page each signed by me, is true to the best of my knowledge and belief and I make it knowing that, if it is tendered in evidence, I shall be liable to prosecution if I have wilfully stated in it anything which I know to be false or do not believe to be true.

Dated the 28th day of April 2016

Signed O J Meadows   Signature witnessed by Herbert Brown

On 19th April 2016 I attended No 66 Portobello Road in Ladbroke Grove, W11, as a result of information received. I introduced myself to a woman who answered the door. I now know her name as Mary Brinda. I informed her she had been accused of theft from the Central Blood Bank. She said, 'I have only just returned from Bath where I have been visiting my father all week.'

I then cautioned and arrested Mrs Brinda. She was then conveyed to Notting Hill Police Station. A search of her handbag revealed a return train ticket from Bath to London dated 14th April 2016 and clipped by a ticket inspector. A check was made with the hospice where Mrs Brinda claimed she had been. Her name was signed in the visitors' book on all days that week except on the 14th of April.

Mrs Brinda then took part in an ID parade and was positively identified.

I was present when she was charged with theft.

Signed O J Meadows   Signature witnessed by Herbert Brown

6

METROPOLITAN POLICE

RECORD OF INTERVIEW

INTERVIEW OF: MARY BRINDA   19/4/16

Age/Date of birth 24/6/77   Occupation Blood tester

Address and Tel 66 Portobello Road, Ladbroke Grove, W11

BY: DS MEADOWS

AT: NOTTING HILL POLICE STATION

OTHER PERSONS PRESENT: PC BROWN

TIME INTERVIEW COMMENCED: 18.15   TIME INTERVIEW CONCLUDED: 18.30

TAPE COUNTER	PERSON SPEAKING	TEXT
0:00		Introductions made, reminded of right to solicitor, then cautioned.
1:55	MEADOWS	Do you wish to say anything regarding the theft of blood from your employer last week?
	BRINDA	You can check the personnel records. I was not working last week—I had booked a week's holiday to spend with my father who is terminally ill.
	MEADOWS	Yes, that has been confirmed. However, you were seen in the building on the 14th by two people and there is no record of you visiting the hospice that day.
5:55	BRINDA	I could not have been seen. They must be mistaken, and obviously my father does not remember my visit as he is delirious from the morphine.
	MEADOWS	There is no record of you signing in at the hospice.
	BRINDA	What difference does that make? I did not sign in on every single visit. Sometimes it is very lax and you can just wander in and out.
8:40	MEADOWS	How do you account for the train ticket that was found in your handbag?
	BRINDA	I have no idea how that got there.
	MEADOWS	Sally Reid has positively identified you at the Bank on 14th April. She even had a conversation with you about the fact that you were stealing blood.
	BRINDA	Sally Reid does not know me and there is no way I would have a conversation with her. She is obviously mistaken. I did not steal anything because I was in Bath visiting my father.

7

TAPE COUNTER	PERSON SPEAKING	TEXT
11:10	MEADOWS	Sally also told us about you feeling aggrieved with the Bank because they owe you some back pay. This was your way of taking what was rightfully yours, wasn't it?
	BRINDA	No, I was in Bath.
14:00		DS Meadows then explained that further enquiries would have to be made. Interview concluded.

IN THE WEST LONDON CROWN COURT

THE QUEEN

v

MARY BRINDA

DEFENCE STATEMENT

Mary Brinda's defence is that:

1. She was on leave from the Central Blood Bank at the time of the disappearance of the blood on 14th April 2016.
2. At the time of the theft, she was staying at a friend's house in Bath in order to be close to the hospice in which her terminally ill father was being cared for.
3. She is unable to call the friend with whom she was staying as a witness in support of her alibi as the friend is abroad.

Horace Pink & Co
81 Kensington Park Road
London W11

9

PROOF OF EVIDENCE

MARY BRINDA WILL SAY:

I am 39 years old and married to Gregory Brinda. He is a Canadian by birth, I am British. We have lived in London for 17 years, all of which time I have worked at the Central Blood Bank. We live at No 66 Portobello Road, London W11. Gregory is currently unemployed.

My husband has gone to Canada to help his father. His father is working in very difficult conditions trying to help his second wife who is severely disabled, and he has been in trouble with the Canadian authorities because they believe he has been involved in black market software piracy. In spite of being a Western state, certain activities in Canada that are seen to be a threat against the Canadian economy carry very heavy sentences. He was arrested about 2 weeks ago, but has since been released.

About nine months ago I discovered I should have been given a pay increase in March 2015 as I had obtained my third stage Blood Testers Certificate. I have worked out they owe me about £2,000. When I discovered this my pay was increased, but I have to apply to the Employment Tribunal to get the arrears. This is proving to be very difficult. If the court decides it was me that took the blood, could I not just say the money was mine anyway?

I have one previous conviction for shoplifting. It was in July 2015 and I was given a conditional discharge for 2 years. If the court does not know about this, I would prefer to keep it a secret. During the week when the theft occurred, I was in Bath visiting my father who is terminally ill in a hospice there. I stayed at the house of a friend who is out of the country.

On 19th April 2016 when I went back to work, I was told I was suspended from work until the matter was dealt with. I am very worried about the effect all this will have on my family.

10

CASE PREPARATION

The Queen v Mary Brinda

Overview

[Initial information from brief to set the conference in context]
Location of Conference: Chambers

Client: Mrs Mary Brinda
             (Instructing Solicitor: Horace Pink & Co)

D.o.B.	—	24.6.1977
Age	—	39 years old
Married	—	to Gregory Brinda for 17 years
Children	—	no mention in papers—check
Occupation	—	Blood Tester (for past 17 years) at Central Blood Bank, employment currently suspended while this charge investigated
Address	—	66 Portobello Road, London W11.

Charge: Theft, contrary to s 1(1), Theft Act 1968. Alleged to have stolen blood (100 pints) to the value of £2,000.00 from employer, Central Blood Bank, on 14th April 2016. PTPH fixed for 20th October 2016 at West London Crown Court.

Preliminary view of client's version of events/background/charge:

Mrs Brinda denies committing the offence as charged. Claims to have been visiting her sick father in Bath at the time of the alleged theft.

Mrs Brinda claims that she is owed £2,000.00 in back pay by her employer (same value as the stolen blood). As a result of passing the third stage Blood Testers Certificate, she is entitled to a pay increase. Pay increase not forthcoming—currently pursuing remedy in Employment Tribunal proceedings.

Appears adamant about her alibi—ie her visit to Bath to see her sick father. Would like to know whether taking property in lieu of back pay owed could be justified as some sort of set-off or claim of right.

Worried about effect of trial (outcome) on her family.

Personal problems predominant: sick father, unemployed husband, trouble in husband's country of birth (Canada), two pending court actions.

Previous conviction for shoplifting (July 2015)—two-year conditional discharge.

Wants to keep previous conviction secret.

Client needs advice on:

- how to plead;
- possible defences;
- adverse inferences which may be drawn;
- likely sentence (if found guilty or pleads guilty);
- effect of previous conviction:
    - can it be kept secret?
    - can the court activate it?
- effect of conviction for this offence (if found guilty or pleads guilty).

Legal analysis

[The analysis necessary to decide the legal framework of case and what areas of questioning will be necessary]

1.   The charge

The charge is theft contrary to s 1(1), Theft Act 1986. It is alleged that Mary Brinda stole 100 pints of blood from her employer, the Central Blood Bank on 14th April 2016.

In order to secure a conviction, in addition to satisfying the jury that it was Mary Brinda who took the blood, the prosecution have to prove, beyond reasonable doubt, that she:

• appropriated	— yes, no authorisation to remove blood, therefore assumption of rights of owner (s 3(1), Theft Act)
• property	— yes, 100 pints of blood valued at £2,000.00
• belonging to another	— 'property of Central Blood Bank'
• dishonestly	— need to check possible defences under s 2(1), Theft Act 1968 and/or defence of claim of right
• intention to permanently deprive	— would seem to be satisfied, ie to what use could the blood be put except one which is treating the property as one's own to dispose of (s 6, Theft Act, 1968)?

2.   Defences

Possible defences to meeting charge on the basis of no dishonesty:

Was Mrs Brinda dishonest (even if she admits to taking the blood)? Two-stage test laid down in *R v Ghosh* (1982) 75 Cr App R 154, CA:

• Was what the defendant did dishonest according to the ordinary standards of reasonable and honest people? [If not, prosecution fails.]

• Did the defendant herself realise that what she was doing was, by those standards, dishonest?

Thus, it seems that if the jury were satisfied that Mrs Brinda was acting in a way that she knew ordinary people would consider dishonest, even if she believed she was justified in doing so, she would be dishonest.

On the facts, it would be an uphill battle to persuade a jury that Mrs Brinda, employed in a senior capacity at the Blood Bank for some 17 years, would not know that removing blood was dishonest.

3.   Claim of right defence

To run this defence, Mrs Brinda must have believed that a right to the property existed in law (even if the belief is unfounded). A belief in moral right to take the property will not suffice: *R v Bernhard* (1938) 26 Cr App R 137; *R v Woolven* (1983) *77* Cr App Rep 231. This is almost certainly a non-runner.

4.   The alibi—the heart of the defence

Defence statement has been served. It contains the bare minimum of information. Consideration must be given to the possible consequences of any changes in the version of events as put forward by Mrs Brinda, or any further evidence upon which she may seek to rely. Adverse inferences can be drawn from a failure to mention when arrested and cautioned any matter later relied upon at trial (s 34, Criminal Justice and Public Order Act 1994), as can any departure at trial from her defence statement (see generally, Criminal Procedure and Investigations Act 1996).

5.   Evidential issues raised

Identification at scene by two witnesses. Prima facie appears to be the strongest evidence for the prosecution. Recognition cases—need to check details of knowledge and familiarity of witnesses. Need for caution/warning if and when case relies substantially on ID evidence. Guideline case *R v Turnbull* [1977] QB 224, CA.

Identification parade—need to check Pre-Trial Identification Procedures (Code D, Police and Criminal Evidence Act 1984) to discover whether any breaches in this procedure, etc. If so, did any of the alleged breaches cause any prejudice to Mrs Brinda, and is there any possibility of evidence being inadmissible? (See eg *R v Quinn* [1995] 1 Cr App R 480.)

Admissibility of train ticket discovered in Mrs Brinda's handbag. If adduced for the truth of an implied assertion, ie that Mrs Brinda did travel Bath–London–Bath on 14th April 2016, then admissible evidence. See *R v Twist* [2009] 2 Cr App R 17, CA; and Criminal Justice Act 2003, s 115.

6.   Sentence (if pleads guilty or is found guilty at trial)

See generally the Criminal Practice Directions: VII Sentencing. The problem is that this case appears to be a 'breach of trust' case in that it is a theft from an employer. The parts of the Sentencing Guidelines Council's Sentencing Guidelines that are most relevant are Part 14 Theft, including Theft in Breach of Trust. In general terms, a high-level community order sentence is likely, but there is some risk of custody should the court consider the degree of trust to be a high one. The circumstances of the offence and the offender need to be analysed.

If custody is considered, the court will take the following factors into consideration when determining the length of sentence to be imposed in breach of trust cases:

- loss suffered by the victim (monetary value and other impacts, if any);
- nature and degree of trust, including the type and terms of the relationship;
- period of time over which thefts were committed;
- use to which property dishonestly taken is put (eg need or desperation);
- impact of the offence on the public and public confidence;
- effect on fellow employees;
- effect on offender herself (but not usually loss of employment and inevitable hardship);
- her own history;
- her personal mitigation.

If custody is decided to be the correct disposal for this offence, the starting point will be one year's custody, with a range from 26 weeks to two years' custody.

Suspending any term of custody. See the Sentencing Guideline Council's Sentencing Guideline, Part 2 New Sentences: Criminal Justice Act 2003, Section 2—Custodial Sentences, Part 2—Suspended Sentences of Imprisonment. The custody threshold must be crossed and it must be unavoidable that a custodial sentence be imposed. Only then will the sentencing judge consider whether or not to impose the custodial sentence.

Community orders. If instead of custody a high-level community order is the appropriate sentence, see the Sentencing Guideline Council's Sentencing Guideline, Part 2 New Sentences: Criminal Justice Act 2003, Section 1, Part 1—Community Sentences.

Breach of conditional discharge. If Mrs Brinda pleads guilty (or is found guilty at trial) she will be in breach of a conditional discharge received following a conviction for theft in 2015. This trial will take place during the currency of the discharge. In dealing with the breach, the court may sentence her for the original offence in any manner in which it could have dealt with her if she had just been convicted before the court for that offence (s 13(6), Powers of Criminal Courts (Sentencing) Act 2000).

Factual analysis
[The analysis necessary to become familiar with the case to identify missing information and clarify ambiguous/conflicting information]

(Client's version of events: Instructions to Counsel and Proof of Evidence p 10.) Date of theft: 14th April 2016.

Mrs Brinda in Bath visiting terminally ill father in hospice. Father too ill to confirm visit. Stayed with friend near Bath—friend now out of the country.

Failed to sign visitors' registration book at hospice on 14.04.16, but signed on every other day.

Train ticket dated 14.04.16 (Bath–London–Bath) found by police in handbag (DS Meadows p 6).

Identified as being in London at work on 14.04.16. Two witnesses (both fellow employees)—Peter Josephs (p 4) and Sally Reid (p 5). Both say she was accompanied to work by a man. Reid claims she recognised the man as Mr Brinda.

Arrested (after caution?) 19.04.16. ID parade—positive identification—charged with theft of blood.

Police interview 19.04.16—denies offence, maintains being on leave in Bath (pp 7/8).

Is apparently in breach of a two-year conditional discharge passed in July 2015. Worked at Central Blood Bank for 17 years. Currently suspended until resolution of matter of theft.

Husband (Gregory) Canadian. Currently unemployed. At present abroad in Canada visiting father who is in some trouble with Canadian authorities. Children/other dependent relatives—no information.

Central Blood Bank failed to increase pay following acquisition of Stage 3 Blood Testers Certificate. Pursuing claim for £2,000.00 through Employment Tribunal. Note: no public funding for Employment Tribunal hearings.

Questions to elicit necessary information
The offence:

- When first heard of it?
- What reaction?
- What sort of bulk is 100 pints of blood?
- Storage—temperature required?
- Removal—how difficult?
- Black market potential?
- Shelf life?

The alibi:

- Exact dates in Bath—when left London/returned to London?
- Leave/holiday from work booked in advance—when?
- Who at work knew leave due?
- Father's illness—how long/prognosis?
- Any possibility of father remembering visit?

- Where stayed during time in Bath?
- Name of friend?
- Where is friend currently?
- Friend available as witness?
- Any other witness—eg nurses/friends/acquaintances at hospice?
- Any other person likely to have seen her at hospice on 14.04.16?
- Usual to sign the visitors' book?
- Explanation for lack of signature in visitors' book on 14.04.16?
- Any other way to confirm presence on 14.04.16?
- Where was Gregory during this week, and especially on 14.04.16?
- Explanation for train ticket discovered in handbag?

Identification (at workplace on date of alleged theft):

- Relationship with Sally Reid and Peter Josephs—how well known?
- Either involved in the pay dispute/either know Gregory?
- Describe layout of workplace?
- Location of refrigerator?
- Describe Gregory.
- Gregory's dates in Canada?

Caution, arrest, ID parade:

- Check details of these—no information in instructions to suggest suspicion of impropriety, but need to check.

Potential defences:

- Explain why thinks taking property in lieu could be justified.
- Pay dispute—contractual right to increase.
- What procedure adopted by employer for pay increases?
- Current stage of Employment Tribunal hearing/what costs incurred?
- Contemplation of this.

Previous conviction:

- Check details: ie only one offence of shoplifting?
- Value of goods/method/plea?
- Confirm date?
- Confirm sentence—two-year conditional discharge?
- Understands the meaning of conditional discharge?

Personal circumstances (mitigation):

- Salary?
- Savings?
- Debts/outgoings?
- Husband unemployed—any prospects?
- Cost of Canadian involvement—trips/support for family?

- Any costs for hospice; father's financial position?
- Cost to date of Employment Tribunal application?
- Any other exceptional factors?
- Confirm 17 years' employment with Central Blood Bank?
- Exact nature of duties?
- Any previous trouble?
- Work history?
- Details of family responsibilities?
- Health?
- Any specific problems/medication?
- Response to problems—Canadian connection/financial difficulties/pay dispute?
- Reaction to current proceedings?

Merits of case (strengths and weaknesses)

[Note: this is only a preliminary conclusion derived from legal and factual analysis of the papers contained in the brief. Merits of the case may change in response to questions asked.]

Prosecution case appears strong:

(a) Alibi weak:
   (i)   apparently no alibi witness;
   (ii)   no record of presence at hospice on 14.04.16;
   (iii) signed hospice visitors' book on other days that week;
   (iv)   train ticket (query admissibility).

(b) Identification at workplace on day of alleged theft:
   (i)   Sally Reid quite strong—knew Gregory;
   (ii)   Peter Josephs convincing on Mrs Brinda, less on Gregory;
   (iii) two positive identifications—compelling evidence.

(c) ID parade:
   (i)   need some instructions in conference to be in a position to attack this evidence—prima facie admissible—strong.

(d) Pay dispute:
   (i)   inference may be drawn that Mrs Brinda stole the blood to recover the money she claims is owing, ie taking the law into own hands;
   (ii)   need instructions on defence of claim of right.

(e) Nature of property taken:
   (i)   blood only of use to someone with knowledge of value/storage;
   (ii)   likely to have been taken by someone with expertise in field;
   (iii) weight/bulk of 100 pints of blood/difficult for one person to move/presence of Gregory to assist;
   (iv)   jury may take a dim view of the fact that the property in question (blood) may be regarded as a precious commodity.

(f) Where is Gregory now? Where was he on 14.04.16? Probably fatal to the case against Mrs Brinda if he is not in the country to give evidence on her behalf.

(g) Without more evidence in support of Mrs Brinda the prosecution case against her looks strong.

Preliminary advice—options available

[Note: depending on instructions received in conference, other options may be available to Mrs Brinda. Similarly, what is the most acceptable course of action to take will depend on answers elicited during conference.]

Option 1
Conference reveals cogent evidence to dispute identification and/or challenge admissibility, and good alibi evidence and/or witness. Advise not guilty plea.

Option 2
Conference reveals cogent evidence to dispute identification and/or challenge admissibility, but no new supporting evidence of the alibi or any witness available to testify. Even without good identification evidence, lack of support for alibi may be very damaging. Advice would depend on the nature of the other evidence in support of Mrs Brinda—eg Gregory—and what kind of witness Mrs Brinda will be and how she will come over to the jury. Advice will depend on these and other possible factors (see Option 3).

Option 3
Conference reveals no new alibi evidence, no challenge to the identification evidence, and no claim of right defence. This complies with initial analysis of the papers and therefore in all the circumstances a plea of guilty would appear to be the most appropriate solution. However, it is vital to remind the client that:

- she should not plead guilty if she did not take the blood;
- despite your advice the decision on how to plead is ultimately hers.

The Bar Standards Board's *Professional Statement for Barristers*, at 1.6, requires barristers to be able to provide clear, concise and accurate advice in writing and orally and take responsibility for it. This includes an ability to convey unpalatable advice where necessary. (See also Section 3: Written Standards for the Conduct of Professional Work, Code of Conduct of the Bar of England and Wales, which permits you to give advice in strong terms.) To support your advice:

- re-evaluate the strength of prosecution case/remind client that it is likely that a jury will convict in the light of the evidence against her;
- remind client of the strong mitigation (effect on reducing sentence);
- explain sentence reduction for plea of guilty (note: this must not sound like a 'carrot' to induce a plea of guilty);
- explain that if there is a guilty plea, the matter can be dispensed with more speedily.

Likely sentence:

(a) Guilty plea: in absence of exceptional circumstances custody threshold reached for breach of trust cases of this nature (see above, Legal Analysis note 6) but with mitigation discount for plea, expect three to six months.

(b) Not guilty plea and convicted: expect 6 to 12 months.

(c) Breach of conditional discharge: sentence will depend on the severity of previous offence. Court may sentence for this offence to run consecutively with sentence for the theft of blood (Powers of Criminal Courts (Sentencing) Act 2000, s 13).

Other points raised

Professional conduct
Does the previous conviction for shoplifting need to be revealed? First, Mrs Brinda should be told that a barrister is not obliged to reveal the previous conviction to the court if the court is unaware of it unless she gives permission to do so or where the court would

pass mandatory sentences (gC12, Code of Conduct). It is for the prosecution to gather and present relevant facts against the defendant at court. On the other hand, Mrs Brinda would not be able to be put forward to the court as being a person of good character. Best advice if Mrs Brinda decides to plead guilty is that it would be in her best interests to reveal the previous conviction to the court in order to get credit for full and frank disclosure and ensure the mitigation on her behalf can be as effective as possible.

Future consequences if Mrs Brinda pleads guilty (or is found guilty)?
It should be pointed out that a finding of guilt on a charge of this theft will mean that she has a criminal record for an offence of dishonesty, and, consequently, job applications will be subject to Rehabilitation of Offenders Act 1974.

5.7 Summary of stages used to prepare sample case

It should be apparent that comprehensive preparation and planning is central to your ability to conduct an efficient and effective client conference. As we have seen, thorough preparation for every conference requires:

- legal analysis;
- factual analysis;
- identification of gaps/ambiguities/conflicting evidence;
- preliminary assessment of likely outcome(s).

At the completion of this stage you should be in a position to:

(a) decide how best, and in what order, to conduct the conference (see **Chapter 4**);

(b) identify all the information you need to elicit from your client (see **Chapter 6**);

(c) provide, in the light of that information, sound advice (see **Chapter 7**).

It will also be apparent that thorough planning often involves preparation of a lengthy document, which could be cumbersome to use during the conference with the client. It is recommended that, in addition to the case preparation undertaken, you draft a top page, a conference plan, for use during the conference. This can, of course, be annotated for easy reference during the conference, to specific areas of questioning, for example. In addition, it is often helpful to 'flag' sections of your preparation for ease of identification and reference. The following is an example of a conference plan in the case of *R v Mary Brinda*.

5.8   Example of a conference plan

CONFERENCE PLAN
The Queen v Mary Brinda

Preliminaries
Welcome/introduction/role of barrister.

Purpose of conference
Deal with the following:

- Advise on merits of prosecution case and evaluate the likely outcome.
- Need to question before being able to advise.
- Cannot advise until full evaluation of facts.
- Need to explain conclusions reached and why.
- In the light of the third item above, advise on plea/sentence.
- Take instructions.
- Advise on next steps at the PTPH.

Area of questioning
Identify:

- the offence charged;
- alibi;
- identification: at workplace, in identification parade;
- pay dispute with employer;
- previous conviction;
- personal circumstances.

Merits of case
Deal with the following:

- Offer a full evaluation of the strengths and weaknesses.
- Identify sources for conclusions reached (her answers/witness statements/evidential rules).
- Explain law and procedure.
- Evaluate prosecution case and likely outcome.

Advise
Advise on the following:

- plea;
- sentence if pleads guilty or is found guilty;
- other consequences.

Take instructions

Emphasise that the final choice is hers [note: see **Chapter 7**]. Check she understands advice. Give client time to go away and consider advice.

Next steps

What will happen at PTPH? Reassure client of further meeting prior to court appearance.

Conclusion

Check/confirm any instructions given. Check whether client has any further worries or questions. Confirm that if any problems or if any further information comes to light contact can be made via solicitor at any time prior to court appearance.

6 Questioning techniques

6.1 Introduction

In **Chapter 5**, we have seen that effective preparation for a conference requires you to plan in advance precisely what information you need to elicit from the client—that is, of course, what questions you need to ask your client. Ultimately your most important source of information is your client. It may appear strange therefore that barristers meet the client on surprisingly few occasions. This is because the solicitor is the first point of contact for the lay client and will continue to be the first line of communication for the client and you during the lifetime of a case. Note that this chapter, like the manual in general, is written on the basis of instruction through a solicitor rather than any form of direct access.

In much litigation the barrister will only meet the client for one, or perhaps two, conferences before the case goes to court. Sometimes it is only at court that the client and counsel finally meet. This is especially true during the early years of practice. This arrangement can be open to misinterpretation by the public, and particularly by clients. The lawyer can appear to be insufficiently interested in the litigant's case, or aloof from it. However, barristers and solicitors work as a team, albeit a rather disjointed one. Different roles are being fulfilled by the two professions. Solicitors prepare and manage the case through its course; barristers offer advice and take the major part of courtroom advocacy.

It follows that in the normal course of events, if the barrister needs further information, he or she can seek it through the solicitor. However, on many occasions as a pupil you will be the first lawyer that the client has had contact with, and the luxury of an instructing solicitor to support you will be all but non-existent. Nonetheless, there are occasions when the barrister requires information of such detail or complexity that it is necessary to invite the client to attend a conference in chambers. This allows the barrister to request information and to take instructions from the client face to face. Clearly, the barrister will wish to make the most of this opportunity to gather sufficient information to be able to advise appropriately and to take the client's full instructions. The key to fulfilling these tasks is effective use of questions.

Naturally both the barrister and the client will wish to discuss the case in detail, but unlike the normal course of conversation the conference questions must be planned in advance. This preparation will establish a clear idea of what type of information is required and how best to obtain that information from the client. The key to this is a sound knowledge of questioning techniques, and what makes an effective conference into a good one is the efficient utilisation of these techniques. The planned questions will enable you to do two things simultaneously:

- to exploit the client as a source of information; and
- to have concern for the client as a human being.

There are some parallels here with the art and techniques of examination-in-chief and re-examination (see *Advocacy* manual, Chapters 21 and 23). Gifted advocates exploit their own witnesses without destroying them. Before investigating the elements that go to make up the techniques of questioning, it will help to have a picture of the different types of questions that are at the barrister's disposal.

6.2 Classes of questions

The following definitions and explanations introduce the major categories of questions. Most will, of course, be familiar to you, but what is important for the barrister is what effect each type of question will have upon the client. With this knowledge you should be able to quickly gather the relevant information whilst controlling the client. In short, the barrister must be familiar with all the available tools of the trade.

6.2.1 Yes/no questions

These are the simplest and perhaps the most limiting form of questions. The only answer expected, indeed at times permitted, is a straightforward affirmation or denial.

EXAMPLE

Q1 Your name is John Smith, isn't it?
A1 Yes, it is.
Q2 Are you married?
A2 No.

Obviously the questioner does not expect much additional information from the client. On occasions, though, the person replying will volunteer more information. For example, the reply to Q2 could have been: 'No, I'm divorced.' Further, the questioner has phrased the question to allow for a confirmation or a denial but that does not mean that he or she is personally ignorant of the truth. For example, questions like Q1 are often designed to confirm information already known to the questioner. However, the question might be a speculative one. The questioner might have a strong suspicion that the person in front of him or her is called John Smith, but requires confirmation of this suspicion.

One important drawback with this form of question is that it enables the respondent to give very limited replies, 'yes' or 'no', without ignoring the question. The full picture may not be revealed because of a desire to be evasive, or a fear of going beyond the limits set by the question, or because of sheer inertia. On the other hand it is, of course, an excellent way of controlling the amount of information that comes from the client and the style in which it is presented. The barrister can control the client further by adding that the answer is limited to a simple 'yes' or 'no'.

6.2.2 Closed and semi-closed questions

This is a large category, of which the latter group forms a subset. They are called closed because to a greater or lesser extent they control the answer that the client will give to the barrister. Answers of a short length are sought; a phrase or a single word will often suffice.

EXAMPLE

Q1 What is your name, please?
A1 Alan Jones.
Q2 When did you leave your wife?
A2 On 16 January.

The first question severely limits the expected response, although it does not suggest the answer. Q2 is another example: this time the word 'when' indicates that only the date is required.

EXAMPLE

Q3 You then moved in with your mother and following that you lived with which brother, David or Geraint?
A3 Geraint first and then David.

The third question is a leading one, as although expressed as a choice, the answer appears in the question itself. It is also a classic example of a closed question. The client, however, went beyond what was asked and offered some additional information. This is not surprising as the client wished to clarify the position.

Clearly, then, closed questions offer guidance as to the sorts of answers expected and indicate to the client the amount of information expected. This will assist the barrister to control the client. However, there are drawbacks. An obvious danger is that the client will limit his or her answers, and it is unlikely that he or she will give you the full picture. What if, for example, the full story was that the client stayed with a female friend (and a possible co-respondent) immediately upon leaving the marital home and before moving in with his mother? Closed questions should be used with caution, and avoided unless you already have the client's version of events.

6.2.3   Open questions

The open question allows the client freedom to speak at some length and on a wide choice of topics. In effect the question invites the client to launch into a narrative or an explanation using his or her own words. Typically, the answers are long and there can be diversions from the original topic. There are, therefore, some inherent dangers, but this form of question can be a swift route to a large amount of information. Consider the likely responses to the following questions.

EXAMPLE

Q1 What was your relationship with your wife like?
Q2 Why do you blame yourself for the breakdown in communication?
Q3 How do you account for the financial problems that you were both facing following the birth of your second child?

Whilst one can imagine a variety of answers, the amount of detail and the honesty with which they are answered depend upon the client's willingness to be open with the barrister. Additionally, the client's knowledge of events will limit his or her answers. On most occasions, if the barrister asks questions of this type, the client will respond with large chunks of information that will require further explanation and expansion.

Open questions do not readily allow the questioner to exert control, and interruptions must be handled with care. Too many interruptions will jeopardise the rapport between client and counsel. If a question is asked, it is only right that the person answering should be allowed to say what they have to say uninterrupted.

6.2.4   Semi-open questions

This class of question can be one of the most useful to the barrister during the conference. It combines the control of the closed and the semi-closed question with the fruitfulness of the open question. The questioner selects and imposes limits upon the answer expected and communicates these to the client through the medium of the question itself.

EXAMPLE

Q1 Please tell me what you were doing on 10 January between leaving work and returning home at 2 am.
Q2 What did you tell your wife in that telephone conversation?
Q3 What did she say to you when you returned home?

Each question gives the client a clear picture of what type of information is sought, but leaves the respondent sufficient freedom to give detailed replies.

6.2.5   Simple questions

This is not strictly speaking a class of question but refers to the form that questions can take. They are also known as single-issue questions. Let us consider two important observations in turn. First, lay clients are rarely used to being interrogated; second, like all of us, they are used to holding a conversation. The former point is worth bearing in mind throughout the conference. You cannot expect the client to answer all of the questions either immediately or satisfactorily. Nor can you treat the client in the same way as you might choose to cross-examine a witness who is damaging to your case and inimical to you personally. This is just common sense, but easily forgotten when a conference is not going as smoothly as planned.

The second point warrants greater attention. Most conversations follow an unplanned and freely structured format. Questions maintain the flow of communication, and the degrees of appropriateness of the answers reflect the formality of the conversation. In this fluid environment, a questioner will often use verbal shorthand to indicate to the other what topic or topics he or she is interested in hearing about next.

EXAMPLE

Q1 Did you enjoy your holidays? Was the weather good?

The questioner obviously wants to know about the trip, but has also singled out the weather for comment. During everyday settings little, if any, confusion is caused by this style of question. During the introductory chat with the client there is nothing wrong with continuing to use these everyday forms. However, consider the next example.

EXAMPLE

Q2 What treatment did the hospital administer to your wounds; were you satisfied by it at the time?

The two topics are both relevant, but this is really two questions rolled into one. First, the barrister seeks information about what actually took place in the hospital. Second, he or she seeks an estimation of the client's satisfaction with that treatment. By addressing these two relevant points at once, there is a danger that the client will either answer one and ignore the other or give inadequate answers to both. Sometimes, however, it is not clear that two issues are being dealt with in the same question.

EXAMPLE

Q3 Who delivered the cash to the banks?

On the face of it this question appears to be a single-issue question, but in certain circumstances it could contain at least two issues. First, who delivered the money and, second, to which banks did the various parties make their deliveries? Unless both questions are addressed separately, important information may be missed and the conference's objective to take full instructions may not be obtained. This in turn could lead the barrister into giving faulty or incomplete advice to the client. The key then is to ask single-issue questions in a logical order. This will assist you to conduct a thorough examination and allow the client to pass on detailed and focused information.

6.2.6 Leading questions

Leading questions appear in several forms, but there are broadly two categories. First, there are those that encourage the client either to agree or disagree with a statement made by the questioner with the express design of putting words into the mouth of the person being questioned—in other words, feeding.

EXAMPLE

Q1 You were not the person whom the store detective saw in the chemist's that morning, were you?
A1 No, it wasn't me.
Q2 Because you would have been in school as it was a Wednesday?
A2 That's right.

Second, a question will be a leading one if it offers a choice of answers. This is leading because the answer again is being suggested in the question.

EXAMPLE

Q1 Were you wearing a red or a green jacket that morning?
A1 A dark green one.
Q2 Did you or didn't you take the train to work?
A2 I did.

The appropriateness of leading questions in examination of witnesses is strictly beyond our concerns here, but they are not usually permitted during examination-in-chief on matters in issue, when the witness should give testimony in his or her own words. Similarly, during a conference, there is little point in suggesting to the client what to say. The client is the source of the information, not the barrister, so avoid leading questions when possible. The advice to avoid leading questions becomes an imperative instruction when you approach the heart of the client's problem. It is unethical and unprofessional to lead a defence to a client when dealing with central issues or new matters. You should never use the following form of leading questions.

EXAMPLE

Q1 So you picked up the bag from the platform?
A1 Yes, that's right, I thought someone had forgotten it.
Q2 What did you do next?
A2 I went home, taking the bag with me.
Q3 Did you intend to take it to lost property before the police came to your house?
A3 Er, yes. Yeah, I thought I'd take it in the next day on my way into work.

In hindsight the danger is clear. The third question should have been neutral, eg 'What did you intend to do with the bag once you got home?' No matter whether the questioner wittingly or unwittingly suggested the course of action, the client exploited the opportunity offered by the leading question and now presents a defence. The prohibition against leading extends to all areas of the law, encompassing the civil as well as the criminal. Thus, it would be quite unacceptable to pose the following set of questions to a client making a claim in personal injury negligence.

EXAMPLE

Q1 Were any of your personal belongings damaged in the crash?
A1 Well, my jeans were ripped and my watch broken.
Q2 OK, how much were they worth?
A2 The jeans were pretty new, so about £45; but the watch was a gift so I'm not sure.
Q3 Well, shall we say £100?
A3 Yes, all right.

As counsel, the Code of Conduct covers all of your professional work. It is quite clear that feeding the client information is unethical in the courtroom and the spirit of this code extends to the conference room. The Code of Conduct rC6 states:

> Your duty not to mislead the court or to permit the court to be misled will include the following obligations:
>   .1   you must not:
>
>   .a make submissions, representations or any other statement; or
>   .b ask questions which suggest facts to witnesses
>
>   which you know, or are instructed, are untrue or misleading.

Rule C9 states:

> Your duty to act with honesty and integrity under CD3 includes the following requirements:
>
>   .4   you must not rehearse, practise with or coach a witness in respect of their evidence.

There are, naturally, less dogmatic reasons for avoiding leading the client. There is little point in asking someone a series of questions if you continually suggest the answers to them: you will be dictating to them rather than investigating the limits of their knowledge. Whilst the other person may adopt your version of events or set of facts, once they enter the witness box it is unlikely that they will either remember them or stick to them. There is nothing quite like a confused witness giving illogical evidence to whet the appetite of an eager, cross-examining counsel.

However, there may be questioning techniques which although technically leading are nonetheless suitable for use in the conference, for example when asking clients confirmatory questions or when seeking their comments on your summary of events. These questions conclude question-and-answer sessions, or seek to double-check the accuracy of information—that is, information which has already been communicated to the barrister by the solicitor. The important considerations are therefore:

- to allow the client to tell you first-hand the information you require without unsuitable prompting;
- to use questions that may be leading ones only with extreme caution.

6.2.7 Conclusion

Clearly, each of these types of questions will be familiar to you through daily use. During the conference, however, one is faced by many concerns and stresses and the selection of the appropriate form of question can become laborious. The danger is that communication between you and the client may become staid or awkward. Two things can assist you:

(a) Practice is essential. Become familiar with the mental process of selecting and utilising different question forms to elicit information. Experience can only come about through some trial and the occasional error. In each conference you will have to assess the client's level of intelligence and spend a short time selecting the most appropriate questioning strategy.

(b) Planning will greatly assist you. Not all questions can or should be planned word for word. Some idea of the type of information that you require should enable you to identify areas for questioning and encourage you to prepare a strategy for extracting this information from the client. If a fundamental question or one requiring caution on your part is identified, it may be worthwhile drafting it out in full. The key to success here is practice and flexibility. The plan should be sufficiently flexible to allow you to adapt to the needs of each conference and the characteristics of each client. (See **Chapter 5**.)

With an understanding of the major categories of questions it is now appropriate to develop knowledge of how to use them during the conference. From the examples used previously you will have already noted one useful technique: the degree of control that can be expected from a closed question compared with an open one. In section **6.3**, we will consider in greater depth the techniques that can be used as part of an overall questioning strategy.

6.3 Selecting questioning techniques

There are many acceptable ways to question a lay client during the conference; indeed, several styles may be adopted during different stages in the conference. The decision to utilise various techniques of questioning will form part of your questioning strategy. To begin with, it is probably worth selecting and planning these strategies in detail as part of your preparation for the conference—but remember, a useful plan will be sufficiently flexible to allow you to adapt your preparation to meet the vicissitudes of the conference. After some practice you will learn to adopt and adapt these techniques with greater ease. In this section we will look in greater detail at the constituent parts that form questioning techniques.

6.3.1   Type of question

Each time you wish to ask the client for a piece of information you should decide upon the type of question you are going to use. We have already seen that each type of question will elicit a different response from the client. Therefore select the type of question that is appropriate to your needs.

6.3.2   Style of questioning

The manner in which you ask your questions will depend upon the type of client, your purpose in asking, and the sort of answer that you expect to receive. Each client must be assessed at the outset of the conference so that you can adjust your style to suit their personality and characteristics. Factors include the person's age, education, and profession, their familiarity with the legal process, and with you. There is little point in adopting an excessively businesslike or legalistic style of questioning with an 18-year-old factory worker experiencing his first brush with the criminal law. On the other hand, it is inappropriate to take an unnecessarily friendly or simplistic style of questioning at all stages of the conference. There is probably room for both styles at the right time. You will have to use your judgement and professional experience to help you to decide when one style is more appropriate than the other. Sometimes it will be clear that your questions ought to be phrased in a sympathetic way, for example if asking the client about injuries sustained in an accident. On other occasions you may have to adjust your style subtly, for example if you believe the client is exaggerating the symptoms. The key is to remain alert to two things:

- the reason why you are asking the individual question; and
- the client's reactions to you and the questions that you are asking.

Both of these will help you to choose and adapt the appropriate style in which you ask the questions.

6.3.3   Strategy

In order to conduct a thorough and effective investigation of the facts, you will need to consider your overall strategy for the questioning section of the conference. This will include not only the right questions to ask, but also the most successful way to present them and the best way to exploit the client's memory. These, and some of the other central questioning techniques, will make up your questioning strategy.

Several factors might affect your choice of strategy: the nature of information that you require; the client's reactions and answers to your questions so far; or the point reached in the conference. An inquisitorial line of questioning, for example, might be selected for a short period to test the client's suitability as a witness. This is a strategic decision that needs careful selection. You will have to take every precaution to avoid upsetting the client and jeopardising the effectiveness of the conference as a whole, as well as to avoid coaching the client as a witness. If, on the other hand, the client becomes upset or confused, you will wish to adopt an explanatory and supportive style and introduce simpler questions, perhaps closed ones. This will help the client to calm down before you resume a more demanding line of questions.

6.3.4   Technique selection

Some of the more common techniques are discussed in the following sections. Several techniques will almost certainly be necessary during the conference: each technique is selected because it is an appropriate route to the necessary information. Remember that you will have to return to different techniques at different times during the conference. No one technique will realise all of the conference's objectives.

6.3.4.1 Confirming and checking information

This will require an indication that you are looking for short answers, mostly in the form of agreement or disagreement and correction. A mixture of yes/no, closed, and semi-open questions would be most suitable for this technique. These forms of questions will enable you to control the client's answers and allow you to move quickly from topic to topic. For example, names, addresses, and other details already indicated in your instructions can be swiftly checked in this way.

6.3.4.2 Inviting the client to give you further, more detailed, information

The point is to allow the client to pass on sizeable amounts of information to you. Therefore, inform the client that you want them to give you details to fill in gaps in your knowledge and make them feel comfortable and free to do so. A series of open and semi-open questions are the most useful forms of question as they give the client freedom to speak at some length. Additionally, the client will probably require some reassurance from you that what is being said is relevant and helpful. So remember to remain interested in what the client has to say.

6.3.4.3 Inviting the client to raise his or her concerns

Some specific open questions will have to be asked to get the client to express any matters that continue to concern him or her. Closed questions or yes/no ones should be avoided. These types of questions will enable the shy client the opportunity to gloss over these points. It may be necessary to combine your open questions with some gentle encouragement. This might take the form of a statement that you are willing to help with additional matters, and that you invite the client to raise them now.

6.3.4.4 Gathering specific details

If you need to gather detailed and complex material, for example a chronology of events, it is useful to combine a business-like style with semi-open and some closed questions. This technique will concentrate the client upon the task in hand. The business-like style will help you to get the client to collaborate with you and enable you to exploit the client's knowledge of the facts. The initial question should be a semi-open one. This will control any answer by setting limits so that the client begins by discussing the relevant issues. You can assist the client further by stating what sort of information you are looking for. Leading questions should, of course, be avoided. Semi-closed questions will enable you to select areas to fill in gaps and those that seek to confirm and complete the answers will settle any ambiguities.

6.3.4.5 Compiling a proof of evidence

When gathering large amounts of information of this nature there is a particularly useful technique that is known variously as the funnel, X, or V technique. These names all describe models which are broadly similar and are widely thought of as appropriate for use at an initial client interview, but can also be useful at other times when you do not have sufficient detail to be able to advise the client. Broadly speaking, this technique is a combination of open, semi-open, and closed questions. Starting with a widely phrased open question, the client is encouraged to tell the story of events in his or her words. At this early stage the lawyer adopts an interested but silent manner. Once the client begins to talk about issues that are relevant to the case the questioner will guide the speaker to focus on them. This is done by use of an ever-narrowing series of semi-closed questions. The lawyer begins to exert control over the choice of topics and over the client. Finally, some yes/no and clarification questions are employed to complete the questioner's comprehension and understanding of the client's version of events. At this stage the lawyer is fully in control and the atmosphere is set for the next stage of the conference, often a discussion of the options that exist for the client.

In almost all litigation the solicitor has responsibility for initial meetings with the client and will usually prepare a proof of evidence. In most circumstances you can therefore expect that the client has already been through this process. However, there will be times when you have to undertake this job yourself. There are many reasons for this—for example, the solicitor might not have had time to prepare a proof, or events may have developed since one was drafted. You should be aware of the dangers attached to using this technique too freely: the client will repeat information that you already know. The result could be that the client will become frustrated with your questions and you may waste valuable time. Caution is therefore required. Check whether you need to gather so much information and consider whether a confirmatory technique would be preferable or one that only gathers specific details. In either event it is a good idea to acknowledge that you know that the client has already addressed these points with the solicitor. Additionally, you should always be in a position to justify any question that you address to the client.

The advantages of this structure are clear: it is client-centred and focused on the issues. The early open questions encourage the client to do much of the initial talking, so the lawyer has the benefit of hearing the first-hand account, and this is why it is more suitably employed by the solicitor. The later closed questions pull the matter to a conclusion that satisfies the needs of both lawyer and client. The disadvantages are that the process is time-consuming and there can be an initial lack of direction. Further, it will require some degree of repetition, by the client, of information already passed on to the professional client. Overall this structured technique of questioning the client is of limited use to you as a barrister.

6.4 Planning questions

How you choose to present the questioning stage in your plan will depend upon personal preference and style. What follows is for your consideration when making some of these choices.

6.4.1 The written plan

Most barristers will follow a written plan to some extent, as few, if any, conferences can afford to rely upon the barrister's memory alone. This is particularly true of the questions as they form the hub of any conference. A complete list of fully drafted questions is rarely necessary and can impede the progress of the conference, as it can be cumbersome and restricting. On the other hand, if the areas for questioning are too vague, important topics may not be investigated and vital questions may be left unasked. A compromise position is often the answer. A combination of bullet points and selected questions is one solution that has found favour with practitioners and students alike. The bullet points for questioning will need to be logically and coherently ordered so that you can conduct the conference in a way that enables the client to appreciate what you are doing at each stage and follow your line of enquiry. Drafting what you want to ask in full will help you with the construction of complex questions or those which require particular care in their formulation and to avoid leading the client. Your performance can therefore be aided by some careful forethought and the plan can act as a useful reminder.

Time is always of the essence during the conference so you will need to prioritise the questions. Some questions are inevitably more central to the objectives of the conference than others. Nonetheless, there will always be a need to ask a number of questions to establish the foundation for the client's knowledge before you gather the relevant information. Once you have established this foundation you can move on to the questions that are designed to elicit the details. Remember that each issue must be introduced within a reasonable amount of time, and adequate time must be allocated to enable you to investigate all the relevant points in turn. All the questions must be asked whilst both you and the client have sufficient energy to move on to the advice stage.

The physical layout of a plan is also important. It is worth remembering that some space for answers and notes can be an advantage. This will save you time during the conference and aid the comprehension of the notes after it. It has already been recommended that all plans have sufficient flexibility to incorporate fresh topics raised in the conference. The unexpected always happens and no one is perfect, so time for some additional questions should be accounted for in the plan. (See **Chapter 5**.)

6.5   Establishing trust and rapport for the questioning stage

Conferences are live events—there are no dress rehearsals; the parties are real people, with lives outside the conference room. Throughout the conference, and especially at the questioning stage, you need to be alert to the subtle changes and adjustments in the rapport between yourself and the client. In many cases the parties will quickly settle into the conference and be able to concentrate on its issues and objectives. You will always require detailed and frank answers to your questions and in order to obtain these you need the client to have complete confidence in you as a lawyer and to feel comfortable with you as a person. A client cannot be expected to give his or her undivided attention to counsel's questions if there is a lack of trust or an unproductive environment. If there are distractions to the rapport you must take the lead and resolve the problems that cause them. (See **3.2** and **4.3**.)

6.5.1   The client's say

A client invariably visits a barrister because there is a problem that he or she has to face. The client has almost certainly formed a view of the case either independently or with some legal or non-legal assistance. Advice may have been offered by a friend or a family member, or with the assistance of a solicitor. Such forethought is to be welcomed and ought to be given due consideration. The client's estimation of the case can indicate its importance to them. If a client has a speech that has been rehearsed on the journey into chambers, allow him or her to deliver it to you. If you display an unwillingness to listen to what the client has to say at this early stage you cannot expect him or her to give you full and accurate answers to your questions later.

6.5.2   Basics that establish trust

Although your client will have a fair or even a good idea of what can be achieved from the conference, you must confirm the purpose and the limitations of the meeting that you have called. When you reach the questioning stage of the conference particularly, you will have to explain to the client that you will require him or her to work with you and to do some deep thinking. Clients who are inexperienced with the law often do not appreciate that they will have to do a great deal of mental work and talking during the conference. To prepare them for this and to encourage cooperation and collaboration you will have to show them the benefits of this labour to their case and ultimately themselves. You may need to return to these points again on several occasions during the conference.

Before you can move clients on to the questions you must make it plain that you are not sitting in judgement upon them or their actions. Clients come to seek the barrister's assistance for a multitude of reasons and the subject matter of the mixed practice will be drawn from every facet of human existence and relationships. Many of these, in the context of both civil and criminal law, can be the cause of emotional pain, personal sorrow, or even shame. Initially your aim will be to alleviate the stress or embarrassment of answering your questions. Later, specific anxieties may have to be met. A timely reminder that you are there to serve the client's best interests will often facilitate openness on the part of the client. The occasional overt offer to assist clients with further explanation will help them to cooperate with you. Clients will not always take up your offers to assist them and will bravely struggle on in the hope that they will not lose face in front of a lawyer. Therefore you must be alert to hesitancy, nervousness, or indications that they do not understand what you are asking them. It is your responsibility to see that the client has complete comprehension of what is taking place and has security of mind. There are, of course, advantages for you too. If the correct atmosphere is established at the beginning of the questioning stage of the conference you will reap the benefits of working with a more relaxed, cooperative, and honest client.

6.5.2.1   Establishing the client's trust

> **How to do it**
>
> (a) Inform clients that you need to ask some questions before can offer any advice or communicate your opinion. Justify why this is necessary.
>
> (b) Invite clients to ask you to repeat or rephrase any questions that they do not understand. Assure them that this is quite understandable, as some of the questions will be complex.
>
> (c) Explain to clients the duty of confidentiality you owe them and briefly explain in realistic terms the effect this will have on the answers that they give to your questions.
>
> (d) Invite clients to adopt a cooperative and collaborative approach by telling them what you aim to achieve for them by asking the questions. Relate this directly to the clients' objectives for the conference.
>
> (e) Periodically thank clients for their assistance and continue to explain the benefit of their answers to the conduct of the conference.

6.5.3   Rapport is a two-way process

Barristers have contact with numerous clients and cannot hope to find it easy to work with them all. You may come into close contact with people with whom you have little in common or whose views on life conflict with yours. The so-called cab-rank rule makes it impossible to be selective about clients, lay or professional. The circumstances governing refusal to accept a brief or instructions and withdrawal from a case are closely governed by the Code of Conduct (see **9.9**). Therefore you will have to learn to surmount personal differences. As the barrister, you are responsible for the conduct of the conference and must take control of it in a professional manner. All clients deserve the same treatment, no matter whether you like them or approve of their past actions or not. It is also your responsibility to encourage clients to put aside their own differences and to cooperate with your questions.

Certain questions may jeopardise the rapport that you have established with the client. Whilst asking questions of an unpleasant or intimate nature you should have consideration for your sensitivities as well as those of the client. If you communicate embarrassment or discomfort the rapport between you and the client will be placed in danger. Your professional duties must be carried out to the best of your abilities. Therefore take care to be alert to any possible dangers of this nature before the conference. There is no excuse for rudeness to a client, but also there is little point pretending that you are fully composed when you are not. As you have responsibility for the conference you will need to appear relaxed and confident. You should be sufficiently in control to be able to assist the client at all times. If, however, you do momentarily lose your self-command, do not simply hope to gloss over it. Rather, break off questioning, apologise to the client, and then briefly review where you have got to in the conference. If you have decided that the question is an important one, resume your enquiry.

However, there are occasions when you will need to assess the client by maintaining an objective eye on the answers to your questions and on what he or she says. This function with time will be a constant one; you must learn to act upon the conclusions you draw without reacting inappropriately. For example, if you suspect that the client is not telling the whole truth you will want to consider a further investigation of the matter whilst not communicating your disbelief. Whether you believe the client or support his or her application is to that extent immaterial.

6.6 Gathering adequate information to advise the client

The overall objective of asking the client questions is to gather the relevant information that will enable you to form an opinion of the case and communicate this in the form of advice. Thus, the information that you gather from the client's answers is not an end in itself. Your preparation ought to have indicated what was relevant and determined the specific objectives of the questioning stage of the conference. However, you cannot view clients as an inexhaustible source of information. Eventually they will become tired or will have told you everything they know. If either of these events occurs there is little point pressing the client further. It is usually time to take stock of what your client has told you thus far. If the client looks fatigued or is unable to answer your enquiries, ask yourself whether the client will be able to assist later, after a break perhaps, or whether someone else has the requisite knowledge.

On the other hand, if the client has assisted you fully, conclude the questioning section. This ought to happen once you have satisfied yourself that there is sufficient information to enable you to move to the advice stage. This means that you have addressed all relevant issues and asked all relevant questions. Again, careful and thorough preparation at the planning stage will assist you to make decisions at this stage. If you set an agenda of questions for the conference in advance, it will be readily apparent when one topic of investigation has been exhausted and it is appropriate to move on to the next.

However, there are some exterior factors that will affect the duration of the questioning stage: time is often the greatest of these. Other factors might include the stage of the proceedings reached, or the state of preparation of the brief. There is, as we have already seen, the limitation of the client's direct knowledge of matters under investigation, or his or her memory or understanding of the facts. To judge the extent of the client's knowledge, consider beginning each section of questions with a couple of preliminary questions. These should be designed to gauge the depth of the client's knowledge, comprehension, or belief. These will establish the foundations for any facts adduced or views held by that client. Before moving from one topic of investigation to the next, or when concluding the questions, take stock of what the client has told you thus far. Ask yourself whether it is sufficient to meet the objectives of the conference. If not, consider which additional questions need to be asked to tie up any loose ends or to clarify what the client has told you so far. Until you are satisfied you should be very cautious about moving on to the next area for investigation. Certainly, it would be unwise to attempt to give any advice.

6.6.1   Show clear understanding of the client's version of events

It is essential that your understanding of what the client has told you accords with his or her version of events. A relatively swift and simple way to do this is to give a précis of what the client has just told you. Clearly indicate to the client what you are doing and why you are doing it. Invite the client to correct your understanding of what he or she has told you and to fill in any remaining gaps. Naturally your summary should not be tainted by your opinion of the merits of the case. Your concern at this stage is merely with the client's version of events and your comprehension of it. It is of paramount importance that you appreciate fully the client's version of the relevant events. This will enable you first to advise appropriately in the light of your client's instructions and, second, to gauge the extent of the client's unassisted knowledge.

6.6.2   Obtain the client's full instructions

Your brief will contain your instructions from the professional client; however, the client's own proof or statement will also reveal much about his or her aspirations for the case. For example, the client may reveal his or her non-legal objectives for the litigation and hopes or fears for the future. Your instructions from the solicitor will, of course, indicate the client's legal objectives and outline the purpose of the conference. Additionally, during the conference you ought to clarify and add to the list of client objectives as the client reveals them to you. You need to address these questions explicitly to the client.

Following your explanation of the situation and the expression of an opinion, the fundamental question will be, 'What are the client's instructions?' Each of the conference's objectives must be addressed. Often there is no further opportunity to meet with the client and so both you and the client must leave the conference fully informed of what will happen next in the case. Therefore, give the client a picture of the current situation and check that you are both confident about what action needs to be taken in the future. You can achieve this by obtaining clear, full, and explicit instructions from the client and by ensuring that you have addressed all the objectives of the conference. Appropriate questions at this stage will include ones to check that the client agrees that all the relevant matters have been addressed. Thus, some open questions to invite further contributions from the client are helpful.

EXAMPLE

Q1 I believe that we've covered all the issues at this stage. What do you think?

Q2 That concludes the questions that I wish to ask you. Have I missed any matters that you think are relevant?

This approach allows the client to air his or her concerns. Some of these may have to be put to one side and addressed at the advice stage, but do not brush aside any expressions of worry or doubt. On the other hand, the client may raise an issue or produce a piece of information of which you were hitherto unaware. A further advantage of concluding the questioning section with this enquiry is that the initiative is with the client. This allows you some extra thinking time before you go on to your advice. (See **Chapter 8.**)

6.7 Listening techniques

6.7.1 Introduction

As we have seen in the introductory chapters, members of the public commonly complain that they feel ignored by their lawyers and that barristers appear distant and aloof. In order to overcome this prejudice you need to be conscious of your responses to the client. In this section we will consider how people indicate that they are listening and what these different forms of listening can tell you about them. This will assist you to use the appropriate techniques yourself and to interpret the client's behaviour better.

There is nothing particularly novel about the methods and styles of listening and communication discussed in this section; indeed, you can apply them to everyday situations such as conversations and the more formal listening patterns of an audience in a lecture theatre. For you as a barrister in a conference it is particularly important to understand how people listen to enable you to communicate effectively with your clients. This understanding will help you to comprehend the clients' reactions better and also to convey your own messages to them.

When a client answers your questions you must, of course, pay full attention to what is said. However, a lawyer needs to be alert to the extent to which a client is listening too. This is important because the different ways of listening and the non-verbal responses of a person communicate a great deal of information. This might include whether the audience is alert or bored, whether it agrees or disagrees with the speaker, or whether it understands what is being said. People obviously perceive what they are listening to with their ears, but they manifest their reactions to what they hear with their faces, body posture, and vocal response.

In the conference, the client and the barrister will be sharing the tasks of listening and talking between them. Both parties will communicate signals that indicate how and to what degree they are listening to the other. You must be alert to the degree to which the client comprehends what you say and be aware of his or her powers of concentration. Whilst it is unlikely that the client will consciously monitor you, it is part of everyday communication between individuals to be sensitive to the responses of a person to whom you are talking. You should pay attention to how you respond to the client, as well as noting the extent to which he or she listens and comprehends what you say. There are subtle ways to communicate your attentiveness or to pass on your emotional responses to what the client says; you might choose to employ them at different stages in the conference.

6.8 Terminology

6.8.1 Passive listening

This is the least responsive style of listening. The listener sits quietly but attentively before the talker and waits to hear what is said. Very few messages, whether verbal or oral, are communicated from the listener to the speaker. There may even be short periods of silence; the listener will not fill these pauses nor add much, if any, encouragement to the speaker. The listener acts only as an audience and merely listens to what is said.

6.8.1.1 Characteristics

- The speaker is unimpeded by interruptions.
- Control over the amount of information and the style in which it is communicated is retained by the speaker.
- Narratives and other detailed information are passed on in logical sequence.

6.8.2 Responsive listening

This is a modified form of passive listening. The listener will add short verbal and physical messages to the speaker without interruption or seeking to control what is being said. Common responses are nods of the head, short agreements, or neutral responses. The point is neither to pass comment upon what is said nor to interrupt the speaker. However, the listener will assist the speaker and can offer limited support, for example by indicating that he or she is interested or agrees with what is said. Silences or displays of difficulty by the speaker can be met with such responses to offer encouragement.

6.8.2.1 Characteristics

- The listener does intervene, but only to a limited degree.
- The speaker maintains control over what is said.
- Responsive listening is a help and a support to the speaker: it maintains the flow of information from the speaker to the audience.

6.8.3 Receptive listening

This is an interventionist form of responsive listening. Again, speakers are free to answer the question as best they can and in their own fashion. When appropriate, however, a listener will offer some emotional response. For example, when a client is recalling a painful incident, such as an accident, some empathy may be expressed, or if the client becomes emotional and falls silent through embarrassment, the listener's sympathy might be communicated.

6.8.3.1 Characteristics

- Interventions are short and mostly verbal, but with appropriate reactions.
- The client is largely free to answer the question in his or her own way, but the listener may affect the flow of information by revealing his or her reactions to what is said.
- The listener becomes personally involved with the speaker at an emotional level—it may be difficult to disentangle oneself from this later during the conference.

6.8.4   Active listening

This is another interventionist style of listening. The listener paraphrases or summarises what has been heard. Whilst the speaker is talking, the questioner listens quietly and then indicates that he or she has paid attention by encapsulating the essentials of what has been said in a précis. This method is used to check comprehension or understanding by the questioner, but it can also be used to invite the client to reconsider the answer to the question asked. For example, by reiterating the answer to the client you can illustrate that the response is illogical or unfeasible. Otherwise it may be used to display interest and attention to the speaker. Caution is required; by repeating what has been said, the listener may add interpretations to what has been said. For example, the summary may be inaccurate and distort what the speaker said or it may fill in gaps that appeared in the original account. This is a danger that few lay people would readily recognise, but it is one to which the lawyer ought to be alert. The client must give you the information that you require and you should guard against adding your own prejudgements and assumptions; there is the further danger that you may inadvertently lead your client. Therefore, remember to allow the client to check the accuracy of your résumé.

6.8.4.1   Characteristics

- The speaker is free to say what he or she wishes largely uninterrupted.

- Although some intervention may take place, the listener reserves most of what he or she has to say until an answer is received.

- An opportunity to respond in turn to the listener's estimation of what has been said is given to the speaker.

- Nonetheless, there will often be a degree of value judgement by the summarising party.

6.9   Selecting an appropriate listening technique

In everyday contact little conscious thought is given to the selection of listening techniques; however, in the conference, the selection of the appropriate method of response can be one of the most effective ways of controlling clients. All the techniques listed previously are already in everyone's repertoire and are used freely, but the lawyer must select and deploy them with care. If you maintain control of the client you will make a success of the conference. Throughout the conference, and particularly during the questioning stage, the selection of styles of listening and appropriate listening techniques will assist you to realise the objectives of the conference. The guiding principle is foreknowledge of what information is required to enable you to advise the client, but the considerate barrister will also wish to cause as little distress to the client as possible and leave him or her with a sense that their counsel has listened to them.

The rapport established between client and counsel is often a delicate one; rarely is either party familiar with the other and, given the subject matter of many conferences, emotions can run high. If someone is talking, they expect their audience to listen to them. This expectation should be met when listening to the client's responses to your question. The type of attention that clients receive will affect the way they respond to you. So, whilst taking the client's instructions, you must respond to the client's needs, however they are expressed. Listen to any concerns the client expresses and respond to their requests for assistance as they are communicated; do not always wait for them to be spelled out.

The conference is a formal occasion and visiting a barrister in chambers or waiting outside court can be a very stressful experience for the client. The conference can also be stressful for the barrister. The final responsibility for the conference rests with you. This means that during the conference the client's welfare, and to some extent his or her well-being is your responsibility. It is worth recalling some differences in the speaker/listener relationship between a conference and other everyday meetings:

(a) Conferences are public rather than private affairs; the barrister is acting in a professional capacity and the client will be seeking legal advice.

(b) In terms of authority the relationship is weighted towards the barrister. Clients often attempt to make the barrister offer solutions early in the conference. The client may need to be reminded that you will need to hear from them before offering advice. (See **3.2.2.4**.)

(c) You and the client will be scrutinising one another. The client may be wholly unknown to you. This can lead to a nervous atmosphere, and can badly affect a person's ability to concentrate and listen properly to what is said.

(d) The outcome of the conference is important and you cannot afford to make mistakes or be mistaken. The need for an accurate understanding of what is said in conference by both parties cannot be overestimated.

(e) The subject matter of conferences is often deeply personal and emotions can run deep. Any lapse in attention can be misread as a lack of concern or a judgement upon what is said.

(f) Constraints are often imposed on the conference. Often time is at a premium. It can be tempting to economise: to cut the client short, or to formulate the next question whilst the client is answering the first, and thus ignoring the answer to it.

Some of these features can be used to your advantage when asking questions. The formal setting and the importance of the conference can help to establish limits within which the client and the barrister are to cooperate. As many clients will expect counsel to take the lead, you can do so without appearing rude or pushy. The style of question can be more formal than that which is acceptable in everyday social intercourse. This freedom to adapt normal patterns of behaviour can be extended to the way you listen to the client. For example, you will be able to interrupt the client more freely than might be thought polite to a stranger and you will be at greater liberty to challenge what is said. And, finally, offers of sympathy and empathy will be appropriate even though you are probably a stranger to the client or might be his or her junior.

Naturally there is no set format or template that can be imposed upon all conferences. Each client must be met on his or her terms, warts and all. You will need to maintain a flexible and practicable approach at all times. It is your responsibility to respond to the client's characteristics and to help and control that client as and when appropriate.

6.10 Barriers to listening

Good communication in the conference can be impeded by forces beyond your immediate control. However, that is not to say that nothing can be done; indeed, a few simple precautions can and should be taken to ensure attentive listening by both the client and the barrister.

6.10.1 Noise and interruption

The physical environment should be free from noise as far as is possible. If the conference is in chambers, avoid interruptions by having telephone calls diverted, mobiles switched off, and displaying engaged signs clearly. To allow the client and yourself to see and hear one another clearly, give some thought to the physical layout of the room. Place chairs close to one another and close doors and windows, for example. If the conference is at court you will want to select as quiet a place as possible: make a friend of the ushers as they can often help you find the quietest locations.

6.10.2 Physical distractions

Hunger, thirst, discomfort, and tiredness all detract from good hearing. You and the client can help to alleviate the first three by the provision of some light refreshment and comfortable seating, but the last is not easily corrected. If the client shows signs of fatigue there is little point in continuing with the conference; a short break may suffice or an additional conference may have to be arranged.

6.10.3 Prejudice

Prejudice is a barrier to listening that is all too often overlooked. If you have preconceived ideas about the case or the client, there is a danger of hearing what you expect or want to hear rather than listening to what is said by that client. Both you and the client can be susceptible to this bad habit. In order to be well prepared you will want to be familiar with the case and may have formed a preliminary view of its merits. However, these preparations should not preclude you from maintaining an enquiring mind. The client may need active encouragement to listen critically to what is said. Phrases such as 'Stop me if you don't understand', or 'Do you agree with the following?' can facilitate and maintain the client's attention. (See further **Chapter 11**.)

6.10.4 Distractions from the speaker

The vocal and verbal characteristics of a speaker can make it difficult for a listener to hear what is said. There can be a variety of reasons for this: an accent or a speech impediment or the use of colloquialisms or jargon can all impede comprehension. Other distractions may be nervous tics or physical disability. Very little if anything can be done about these sorts of distractions, but it is important to be aware of them as potential barriers to comprehension. The extra time and effort that are necessary to overcome difficulties of this nature must be incorporated into the conference and you must be alert to the needs of the client.

6.11 The signs of good listening

The following list is designed to help you to be aware of the physical and verbal indications that might be communicated by someone paying full attention to a speaker. The list is not exhaustive and you might wish to add to it.

6.11.1   Spotting good listening in others and yourself

> **How to do it**
>
> - Body language that reflects cooperation, such as appropriate body shadowing, ie when the listener apes the posture of the speaker.
>
> - Verbal responses from the listener are logical and natural, eg the respondent indicates agreement with the speaker readily.
>
> - Comfortable eye contact is maintained for long periods of time.
>
> - The listener gives short nods of the head or verbal signals to indicate encouragement.
>
> - The listener seeks further information with interventions and questions that are on the same subject as that of the speaker.
>
> - There is an atmosphere of cooperation between audience and speaker, eg the listener seeks to aid and assist the speaker rather than to dominate.

6.12   Keeping a record

If you ask the appropriate questions and listen carefully to the client's replies, you will also need to keep a written record of the conference. This will usually be made contemporaneously. As a pupil you may be asked to take a note for your pupil supervisor during the conference. Occasionally barristers are confident that they can use the solicitor's notes of what is said in the conference. But most often barristers will make their own notes. Whilst there are alternatives to written notes, such as digital voice recorders, few barristers have time to type up recordings of the conference. Indeed, in the early years of practice as a pupil or recently qualified barrister, you will conduct conferences unassisted and in circumstances that will preclude the use of anything more sophisticated than a pen and paper.

It is a waste of the client's and your time if the usefulness of the conference is squandered because of an insufficient record. For example, information to plan examination or cross-examination should be gathered thoroughly at the conference. If an inadequate note is taken at the time, you will have to pass notes in court or go to the dock for instructions. These are habits that rightly attract criticism from the Bench. Inevitably, though, no notes will be perfect and a limited amount of courtroom communication between client and counsel is necessary. However, a reputation for being under-prepared will soon lose you not only your reputation with the judge but also clients. During a negotiation the damage can be even greater. Your opponent will soon spot your unpreparedness and seek to exploit your ignorance and poor memory. (See the *Advocacy* manual.)

6.12.1   The plan and notes

If you identify the purpose of the conference in advance and plan on how to meet its objectives, you will find the process of keeping a note much easier. On the other hand, a plan which is excessively detailed or too tightly structured will inevitably narrow the horizons and impede the assimilation of fresh facts both during and after the conference. The client's full instructions must be taken and this requires counsel to maintain an open and flexible mind. This will enable you to incorporate new information and instructions from the client. For example, if your client's answers are recorded next to the questions on the plan the notes will be easily understood. Additionally, the word count is reduced, so you can pay more attention to the client, and vital questions that have been planned are less likely to be overlooked.

6.12.2 What form should the notes take?

Time is usually of the essence and you do not want to stop the client continuously to take a note. Also, written notes or those made on a computer can be a major distraction for the barrister in conference. The interviewer's mind can easily be concentrated too much on writing or typing and not enough on listening. One way to save time and unnecessary effort during the conference is to use some form of notation or shorthand. Each writer has his or her own particular brand of notation. The primary concern is that the notes are of use to you personally. However, if for some reason you cannot fulfil your obligations to the client another counsel may have to pick up your brief at short notice and take over your notes. Therefore, uncommon forms of notation ought to be avoided and handwriting and layout ought to be kept reasonably neat and easily comprehensible.

It is only common sense to state that it is impossible to take a verbatim note of what is said during the conference. However, of course, it is undesirable to take too few notes. A helpful guide is to consider if your notes will be an accurate and adequate source of information for the next time that you work on the case. This next step in the life of the case might be in court before a judge or in chambers drafting a pleading or writing an advice. So bear in mind what the next stage in the litigation is and during the conference keep notes that will assist you to execute that task. The notes cannot be adequate preparation in themselves—they will need to be adapted and added to—but they will be a major source of information and instruction.

6.12.3 The client and note-taking

At the outset of the conference you must seek the client's permission to take notes of what they tell you. Clients will notice when you actually begin to take a note. This can be a mixed blessing. On the one hand, they may slow down to enable you to take a full note. But on the other hand, the client can misunderstand why you are taking a note of only part of what they say. He or she may think that when you do not note something that what has been said is not important and so will close the topic. The speculative client might attempt to tell you something that they hope will be of great enough significance to warrant a note. A short introduction of what and why you are noting should therefore be given once you begin to record the answers. Remind the client of this when you reach a point during the questions that demands a note of particular detail.

Inevitably, the physical and mental processes of writing or typing something will distract you from the client and what they have to say. It might be appropriate to ask the client to pause at that point to allow you to take a full note of what is being said. Remember also that when looking down to take a note you will not be giving the client the benefit of your full attention. There will be a break in eye contact and perhaps a turning away. This is usually only momentary and quite acceptable in most circumstances. However, consider the effect this can have on a client who is speaking about something that is deeply personal, painful, or important to them. You should take care in such situations. Allow the client to see that you are concerned for their well-being; alternatively, display some understanding or empathy with their predicament. However, do not allow these sensitivities to distract you from recording relevant information. Ask the client to repeat the last answer if you decide that a full note is necessary.

6.12.4   Use of notes from the conference

Your notes will be useful to you during the conference itself. They can assist to confirm and clarify what you believe you have heard; this can be particularly useful when paraphrasing. You will certainly need to use your notes when advising as they will contain detailed information that will form the basis of your advice. They will also assist you to ensure that you have dealt with all the client's objectives and asked all relevant questions. This is particularly the case if you keep a note on your plan.

Following the conference, any decisions taken should be recorded in detail and where necessary or advisable the client should be invited to endorse the brief. Alternatively, if the client is unable to answer any of your questions or is not able to make a decision, then make a note of these outstanding matters. In this way, your notes will provide a record of the client's decision and a useful checklist of tasks to be completed before tackling the next step in the case. When you come to plan and execute that next stage your notes will also provide a vital source of information, thus it is important to keep them safe and that you observe best practice regarding client confidentiality. Particular care should be taken when using removable devices such as laptops, removable discs, CDs, USB memory sticks, and PDAs. Such devices should be used to store only information needed for immediate purposes, not for permanent storage. The Bar Standards Board in its 'Confidentiality Guidance' advises that information on them should be at least password protected, and preferably encrypted. Barristers are also warned to take great care in looking after the devices themselves to ensure that they are not lost or stolen. As was noted earlier, a fellow member of the profession may have to use your notes if he or she takes over the case, and therefore you should be able to retrieve your notes easily.

6.12.5   Taking a good note

> ### How to do it
>
> - Have agendas and questions planned in advance to allow time for note-taking during the conference.
>
> - Ensure that you have sufficient pens and paper, or leave sufficient room on the plan for answers to questions.
>
> - Explain to the client that notes will be taken, why this is, and what use will be made of them.
>
> - Be economical when taking notes; for example, do not record information that already appears in the brief, instructions, or Representation Order form.
>
> - Use a logical, easily understandable form of notation.
>
> - Take a detailed note of important details and double-check this with the client for accuracy.
>
> - Use diagrams, sketches, and other visual aids when appropriate and encourage the client to draw these for you.
>
> - Read over the notes briefly towards the end of the conference to check completeness and accuracy.
>
> - Keep notes in a safe place, separate from the brief for future use.
>
> - Never allow your note-taking to be a distraction from the client personally.

6.13 Problems encountered during questioning

6.13.1 Introduction

In this part of the chapter, we will consider some of the common problems encountered in conference whilst questioning the client. First, we will look at testing and assessing the client as a potential witness. Second, we will investigate how to utilise and exploit documents and objects in the conference.

6.13.2 Testing the client's answers

Establishing the issues and identifying any gaps and ambiguities in the client's case forms an important part of the preparation for any conference. This will enable you both to advise the client in the light of full instructions and to put forward a watertight case later in proceedings. Naturally, this will involve an investigation and assessment of the answers that the client offers you in conference. To achieve this it will be necessary to maintain a critical, professional detachment from the case. But whilst taking an objective approach to the case, you should display a lively concern for the client; ultimately, the outcome of the case will have an effect upon the client.

In order to test the answers properly, you may have to question the veracity or fullness of any replies offered by the client. Do not always be satisfied with the first answer from the client: seek clarification or justification for it. You should constantly assess the type and quality of answers given by the client. When the client's replies appear to be evasive or clouded by vagaries and irrelevancies, you may decide to take an objective line of enquiry or play devil's advocate. This can be done in many ways—for example, by putting the other side's case to the client and inviting comment, or by taking on the role of the opposing party's counsel and simulating a piece of cross-examination.

6.13.2.1 Testing the client's answers

> ### How to do it
>
> - Always explain what you are doing and demonstrate the benefit of this exercise to the case and ultimately to the client.
>
> - It is sometimes advisable to inform the client of the general confidentiality of the conference and that you are always acting in his or her best interests.
>
> - Introduce the critical questions at an appropriate point in the conference, and always after you have established the client's trust.
>
> - Inform the client that you are adopting a critical or testing strategy and tell the client why you think that it is a useful and important exercise.
>
> - Adopt an appropriate questioning style but remain polite and do all you can to protect the rapport that you have established.
>
> - Select the necessary questions with care. Have them prepared in advance, if possible, to save time and ensure efficiency.
>
> - Once you have completed this section of questions, make it clear to the client that you are moving on to another stage.

6.13.3   Assessing the client as a witness

Upon receiving a fresh brief, one common consideration is to decide whether the case will go to trial. The vast majority of both civil and criminal cases do not. (Refer, for example, to the *Criminal Litigation and Sentencing* manual.) However, if in your opinion trial is likely, you will have to consider whether the client ought to give evidence or not. The prospect of giving evidence can be a source of great anxiety for the client, who already has to cope with the usual worries of litigation. It will be part of your preparation to consider whether you will call the client to give evidence in the case. Whether or not you broach the subject in the conference itself will depend upon the stage of the proceedings and the purpose of that particular conference. Civil cases usually go through numerous interim stages before final trial; indeed, the case may well settle between times. On the other hand, because of the nature of criminal cases, a decision as to plea at an early stage may well finally decide this issue. Remember, however, that it is not uncommon for the client to give evidence following a guilty plea as part of his or her mitigation in what is commonly called a Newton hearing. (See the *Criminal Litigation and Sentencing* manual and the *Advocacy* manual.)

The formulation of your opinion as to whether your client will make a good witness should begin with your first impression of him or her. This is a very important consideration as the advocate ought to avoid being surprised in court, particularly by his or her client. Time spent now considering the client's suitability as a witness, or the type of testimony that he or she will give, can help to alleviate anxiety during the trial.

It may be appropriate to put the client in a similar position to that of a witness in court under the pressure of a cross-examination. You might choose to adopt a similar method to that outlined at **6.13.2**. Of course, great tact and care are necessary, as well as an awareness of the inherent danger of coaching the client. As it is the client's case, it is only right that you ask him or her directly whether he or she wishes to give evidence. As with any advice that you give to the client, your advice on this issue ought to be preceded by an investigation of the client's suitability as a witness and an explanation of the advantages and disadvantages of giving evidence.

6.13.3.1   Assessing the client as a witness

How to do it

- Consider the merits of the case and assess the likelihood of the case proceeding to trial. (There is no point overburdening the client with making decisions that will have no effect.)

- If appropriate, test the client as a potential witness, especially as one under cross-examination, by adopting the techniques enumerated at **6.13.2**.

- Explain to the client that the choice is his or her own to take, adding that you can give your opinion to help him or her come to a fully informed decision.

- Isolate and identify the advantages and disadvantages to the case if the client does or does not give evidence in the trial.

- Always confirm that you have the client's full instructions and keep a clear record of any decision not to give evidence on the brief signed by the client.

6.13.4   Characteristics of a good witness

To assist you to reach your decision it is helpful to know which characteristics make a good court witness. As you can see, much information about the client's probable demeanour in the witness box can be gathered from non-verbal indicators as well as his or her verbal eloquence. Naturally, what follows is not an exhaustive list.

6.13.4.1   Spotting potentially effective witnesses

How to do it
• Dispassionate, though not disinterested.   • Physically calm and orally coherent.   • Eloquent and concise.   • Listens well to questions and responds appropriately.   • Well versed in the relevant facts.   • Reacts well to pressure by maintaining equilibrium and suppressing emotions of anger, fear, etc.   • Confident and slow to display doubt or admit mistakes.   • Apparently honest and truthful, ie convincing.

6.14   Documents and real evidence in the conference

In many conferences, you will want to invite the client to consider the contents of a report or a statement, or you may wish to show him or her a piece of evidence found at the scene of a crime or which forms the subject matter of a civil claim. Once your attention is focused upon documents or specific objects, there can be difficulties. In this section we will consider some of them and make suggestions to help you to exploit your time.

6.14.1   Written documents

A great number of documents are added to cases as they proceed. Some of the material will be generated from the client and some from the opposition, whether the prosecutor, or the opponent in a civil case. In either case, the tyranny of the printed page must be faced. Written material, especially in a typed or printed format, will often carry authority in the reader's mind that is unwarranted. If something is in black and white, its contents are not necessarily truthful, nor telling the full story, and therefore each document must be considered critically. Whilst most people can tell when something is clearly wrong, it is well known that the printed page can convince people more readily of the truth of its contents than the spoken word. As professionals specifically trained to develop their critical faculties, lawyers will be alert to this fact. Many lay people, on the other hand, are not so willing to question the apparent authority of documents.

Having noted that clients can more easily fall into the thrall of documents it will be obvious that the client may be less willing to contradict them than you are. You should seek to encourage the client to investigate the deeper meaning and truth behind what is on the page. It is part of your function to ask the client questions about the contents of the document to confirm their veracity and relevance. This investigation must be a thorough one; do not stop until you are satisfied. Pre-planned questions and areas of investigation will assist you to decide when you have fully investigated each page or document.

Another feature of written documents in conferences is that they can be impediments to good communication between client and counsel. If placed between yourself and the client it is all too easy for a listener to start reading what is on the paper. This will distract your client from what you are saying. It might even draw your attention from the client. With fewer distractions, both parties will enjoy deeper concentration. The client will often have his or her own copies of papers provided by the solicitor, or may have brought other documents to the conference. In these circumstances, it will be necessary to ask the client to cooperate with you to avoid distraction; for example, give the client a gentle suggestion to put their papers to one side.

It is often appropriate to spend a little time explaining the nature, status, and nomenclature of each document as an introduction to your questions on them. This ability to place the question in context and offer some preliminary explanation of any technical terms is part of the general skill of asking questions. If you have asked the client to read something, it may be necessary to check his or her comprehension. It is only good manners to give the reader time and silence in which to read and absorb the information, but some additional, tactful questions or remarks may be in order. Clearly, to get the most out of the conference an atmosphere of openness and clarity of understanding is desirable. The client should feel free to seek assistance from the barrister without a sense of embarrassment or without the risk of losing face.

6.14.1.1 Testing the client's answers

> **How to do it**
>
> - Explain the importance and relevance of the document at the same time as encouraging the client to adopt a critical approach to it. Justify why this is necessary.
>
> - Focus the client's attention on each issue relevant to the document as it arises.
>
> - Use specific, planned questions related to the content of the papers to save time and to control the client.
>
> - Select documents carefully and show them to the client sparingly. Once they have served their immediate purpose, remove them from sight or put them to one side.
>
> - Read highlights to clients or direct them to selected or marked passages to concentrate their mind on the relevant details of the document.
>
> - Make these tasks definite and justifiable movements, not vague and disjointed shuffling. By illustrating a command of the papers the barrister will win the trust and respect of the client.
>
> - Be prepared to offer explanations and definitions where appropriate.

6.14.2   Maps, diagrams, and photographs

A picture is worth a thousand words: the mind absorbs a greater amount of information more swiftly through the eye than the ear. Visual aids are particularly useful during the questioning stages of the conference as they communicate a great deal of information swiftly and simply. The technical ability to draw a map of great detail is not required, nor is any artistic flair. A little can go a long way. For example, no great draughtsmanship is required to draw a plan of a road junction, as a simple sketch will facilitate clear understanding between you and the client. A plan will also assist you and the client to understand the different accounts of the events contained within the statements and the client's proof. A word of warning, however: diagrams and photographs are even more distracting than written documents, so once they have served their purpose remove them.

There are a couple of dangers to avoid:

(a) Testing clients' recollection and gathering their account of events is central to the conference, so remember to avoid asking questions which lead clients to draw the plan you imagine being correct. It is often preferable to have clients draw the plan for themselves, or at least fill in the important details such as marking the locations of cars and people. In this way you will hear or see a client's account in an unadulterated form.

(b) Before investing too much time or effort on the diagram, consideration should be given to whether and how you might produce any visual aid in court. (See the *Evidence* manual.)

6.14.3   Objects and artefacts

When physical objects form the basis of your questions similar considerations to those already discussed may apply. Any objects that form part of the evidence of the case ought to be handled with great care; this includes seals and exhibit number reference cards. Artefacts can be just as distracting as printed pages or illustrations, so put them to one side once you have done with them.

If you desire to retain what the client produces in the conference, it is preferable to have the client surrender it to the solicitor, who can provide a receipt. A good photograph of an object may be sufficient for the preparatory stages and save the client inconvenience or concern.

6.14.4   Physical examination

In many areas of practice it is necessary to inspect a part of the client's body, whether it is to view wounds, injuries, or diagnostic scars or tattoos. Photographs are often provided but it is rare for them to be sufficient of themselves. So you may wish to ask the client questions about his or her health or for a description of physical characteristics, and this can involve an inspection for yourself.

Given that an examination of someone's body is an invasion of privacy, give careful thought before requesting such an inspection. Generally it ought to be requested only when there is no alternative. Consider, for example, whether a medical examination would be preferable or if a photograph would suffice.

6.14.4.1   Physical examinations in conference

How to do it

- Allow the client to begin to build up a rapport with you before moving to this stage in the conference.

- Explain clearly to the client why you are asking these intimate questions and seek his or her express permission to view the relevant part of the body. Be prepared to justify yourself.

- It is desirable for another person to be present. This person ought to be of the same sex as the client and be approved by him or her as suitable.

- Close doors and draw blinds and provide adequate lighting.

- Request the removal or loosening of only the minimum of clothing and only if vital to the examination.

- The inspection should be as brief as possible.

- Do not touch the client. Rather, ask him or her to point to the relevant area or to demonstrate the effect of injury, etc.

- Allow plenty of time for the client to dress and settle before adjusting the blinds and so on.

6.15   A worked example

To illustrate and consolidate what we have learnt from this chapter, let us take an example of a conference with a client who is facing a criminal charge in the magistrates' court. First, read the papers in the brief and then follow the development of the case analysis and the preparation for the questions on the conference plan. The plan is a detailed one; this is to enable you to see an overview of the strategies and techniques that are suitable for this type of conference.

IN THE WOOD GREEN MAGISTRATES' COURT

CROWN PROSECUTION SERVICE

v

CLAUDE RANSOME

INSTRUCTIONS TO COUNSEL TO
ADVISE IN CONFERENCE

Legal Aid

Larkins & Co
Holloway Road
London N7

IN THE WOOD GREEN MAGISTRATES' COURT

CROWN PROSECUTION SERVICE

v

CLAUDE RANSOME

INSTRUCTIONS TO COUNSEL TO ADVISE IN CONFERENCE

Counsel has herewith:

1. COPY OF CHARGE
2. PROSECUTION WITNESS STATEMENTS
3. DEFENDANT'S PROOF OF EVIDENCE

The defendant is charged with driving whilst disqualified. He is currently unemployed. Instructing Solicitors are aware there may be a job offer, to begin in two weeks.

The defendant has denied the charge and states he was at a job interview. There are no details at present. What is to be done about this?

Apart from the disqualification, Mr Ransome has three previous convictions, the last one in August 2014, for which he received a two-year community order.

Instructing Solicitors are aware that on the last appearance regarding this matter, when the case was adjourned, the CPS represented to the court that Mr Ransome was of good character. If this is not corrected by the next appearance, what is the position? Do we have to tell them? Instructing Solicitors have included a list of the defendant's previous convictions as we are aware of them.

Counsel is instructed to advise Mr Ransome in conference in chambers on plea and likely sentence if Mr Ransome pleads guilty or is found guilty at trial.

It seems that Mr Ransome has considerable mitigation in any event.

The case is listed for a not guilty hearing on 7th March 2016.

IN THE WOOD GREEN MAGISTRATES' COURT

CROWN PROSECUTION SERVICE v CLAUDE RANSOME

CLAUDE RANSOME IS CHARGED AS FOLLOWS

STATEMENT OF OFFENCE

Driving whilst disqualified, contrary to section 103 of the Road Traffic Act 1988.

PARTICULARS OF OFFENCE

Claude Ransome on 8th December 2015 drove a motor vehicle on a road, namely Wood Green High Street, while disqualified from holding or obtaining a driving licence.

IN THE WOOD GREEN MAGISTRATES' COURT

Statement of Witness

STATEMENT OF   SAMANTHA LONG

Age of Witness (date of birth)   Over 21

Occupation of Witness   Financial Consultant

This statement, consisting of one page each signed by me, is true to the best of my knowledge and belief and I make it knowing that, if it is tendered in evidence, I shall be liable to prosecution if I have wilfully stated in it anything which I know to be false or do not believe to be true.

Dated the 16th day of December 2015

Signed S P Long   Signature witnessed by Alison Leaf

On Tuesday 8th December 2015 I was on Wood Green High Street looking for a specialist tile shop. I had been told that it was next to the Town Hall. I was asking a constable for directions to the Town Hall when he began staring at a dark-haired young man in a Mini.

I looked at the man in the car as he was stationary at a pedestrian crossing. He looked over in the policeman's direction before driving off. As he did so I got a very good look at his face and he was staring in my direction. The policeman asked if I would recognise him again. I said I would. He then took my name and address.

The next Friday evening I was contacted to attend an identification parade at Wood Green Police Station. I attended and identified the man in position No 4. It was definitely the man I had seen on Tuesday driving on Wood Green High Street.

I am willing to attend court and give evidence.

Signed S P Long   Signature witnessed by Alison Leaf

Statement of Witness

STATEMENT OF   RYAN JONES

Age of Witness (date of birth)   Over 21

Occupation of Witness   PC 411

This statement, consisting of one page each signed by me, is true to the best of my knowledge and belief and I make it knowing that, if it is tendered in evidence, I shall be liable to prosecution if I have wilfully stated in it anything which I know to be false or do not believe to be true.

Dated the 22nd day of December 2015

Signed Ryan Jones PC 411   Signature witnessed by Alison Leaf

On Tuesday 8th December at around 11.30 am I was on duty on Wood Green High Street. A young woman had asked me for directions. While giving these I was pointing towards the Town Hall. I saw Claude Ransome leave the multi-storey car park in a Mini car. The multi-storey car park is just in front of the Town Hall.

He then drove in my direction, stopping about 10 metres in front of me at a pedestrian crossing. He looked in my direction then drove off. The young woman asked me why I had been staring at the man in the Mini. I asked her if she would recognise him again. She said 'Yes, probably.' I then asked her if she would attend an ID parade. She again answered 'Yes.' I took her details and finished giving her directions.

I recognised Claude Ransome because in September this year I stopped him in his Mini, registration number CRO 123W, for a road traffic offence of speeding. He was travelling at 70 mph in a 30 mph zone. He was very argumentative and aggressive as he said he already had nine points on his licence.

After pleading guilty he was disqualified from driving for nine months, having accumulated 12 points.

On 11th December I attended 17 Seven Sisters Road. The door was answered by Claude Ransome. I informed him he had been seen driving whilst disqualified. I then cautioned him and conveyed him to Wood Green Police Station, where he was interviewed and gave his consent to an ID parade.

At the station he emptied his pockets and a receipt was found for the Wood Green multi-storey car park dated 8th December 2015.

Throughout the interview he denied the offence.

He was then positively identified by Miss Samantha Long.

I was present when he was charged with the offence. I am willing to attend court to give evidence.

Signed Ryan Jones PC 411   Signature witnessed by Alison Leaf

METROPOLITAN POLICE

RECORD OF INTERVIEW

INTERVIEW OF: CLAUDE RANSOME   11/12/15

Age/Date of birth 22/10/92 Occupation Unemployed

Address and Tel 17 Seven Sisters Road, London N7

BY: DS BENSON

AT: WOOD GREEN POLICE STATION

OTHER PERSONS PRESENT: PC LEAF

TIME INTERVIEW COMMENCED: 20.10 TIME INTERVIEW CONCLUDED: 20.21

TAPE COUNTER	PERSON SPEAKING	TEXT
0:00		Introductions made, reminded of right to legal advice, then cautioned.
	BENSON	Would you like to say anything regarding your arrest for driving whilst disqualified?
	RANSOME	It is all a big mistake. I have not driven my car since I was banned. My brother borrowed my car to do some shopping.
	BENSON	Will your brother be able to verify that?
5:00	RANSOME	No, he has emigrated to Australia.
	BENSON	That is very unfortunate. So can you prove you were not in the car on Tuesday morning?
	RANSOME	I was at a job interview in South-East London on Tuesday morning, but I can't remember the name of the firm as I have been to loads of interviews recently.
7:50	BENSON	How many interviews then?
	RANSOME	About half a dozen or so.
	BENSON	That is hardly loads, is it Claude? Can you remember whereabouts in SE London?
	RANSOME	I'm not 100% sure; it may have been Camberwell or Peckham. I don't know South London very well.
9:10	BENSON	We have two witnesses who saw you driving a Mini reg No CRO 123W, which is the registration number of your car, isn't it?
9:50	RANSOME	I told you before, my brother borrowed my car on Tuesday.
	BENSON	How do you account for the ticket in your pocket for the car park?
11:00	RANSOME	My brother must have borrowed my jacket.
		Ransome then refused to answer any more questions put to him. Interview terminated.

PROOF OF EVIDENCE

CLAUDE RANSOME WILL SAY:

I am 23 years old and live at 17 Seven Sisters Road, London N7; I have been unemployed since losing my driving licence in October 2015. I was a delivery driver.

I have lived at 17 Seven Sisters Road for two years, with my girlfriend. My girlfriend gave up work in December as she is expecting our first child in April. With both of us unemployed I am extremely worried about our financial situation. I am applying for jobs at the moment and have had several interviews for work as a security guard.

Even this is a financial strain, as the travel costs are rarely reimbursed.

I do own a Mini car, reg No CRO 123W. As I will get my licence back in July 2014 I have kept it. My girlfriend cannot drive but I intend teaching her when I get my licence back. My brother borrowed my car to do some last-minute shopping, as he was emigrating on Tuesday evening to Australia. My brother is very similar in appearance to myself, except that he wears glasses.

I was taken to the police station on 11th December 2015 by PC Ryan Jones. I then attended an ID parade, which I had consented to. I was positively identified and charged with driving whilst disqualified. I have no idea how the multi-storey car park ticket came to be in my pocket. My brother could have borrowed my jacket.

I was in South-East London on that Tuesday morning. I was attending an interview for a security guard job. However, I cannot remember the name of the firm or where it is, as I had been to about six interviews in the last two weeks.

I have three previous convictions as well as the disqualification. The last one was in August 2014. I received a community order for two years for theft. I am therefore very worried. I believe the court is unaware of my previous convictions and I feel it should remain that way.

PREVIOUS CONVICTIONS

RANSOME, Claude

DATE	COURT	OFFENCE	SENTENCE
3.4.11	BOW MAGS	DRIVING WITHOUT INSURANCE	CON. DIS. 12 MTHS
3.6.12	TOTTENHAM MAGS	THEFT	FINE £50
10.8.14	TOTTENHAM MAGS	THEFT	COMMUNITY ORDER TWO YRS
28.10.15	BRENT MAGS	SPEEDING	FINE £100 DISQUALIFIED NINE MTHS

CPS v CLAUDE RANSOME

Plan

Legal and factual analysis

Offence

Driving whilst disqualified, contrary to s 103 of the Road Traffic Act 1988.

- Summary offence only.
- Punishment: six months' imprisonment or level 5 fine (£5,000).
- Disqualification is discretionary but endorsement of six points is obligatory.

Key issue: identification

Proposed defence—denial supported by a two-pronged alibi:

- Ransome maintains that it was his similar-looking brother who drove the car on 8th December 2015;
- Ransome states that he was at a job interview at the relevant time of the alleged offence.

Prosecution case—the evidence against this defendant is strong:

- positive identification by two people:
  - PC Ryan Jones, who recognised Ransome at the time,
  - Samantha Long, confirmed by her at the identification parade;
- circumstantial evidence: the parking receipt dated 8th December 2015 revealed by a search of Ransome's jacket.

Other issues

- CPS is unaware of Ransome's previous convictions.
- Possible mitigation, if appropriate.
- Likely sentence, if pleads guilty or found guilty.
- Next steps in litigation.

Objectives of conference

- Question client to:
  - confirm instructions;
  - investigate the strength of the alibi; examine briefly if there are any other defences.

  (Note: will inform client why notes are taken of what he says.)
- Advise client on plea in light of these investigations with a clear and unambiguous explanation of the strengths and weaknesses of his position.
- Advise the client (if appropriate on instructions received) on the advantages of pleading guilty.
- Question client to collect all useful and relevant mitigation.
- Prepare client for the consequences of pleading guilty or not guilty, with discussion of likely sentence and/or next steps for trial preparation.

Agenda to be shared with Ransome

- Introductions, explanation of my role, and purpose of conference.
- Notes: invite Ransome to participate and seek clarification.
- Questions to close gaps in my knowledge.
- Take Ransome's instructions on plea.
- Questions may follow to decide how best to proceed.

Note:

- Be alert to the danger of leading Ransome when questioning.
- Avoid mentioning mitigation and sentence at this stage, but allow time for these topics and fresh matters that might be raised by Ransome.

Gaps and ambiguities

There are many gaps in Ransome's version of events. His account to the police has a beginning, a middle, and an end but the details are all missing. This makes his account highly suspect, especially given the dogmatic statements in the police interview about where he was at the time. His insistence that his brother borrowed the car must be supported by evidence.

Strategy: take a matter-of-fact approach with the questioning initially, but ensure that Ransome gives full answers. Control and encourage him to speak about matters specifically; note how short and non-committal many of his answers were to the police.

Ransome's brother

(Note: must explain to Ransome the importance of brother's evidence to support the alibi and the defence.)

- Name and current address in Australia.
- Date of departure. Flight and emigration details.
- Address at time of offence.
- Physical description.
- Do you think that he would be willing to give evidence on your behalf?

Arrangement to borrow car on 8th December 2015

- Where were you when your brother took it?
- Where were you when the car was returned?
- Did your brother return it?
- Why did he borrow your car?

The jacket in which the parking receipt was found

(Note: Ransome was vague about this during police interview and only surmises that brother borrowed it.)

- Whose jacket is it?
- Who wore it on 8th December?

- If not you, when and where did you last see it before that day?
- Did anyone wear it between 8th December and 11th December?
- At what time on 11th December did you put on the jacket?

The job interview

(Note: Ransome was unhelpful on these matters during police interview. If he has a poor memory impress upon him importance of this information to his alibi. Encourage him to think again and to give thought to any evidence to support his account of events.)

- Name and address of company.
- How and where job advertised.
- Time and place of interview.
- Details of when Ransome left for interview and journey to it.
- Did anyone observe him or accompany him during this period?
- Duration and details of interview; name of panel, etc.
- What was the outcome of the interview?

The police interview

- Why did Ransome refuse to answer further questions?

Material to challenge prosecution witnesses

Samantha Long

- Do you know this woman?
- Did you recognise her at the identification parade?
- What took place at the parade? Note: deal with this briefly; there is no suggestion of irregularity.

PC Ryan Jones

- Details of speeding offence.
- Why should he remember you and purport to recognise you?

(Note: care needed to avoid alienating client with the suggestion that the PC did in fact see client.)

Advice on plea

At this point it will be appropriate to give advice on the plea. Unless Ransome can give the necessary details to support his alibi and defence he will be best advised to plead guilty.

- Invite Ransome to raise other matters of relevance to advice on plea.
- Remind him that the final decision is his, but that I will give my professional opinion.
- Briefly summarise:
  - Prosecution version of events;
  - Ransome's version of events from brief and answers just given. Note: do not pass comment but check accuracy with him.

- Explain the strengths and weaknesses of his chances of success on a not guilty plea.
- Explain the advantages and disadvantages of a guilty plea.
- Seek an explicit decision either way.

Mitigation

Resist temptation to answer Ransome's questions about probable sentence before collecting details of his mitigation.

(Note: Ransome has left his guilty plea till late in the proceedings and he told the police lies in his interview. Further, he has put Long to the trouble of making a statement to the police and attending an identity parade.)

The disqualification was in October 2015 and the offence took place on 8th December 2015, which is only two months into the ban.

The driving

- Where had you been on the morning of 8th December?
- What were you doing?
- Why use a car to do it?
- Where had the car been since the disqualification? Note: danger that the client may admit having used the car on other occasions.
- Why did you deny the offence to the police?
- Why did you go through the identity parade procedure?

Personal circumstances

- Employment status, qualifications, job prospects.
- Girlfriend's pregnancy and expected date of birth.
- Relationship with girlfriend and family.
- Income and benefits.
- Outgoings and debts.
- Health.
- Check if other personal details in proof are current.

Criminal record

- Explain likelihood of CPS having full record at next hearing.
- Set out limits placed on mitigation if I do not mention it.
- Explain my duty to him and to court.
- Questions to gather: history of past offences; progress of community rehabilitation order.

Likely sentence

- Help Ransome to appreciate the seriousness of the offence; explain why the court takes a dim view of those who breach its orders.
- Give him a realistic idea of the impact his mitigation will have upon sentence.
- State likely nature and length of sentence.
- Check he understands this advice.

Conclusion

- Summarise advice and instructions briefly.
- Double-check Ransome's comprehension and that he knows what will happen at the next hearing.
- Question whether I can assist him with any other matters.
- Reassurance and farewells.

7

Advice

7.1 Introduction

As a barrister you hold yourself out as a specialist in various fields of practice and offer your professional expertise and experience in a way that should benefit the client. Commonly the client comes to the lawyer because he or she has been unable to resolve a problem alone. It is likely that this problem is a complex one and almost certainly of great importance to the lay client.

From the outset it is important to recognise that the term 'advising the client' has many connotations. The type of advice you give varies to meet the needs of the different stages of the client's case. You will continue to advise the client throughout your professional involvement, not just at the initial conference. Consider the many decisions that remain to be made by the client during the rest of the litigation process: the pre-trial negotiation, the trial, and in the post-trial period sentencing and enforcement, etc. At each stage you will have some contact with the client, and naturally questions will have to be asked and the issues of the case thoroughly investigated. The additional information thrown up by this process will have to be assimilated with any existing knowledge of the case and its issues. Any preliminary conclusions will have to be adjusted to reflect this new, informed picture of the case. It is only at the end of these steps that you will be able to offer the client some concrete advice on the issues in the case. It is crucial that the client not only finds this advice satisfactory and of practical benefit at each stage but that he or she has a thorough understanding of its consequences. In order to meet these requirements you will have to appreciate the client's level of comprehension and be sympathetic to his or her level of education, age, background, and so on, as well as having an understanding of the legal and factual issues in the case.

The Bar Standards Board's (BSB's) *Professional Statement for Barristers*, at 1.4, requires barristers to 'Have an awareness of the wide range of organisations supporting the administration of justice'. This includes an understanding that the system for administration of justice comprises more than the judicial system alone and the need to have an awareness of the other elements wherever they are relevant to their work. Thus you will need to gain this understanding as well as an awareness of the other sources of advice (eg your professional client) and funding available to your client's case.

The steps that go to make up the advice process are recorded in **7.2**. Whilst at first glance they may appear mechanical, after some practice the process will become more natural.

7.2 Advising: a step-by-step guide

(a) Identify the objectives of the conference and isolate all the legal and factual issues of the case. Compare the two to isolate the relevant issues that require your advice in the conference. (**See 5.4.**)

(b) Gather all necessary information from the papers and ask the client questions as necessary to complete your knowledge of the case. (See **6.6.**)

(c) Assimilate the new information into existing knowledge by filling the gaps and clarifying any ambiguities.

(d) Analyse the legal and factual issues in the case, considering the new information and your revised view of the client's instructions.

(e) Consider the merits of the case, application, and so on with the benefit of this additional legal and factual analysis.

(f) Adjust as necessary any preliminary view that you formulated before the conference.

(g) Formulate your opinion and advice so that it is both practical and appropriate to the needs of the client and the requirements of the case.

(h) Consider how best you may communicate your conclusions to the client by using appropriate language and sufficient explanation.

(i) Identify all the strengths and weaknesses of the case for the client.

(j) Articulate your opinion to the client in a way that he or she can understand.

(k) Take the client's final decision and any further instructions.

7.3 Terminology

Before continuing to discuss the advice stage in greater detail it will be helpful to give some explanation of the terminology used in the study of advising clients on legal matters.

7.3.1 Advice

This term can be used in a general sense to include the whole process by which a barrister communicates information to clients and assists them during the conference. The information and help may take the form of one or more of the processes described elsewhere in this section. However, the term 'advice' may also be used more narrowly to include the barrister's particular instructions and detailed suggestions for action given to the client. Some commentators on the role of lawyers in conferences suggest that giving specific advice is not appropriate as it imposes the view of the lawyer on the client. However, on many occasions barristers in England and Wales do give overt advice to their clients. Indeed, some would argue that this is what they are engaged to do; in short, it is what the client is paying them for.

7.3.2 Opinion

Used in the context of a conference an opinion is a discussion of the merits of the case by the barrister. For example, this might include the chances of success should the case go to trial or the likely outcomes and consequences of a negotiated settlement. In a broad sense this term is also applied to suggestions for future action made by the barrister to the client, but always following an evaluation of the strengths and weaknesses of the relevant features of the case.

7.3.3 Counselling

This is a specific method of advising clients employed by some legal advisers and there is much debate amongst commentators about its various merits. It is designed to be used by the lawyer to advise the client of the full range of options, and the client is invited to take the initiative. This involves the selection of a range of options that best suit the client's identified needs and personal characteristics or that accord with the emotional demands of the client. (See **7.16** for a full discussion of this method.) This method of advising should not be confused with psychological support. The sort of counselling that might be offered by a qualified counsellor is not an appropriate method of advising in a legal conference.

7.3.4 Explanation

This is a neutral method of assistance used to give the client definitions, descriptions, and explanations. The lawyer acts as a guide and interpreter of the legal process and it may include explanations of legal terminology. Thus, although statements of personal preference and suggestions of best choice are not relevant, various and numerous explanations will usually precede another form of advice-giving.

7.4 Standard of advice

No matter what style or method you use to advise your client, as a practising barrister you must reach the standards set by the profession. A stated outcome in the Bar Code of Conduct, C3 You and your client, is that:

oC13 Clients know what to expect and understand the advice they are given.

The standard is a high one, and rightly so, as you will be helping people to make some of the most important decisions in their lives. There are three key objectives for the quality of your advice that can be identified from this outcome of the Code:

- Your advice should be practical.
- Your advice should be appropriate.
- Your advice should be expressed in a way that your client can understand.

In this chapter we will discuss the advice process in detail and investigate the skills you need to develop to meet the standard set by the profession.

When in pupillage and practice you should periodically refresh your memory of the duties you owe your lay and professional clients and the court. Regular reference should be made to the Bar Code of Conduct. The Code and the BSB guidance documents are not merely collections of professional ethics, but also offer clear guidance on good practice. Sometimes the Code deals with very specific circumstances, but it also indicates the outcomes expected in client care and the execution of the barrister's professional duties. For these reasons the Code's contents should form part of every barrister's general knowledge. (See **Chapter 9** and the *Professional Ethics* manual.)

7.5 Reaching the advice stage: assimilating new information

The questioning stage of the conference will only conclude once you have gathered all the information necessary to enable you to advise your client. Before completing that section of the conference you ought to check with the client that you have addressed all the relevant issues in the case. Next it will be necessary to assimilate this extra information into your existing knowledge of the case and the preparation that you carried out beforehand. When considering your preliminary view of the case you must remember that it was based upon facts that might now have to be revised, changed, or rejected altogether. Further, this provisional opinion will be based to some extent upon guesswork and speculation. In other words, you will have passed judgment before you were in full command of all the relevant facts. If necessary you should adjust this prejudged view so that it is suitable to the circumstances of the client as they now appear. Finally, you must take into account your impressions of the client formed from listening to his or her concerns and expectations. This will enable you to formulate advice that is both appropriate to these circumstances and practical to the needs of the individual client.

This process is not time-consuming, laborious, nor mechanical. Indeed, you cannot afford to be dilatory when a client eager to hear your advice is in front of you. With practice and the experience that it brings this process will become swifter and more natural.

Throughout the conference you must analyse the legal and non-legal options open to your client. At various times during the questioning stage take an opportunity to collect your thoughts. Consult your notes briefly and consider the client's instructions in the light of your preparation.

A practical and thorough plan with a clear layout can be your touchstone in the conference. Such a plan will highlight gaps in your knowledge and contain the appropriate legal research, and suggest your preliminary view of the case.

7.6   Preparing for your oral advice in the conference

To give your opinion of the case you will need to be fully prepared beforehand. This is because you will have little opportunity to consider the case in depth during the conference. The mental and social tasks that are part of the conference itself will occupy your mind most of your time. However, new information and perhaps a revised view of the case will materialise during your discussions with the client. Therefore you will have to rely upon your preparation whilst doing some thinking on your feet or seat. Only rarely will there be the chance to consult legal works or seek assistance from colleagues. The client's responses to your questions must be assimilated, analysed, and compared with your preliminary view of the case. The client may introduce additional facts and instructions that will demand additional analysis and broaden the areas upon which the client will require advice. All this will have to be done whilst the client and solicitor are with you. The client expects and is entitled to professional advice that will help to resolve the problems he or she is facing. The lay and professional client may wish to participate and add to your comments, questions, and opinion and you must listen to these interruptions and deal with them appropriately and tactfully. Always remember that the needs of the client are immediate and real; the person in front of you is the individual experiencing the difficulties first-hand.

7.7   How and when to give the client advice

Special care is required when you communicate your advice to the client. A common question is, 'When is it appropriate to inform the client of your advice?' In the majority of conferences some, if not all, of your advice can be communicated orally and immediately. However, on certain occasions there will be a reason to delay the advice, if the client needs time to consider the options further or because you need to carry out additional research. A choice arises whether to telephone through this delayed advice to the solicitor or to put it into a written form. In either event it is important to let the client know when to expect your advice. However, if you have fully researched the law and understood the brief and received full answers to your questions you should be able to offer the client your advice at the conference itself.

When you are about to communicate your opinion let the client know that you are doing exactly this and ensure you have his or her undivided attention. Check that the client understands that you are moving to the advice stage. This will not only ensure that the client is listening attentively to what you have to say but also maintain your control of the conference.

To avoid confusing the client by delivering ill-informed advice you must exercise control over the conference. A logical order must be maintained. Ensure that you have covered all the issues with the client and that all relevant questions have been answered. Further, you ought continuously to monitor the progress of the conference: keep an eye on the time and how efficiently you are addressing the issues of the case and achieving the objectives of the conference. It is your responsibility to decide when it is appropriate to give your opinion of the case to the client; this can only follow a thorough assessment of the issues by you. However, it does not follow that your advice will be at the end of the conference. If it is communicated too late there will be insufficient time to address the consequences of the client's decision. Often there will be many issues to address and several areas to advise upon. On each instance you will need to gather information on various topics, analyse the facts against the law, and formulate and present your opinion. Of course, if you have adequately planned in advance, these tasks will be dealt with more efficiently and fully.

7.7.1   Giving advice

> **How to do it**
>
> (a)   Any conclusion reached ought to be clear to yourself so that you appear confident and are able to justify your advice.
>
> (b)   Formulate the advice in language that is readily comprehensible to the client. Remember to be precise and practical, not vague or patronising.
>
> (c)   Explain how you have reached your conclusion and set out the strengths and weaknesses of its consequences for the client personally.
>
> (d)   Check that the client has correctly heard your advice and understood it.
>
> (e)   Finally, it is of the utmost importance that the client is aware that the final decision is his or hers. Remember, your opinion is merely offered; the client has the freedom to accept or reject it.

7.8   Making your advice clear to the client

The BSB's Professional Statement for Barristers, at 1.6, requires barristers to be able to provide clear, concise, and accurate advice in writing and orally and take responsibility for it. This includes an ability to convey unpalatable advice where necessary. A measure of the acceptable degree of conviction with which you can express your advice to the client was given in an annex to the old Code of Conduct. Although it dealt specifically with a conference with a defendant in a criminal case, it may be applied generally to civil and criminal cases. Paragraph 11.3 of the Written Standards for the Conduct of Professional Work in Section 3 of the Bar Code of Conduct stated:

> A barrister acting for a defendant should advise his lay client generally about his plea. In doing so he may, if necessary, express his advice in strong terms. He must, however, make it clear that the client has complete freedom of choice and that the responsibility for the plea is the client's.

As is clear from the old Code, the client always had freedom to accept or reject the advice that was given—nothing about that has changed with the new Code. Thus you must make this freedom to choose explicit. This should be done in a way that encourages the client to accept the responsibility rather than in a tone that might suggest that your interest in the conference ends with the client's decision. At this crucial stage of the conference, when the client is on tenterhooks to hear your opinion of the best course to take, you must proceed with the utmost caution and sensitivity. It is unacceptable, for example, to state your advice boldly in the following way:

> What you've just told me suggests that a guilty plea would be appropriate and I must warn you that the maximum sentence for violent disorder is five years' imprisonment.

Imagine the devastating effect of such a bombshell on the client! Also, in part at least, this advice is misleading.

The suggestion to plead guilty may well be founded on a realistic analysis of the client's position and therefore be justifiable in the circumstances. However, there is a world of difference between robust advice presented with justification to the client and an insensitive instruction to take the course of action that you as the lawyer have decided upon. Further, the bold and intimidating advice on possible sentence is incomplete and therefore erroneous. The maximum sentence is only ever used in those rare cases where the offence is at the top end of the bracket—that is, it contains many aggravating features and few, if any, mitigating ones. There is always something that can be said in the defendant's favour, and in the majority of cases a sentence well below the maximum can be expected. To overburden the client with the shadow of five years in custody is both inhuman and unprofessional.

7.9 Warning the client of the consequences

Clients may not always fully appreciate the consequences of any decision that they take, for example the implications it might have on costs, the ensuing delay, inconvenience, or litigation stress. Some side effects are of great importance to the individual client. Consider, for example, the effect of having a criminal record if the client is a wage earner looking for a new job, or the effect of receiving a bad credit rating if the client is setting up a business. Certain consequences will have a less tangible but equally devastating effect. The social effects of being convicted for a violent sexual crime, or the loss of face when an employer loses a case of discrimination are two examples. It is therefore part of your duty to offer advice in the light of the consequences of the decisions that the client has made. This advice on collateral issues may include non-legal considerations as well as the usual advice on the legal consequences of your client's decision.

7.10 Giving the client the full benefit of your services: time management

It will be rare for you to receive instructions to hold a conference that covers only one area for advice. If there are several areas to advise upon, time can be scarce during a conference. Clearly, you are required to meet all the objectives of the conference to the satisfaction of both your lay and professional clients. However, there are limits upon the powers of concentration of both you and your client. Therefore it is legitimate to recognise that some of the issues faced by the client are of greater importance than others.

The *Professional Statement for Barristers*, at 1.3, requires barristers to have a knowledge and understanding of the law and procedure relevant to their areas of practice, and to have a good understanding of, and be up to date with, recent cases and developments in the areas of law in which they practise. This includes a good understanding of the rules of practice and procedure operating in courts relevant to their areas of practice. The rules relating to jurisdiction, evidence, disposals, financial orders, and costs are particularly highlighted, and so too are processes by which disputes can be resolved outside court, such as arbitration and mediation. In each case it is necessary and possible to construct a hierarchy of issues that require your advice. Some issues will have priority over others. Some are easy to prioritise, for example those identified for you in the brief by your solicitor. The relative urgency of other issues can also assist you to decide whether they can be left until later, hence the need for a sound knowledge of the rules of procedure and the various time limits imposed on litigation. Non-legal considerations that do not have a direct influence on the case may form part of the secondary issues and so may be left until later. Those that are at the heart of the matter, however, cannot. These will be the issues that are priorities in the case, issues that must be addressed and resolved as a matter of urgency or which take precedence over other peripheral issues.

It is not possible to make a list of priorities in the abstract. Only the individual circumstances of the case and the client will be able to tell you which needs are of greater or lesser importance. It is your responsibility to find out from the client what the central issues are. It is always worth considering which areas to give priority to and which to deal with either later or at another meeting. No one is superhuman, so you must make a realistic estimation of your powers of concentration and those of the client before and during the conference.

If you are really pushed for time it may be appropriate to prioritise the issues upon which you intend to give your advice based upon your brief fee. You are only paid for that for which you are instructed and it is legitimate, but not automatically appropriate, to emphasise the legal function of the barrister. In any event non-legal advice, as opposed to consideration of non-legal options, may be more suitably given by another professional. For example, if a client instructs you to represent him or her in a personal injury case you might suggest an application for State benefits and even give an estimation of the likely financial award. However, it would be negligent not to add that the client should seek professional advice from a benefits officer or a financial adviser working for a disability charity if appropriate.

7.11 Helping the client to understand your advice

The lay client cannot be expected to understand the legal process or the legal context of their case to the degree of sophistication that you do. It is therefore common to spend a significant amount of time explaining in everyday language the effect of the law on the client's case. Legal terminology and the court procedures that surround the case will also need to be explained. Further, some extra time may have to be spent explaining to the client why court litigation takes a certain route and warning him or her how to avoid delays. There are two objectives when you communicate your advice. You will obviously want the client to make a decision fully informed of all the consequences of that decision. And you will wish to pass on your advice to the client clearly and comprehensibly.

In part you will realise these objectives if you ensure that the client appreciates the legal context of the decision. This might include the finality of the decision, its consequences for the future, and the financial obligations that surround litigation. It is your responsibility to guide the client through the labyrinth of the law.

7.11.1   Checking for comprehension

You must avoid prejudice and preconceptions when evaluating your client's apparent intelligence, but you should observe and appraise the client's level of comprehension. His or her formal education alone will not be an adequate indicator. Many clients will feel intimidated or overawed by the complexity of their case even though they have a wide experience of life apart from it. Therefore be patient with the client. This does not mean that you need to be condescending or unnecessarily simplistic in your explanations. For example, an illiterate defendant with a long record will not be able to read the charge sheet but he or she may know a lot about Bail Application procedures. Further, although the client may appear bewildered to be in a road traffic court, his or her 30 years' experience as a driver has probably given some insight into what is and what is not safe driving. It is easy to belittle clients inadvertently by forgetting that they are capable of contributing their knowledge or experience to assist themselves. Apart from making for poor manners, this lapse of common sense can seriously disrupt the rapport established between you and the client. If you treat clients as slow, unintelligent beings, why should they take an active part in the conference? Further, how can you be surprised that they will not trust your judgement or integrity?

An observant stance and a carefully selected vocabulary are the keys to intelligent and considerate explanations. Gauge what you have to say to the client. Avoid clichés and pat phrases; they rarely have a long shelf life. Remember that what is comprehensible to one client is not always understood by the next. So try to adapt your approach to suit the individual in front of you after you have learnt something about their personality and level of intelligence.

If asking a question to confirm understanding, it is often wise to avoid leading or simple yes/no questions. Attempt to encourage the client to repeat back to you what you have explained or methodically investigate the client's comprehension with a series of open and closed questions. Illustrate to the client why it is in his or her interest to understand what you are explaining. By showing the benefit of this additional knowledge you will facilitate greater powers of concentration and interest. If the client fails to see the benefit, ask yourself whether this information is wholly relevant. There is little point in overburdening the client with material of little relevance or import to his or her case.

7.11.2   Explaining the law

At different stages in the life of the case the relevance of the substantive law to the client's case will be greater than at others. It can be expected that by the time the client comes to see the barrister in chambers he or she has some idea of the legal principles of the case. This is usually formed with the help of the solicitor. However, there can be no guarantee that this will always be so. The initial meeting may have been a brief one, the solicitor might not have explained the law sufficiently clearly, or the client might simply have forgotten what he or she has been told.

In some circumstances you will be the first lawyer to discuss the case with the client. For example, at a magistrates' court first appearance hearing after a night in the cells the client may be totally ignorant of the legal basis of the charge. A similar position in a civil setting is an urgent without notice injunction, for example. It is always wise to check with the client personally how much they understand, with some open questions inviting a statement in simple terms of the case. This knowledge, no matter how rudimentary, can be built upon. If it is wide of the mark then some tactful re-tracking may be called for.

Always concentrate on the specific case and avoid taking a textbook approach to the law. The average lawyer spends three years studying his or her subject at university and the lay client cannot be expected to follow lengthy explanations of the law of evidence or intent. By using the client's case as a starting point you will focus your mind and help him or her to grasp the essentials of the law as it relates to the case. As part of your preparation you should consider what law needs to be explained to the client and how you are going to do this. As well as being relevant and pithy, your explanations should avoid legal terminology where possible and always be free of lawyers' jargon and slang. (During your pupillage you will soon discover how barristers derive great delight from using their own dialect and shorthand when discussing a case with one another, but how this argot is usually dropped once they meet the client and address the court.)

7.11.3   Explaining procedure

Clients are often unaware of the procedural context of their case. The lack of an appreciation of the need for the numerous stages of litigation is illustrated by the common complaint that the law is oblique and unnecessarily slow. This is hardly surprising as it is the solicitor who prepares the papers in the case and during the initial stages of litigation the client is not always informed of developments that do not have immediate effect upon the conduct of the case. Also, in the early life of a case there are many stages in which the client is not personally involved—interim applications or solicitor-to-solicitor correspondence, for example. Lawyers, on the other hand, are only too aware of the mundane, run-of-the-mill stages through which both civil and criminal cases go. Therefore lawyers can easily overlook the fact that the client will not understand their purpose or indeed the necessity for each step in the litigation process. Your client has a right to a full explanation of what is taking place. There is an advantage for you too: the informed client will more readily take an active role in the case's progress. Thus, apart from the tactical advantages of a thorough understanding of the litigation processes, this knowledge is essential so that you can assist your client with clear and accurate explanations of civil and criminal litigation.

When explaining procedure to the client think carefully about how much detail he or she needs at this stage. Your concern is not to protect an arcane system, but rather to keep the client's attention on the issues that are important to the conference. The test is one of relevance: does the client need to know? When the client is being asked to make a choice or take a decision, obviously it will be necessary to a greater or lesser degree to inform him or her of the procedural implications, for example the following:

- What delays might be met?
- How long does the client have before he or she must act?
- What are the cost or Legal Aid considerations?

Whilst not advocating the 'You needn't worry yourself about that, leave it to the lawyers' approach, you will need to consider how much time you can allocate to any explanation of procedure. Further, you must consider how easily the client will comprehend and how long he or she will be able to remember this information. Nonetheless, the client who is fully informed will be less anxious about the future and will feel more in control of the destiny of the case. The benefit to you is that you will find that the client is more willing to collaborate with you. Most importantly, once people understand what is happening or likely to happen to their case they are better placed to take decisions for themselves and feel confident about the future. The fear of the unknown can be a great impediment to the successful conclusion of the conference.

7.11.4 Explaining financial costs of the case

The question of money, and indeed figures generally, will arise in most conferences and it is always wise to carry a pocket calculator and have an understanding of rudimentary arithmetic. What follows is merely an outline to assist you to think about the difficulties that you and the client can expect to face. (See further the ***Opinion Writing and Case Preparation*** manual.)

7.11.4.1 Fees

The barrister, working on a referral basis, never accepts money or other forms of payment from the client personally. The solicitor will deal with the financial affairs of the client and your clerk will negotiate any fee on your behalf. Great circumspection is therefore needed when discussing fees with a client. Nonetheless, when advising the client on possible future action the financial costs must be discussed. No precise figures can be offered, but a sensible range should be given where possible to give the client an accurate estimate of the financial cost of any legal help they seek. This projection will be based upon your experience as well as your knowledge. It may be some time before you feel confident enough to give this advice to the client without some assistance. If you feel unable to advise yourself it may be appropriate to refer the client to the solicitor. Indeed, it is your professional client who has the final responsibility of collecting the fees from your lay client.

7.11.4.2 Costs

In civil cases some costs can be stated with a greater degree of certainty than others, but many will be liable to assessment by the court. Remember that whilst most costs follow the event there are numerous exceptions, particularly at interim hearings. (See CPR, rr 44.13–44.17.) In any post-hearing conference you will have to be prepared to explain the effect of the order as to costs. Following a finding of guilt or a plea of guilty the prosecution may request that the defendant pays some of their costs. If advising in personal injury cases, you should be aware of Qualified One-Way Costs Shifting (QOCS), which is a civil litigation funding device that bars a defendant from recovering its costs from an unsuccessful claimant. Care should be taken to discover from the prosecution what costs they are seeking from the defendant if there is a conviction. Note that these are often in addition to any fine or compensation that the court might impose. Again, a range can be given based upon experience and knowledge of similar cases.

7.11.4.3 Public funding

In both civil and criminal cases the Legal Aid Agency may require a financial contribution from the client and in these circumstances the cost of litigation can be a real concern for the client. The solicitor should include information about the level of the contribution and the extent and terms of the public funding. Obviously, the longer the case goes on, the greater the total sum the client will have to pay. In civil cases there is the added danger that the successful client, whether a claimant or a defendant, may have to repay the total amount of public funding received through a process of recoupment. Indeed, civil public funding has been described as being more in the form of a loan than a grant. All of these implications will need to be explained to the client and he or she will also need to be reminded of them at the appropriate times.

7.11.4.4 Legal Aid Agency

The Legal Aid Agency provides both civil and criminal legal aid and advice in England and Wales. It aims to offer a fair, effective, and efficient service to the civil and criminal justice systems. It is a delivery organisation which commissions and procures legal aid services from providers (solicitors, barristers, and the not-for-profit sector). The Legal Aid Agency is an executive agency of the Ministry of Justice. It came into existence on 1 April 2013 following the abolition of the Legal Services Commission as a result of the Legal Aid, Sentencing and Punishment of Offenders (LASPO) Act 2012. LASPO 2012 created the new statutory office of the Director of Legal Casework. The Director takes decisions on the funding of individual cases. Processes have been put in place to ensure the Legal Aid Agency is able to demonstrate independence of decision-making.

With the introduction of more stringent merits and means tests, the availability of public funds for private litigation has become increasingly rare. Public funding has effectively been abolished in the majority of civil litigation cases. In many cases conditional fee agreements (CFAs) have filled the gap. Nonetheless, legal aid could help pay for legal advice, family mediation, or representation in court or at a tribunal. Clients can get help with civil legal aid for: benefit appeals; debt, if their home is at risk; special educational needs; housing discrimination issues; help and advice if he or she is a victim of domestic violence; and issues around a child being taken into care.

A grant of Criminal Legal Aid is subject to the Interests of Justice (IoJ) merits test and a means test; both tests are subject to revision and the calculation rules are complex—what follows is merely an overview. In the magistrates' court, if your client passes the Interests of Justice test and the means test they will receive free legal aid. In the Crown Court, similar considerations will be taken into account in an application for legal aid. If your client is ineligible, he or she will be required to pay all of their legal costs privately. If your client is eligible for legal aid, then the means test will consider the client's income and other circumstances and they may be liable for contributions towards costs either during the proceedings or at the end of their case.

7.11.4.5 Conditional fee agreements, damages-based agreements, and third-party funding

Conditional fee agreements, commonly known as 'no win, no fee' arrangements, are a modern way to fund civil litigation. They were initially introduced in personal injury cases but are now widely available in civil litigation (but not family cases). They have been introduced to encourage 'middle-income' clients to pursue cases where they are not eligible for public funding but not sufficiently wealthy to bear the risk of litigation personally. Under a conditional fee agreement the solicitor will not charge the client a fee for his or her services if not successful—hence the popular name 'no win, no fee agreements'. However, there is a price to pay, or rather an additional risk to bear under the scheme. When a client enters a conditional fee agreement, the client will have the risk of paying an additional 'success fee' to his or her lawyers if the case is won. The success fee is charged over and above the solicitor's 'basic costs'. The client will also enter into an insurance scheme to support the conditional fee agreement. So, if the client wins, he or she will be able to claim the following from the unsuccessful opponent: damages; his or her own solicitor's cost, plus VAT; disbursements; and the success fee and the insurance premium. If the client loses the case, he or she will only have to pay the following: any disbursements that the solicitor has incurred (but no fees—remember, no win, no fee); and the opponent's costs. These are usually met by the insurance cover.

However, note that it is possible for a successful litigant to be awarded damages but also be ordered to pay some or all of the opponent's costs and not be able to recover all of his or her own costs. (An example of such a situation is where the claimant refuses to accept a Part 36 offer and fails to beat it at trial.) In such an event the insurer will only pay any outstanding costs and disbursements to the extent that they exceed the damages that the client is awarded.

Clearly, conditional fee agreements are a common feature of civil litigation. You will need to be aware of the risks for the client when advising on settlement and trial. You will also need to be aware of the risks to yourself when entering into such an agreement—if you lose the case you don't get paid! (Remember 'winning' means any money settlement or judgment in favour of the client.) It is very important that you understand the professional and ethical issues that are relevant to these new arrangements. Make sure you consult the Code of Conduct and seek advice from experienced counsel. LASPO 2012 has abolished the recoverability of success fees against the losing party as an element of the usual order for costs to follow the event.

A damages-based agreement (DBA) represents another alternative funding model. Under DBAs the client agrees to pay the lawyer a percentage of sums recovered in a claim. If the client were to lose, the lawyer would not receive any fee.

Third party funding (TPF) is the provision of funds by those who have no connection with the litigation in return for a share of the proceeds. It is available for litigation, arbitration, and other forms of Alternative Dispute Resolution. It is legal so long as the funder does not exercise control over the dispute. TPF-supported litigation is typically large-scale claims, and funders tend to be institutional investors, private equity funds, hedge funds, and private investors. A funder's fee comes out of the damages; it is not a recoverable cost of litigation.

7.11.4.6 Non-legal financial considerations

Clients will often be under financial strain besides the cost of litigation. This may be because they are prevented from earning a wage following imprisonment or because of the demands that the litigation is making on their time. At the early stages of proceedings the client may not appreciate the degree of impact that the case will have on his or her time or purse. You have a duty to keep the client aware of the cost of litigation and this will include the non-legal costs. Some clients will lose their livelihoods as a result of their involvement with the criminal courts or by becoming embroiled in civil proceedings. You should not only alert the client to these possible consequences but also offer some practical advice. Suggestions of the non-legal options, or references to other professionals who will be able to offer assistance, ought to be made when appropriate. A working knowledge of the welfare benefits system is essential if practising family or criminal law, where the means of the parties are often of interest to the court itself. (See *Remedies* manual.) Once again, when dealing with figures, it is best to think in terms of ranges and to admit uncertainty if it is appropriate to do so. Remember that most welfare benefits are discretionary so there can be few guarantees.

7.12 Dealing with conflicting advice

Occasionally the advice that you believe is appropriate will differ from that already communicated to the client by the solicitor or a counsel who previously held the brief. Two or more lawyers looking at the same case may hold differing, sometimes conflicting, opinions. This is not as uncommon as some lay people may expect. Indeed, in an adversarial system there is rarely certainty when applying the law to a set of facts or identifying the strengths or weaknesses of a case. The particular difficulty for the barrister in a situation such as this is that there are two clients and three duties. There is a professional client and a lay client, with separate duties owed to each and a third duty to the court. For the newly qualified lawyer this three-way pull can be the source of great anxiety. This is particularly so when there is the nagging feeling that any upset caused to either of the clients or the court will be reported back to chambers. In this part of the chapter we will look at this dilemma and offer some suggestions to assist you to overcome it.

The Code has set out some clear guidance and rules to assist in such difficult circumstances. The relevant paragraphs are quoted below, but the gist of the rules is that your primary duty is to your lay client.

rC15 Your duty to act in the best interests of each client (CD2), to provide a competent standard of work and service to each client (CD7) and to keep the affairs of each client confidential (CD6) includes the following obligations:

.1   you must promote fearlessly and by all proper and lawful means the client's best interests;

.2   you must do so without regard to your own interests or to any consequences to you (which may include, for the avoidance of doubt, you being required to take reasonable steps to mitigate the effects of any breach of this Handbook);

.3   you must do so without regard to the consequences to any other person (whether to your professional client, employer or any other person);

.4   you must not permit your professional client, employer or any other person to limit your discretion as to how the interests of the client can best be served.

There is also the danger of confusing the client by offering an opinion different from that already indicated by the solicitor. This can be merely irksome to the client or place additional stress on him or her at an already stressful time. In most circumstances the client will only have received a preliminary view of the possibilities from the solicitor. The alert client will appreciate that you are a specialist to whom they have been referred for more certain advice. If the client shows a reluctance to accept your view rather than the solicitor's, you must take control and justify why your views differ. Often the easiest way to support your view is to highlight to the client the additional information that you have gathered at the conference and explain how this affects the legal analysis of their case.

7.12.1   Dealing with conflicting advice

> **How to do it**
>
> If your view of the case leads you to give advice that, if followed, would alter the litigation to a great degree, you may wish to consider the following suggested approach:
>
> - Avoid confusing clients or undermining their faith in their solicitor unless strictly appropriate.
>
> - If possible, speak with the other lawyer with whom you disagree to discuss his or her views. That lawyer may know something that you do not.
>
> - If appropriate and practical, review the process by which you reached your advice to double-check your conclusions.
>
> - Highlight to the client your advice and identify its strengths and weaknesses.
>
> - Allow clients to make their decision, reminding them if necessary that the final decision remains theirs.
>
> - Inform clients of the effect of any change or adjustment that will result (eg extra costs, effect on procedure).
>
> - Inform the professional client of any changes—be prepared to explain and justify what has taken place.
>
> - Ensure that the court is informed of any developments and material changes.

7.13   Expressing risk to the client

This section introduces various methods by which you might express the risk involved in litigation to the client and considers the strengths and weaknesses of these methods. It is important to communicate the degree of chance directly to the client, who can then make a decision in the full knowledge of the attendant risks of litigation. There are few certainties in law; trials, for example, are not so much investigations of the truth as testing of conflicting testimonies to ascertain which is more believable. The verdict is guilty or not guilty rather than guilty or innocent. Likewise, the levels of damages to be awarded for personal injury are not scientifically assessed but approximated. They are often only a symbolic sum to reflect what was suffered by the injured party. The client, however, will want to know what is going to happen: what the chances are of success at trial, and how the damages will be assessed and at what level. Clearly, it is part of the lawyer's role to give estimations of these risks and chances.

7.13.1   Preliminary considerations

You should always attempt to be practical and realistic: do not forget the specific problem faced by the client before you. Any expression of risk will have to be effectively communicated to the individual client: will he or she be able to comprehend what you are saying? There are several methods and styles of expressing risk; which one you choose will depend upon your preference and its suitability for the issue in question. It may, of course, be necessary to experiment, particularly in the early stages of practice. Much can be learnt by observing other members of the profession, and these lessons can help to develop your repertoire.

7.13.2   Introducing risk analysis to the client

How to do it

- Check that the client is fully satisfied that he or she has sufficient information about the strengths and weaknesses of the case.
- Allow the client to raise any additional concerns, if appropriate.
- Ask the client to consider how the risk of failure/success is affected by these strengths and weaknesses.
- Invite the client to estimate whether the relevant risk is high, low, or next to nothing.
- Ask the client to state explicitly whether he or she is willing to accept that level of risk of failure/success.

7.13.3   Use of language

The most common way of expressing a risk is to use everyday expressions: 'x is less risky than y'. Alternatively, phrases such as 'there's a good chance that . . . ', or 'such and such is unlikely to succeed' also give a measure of the risks involved. When adopting such expressions the speaker is attempting to pass on his or her judgement as swiftly as possible.

Difficulties soon arise, however, once the recipient of this information requests explanation or justification of the estimate, or a clearer statement of what the precise risk is. Sometimes the answer may be that the lawyer runs through the strengths and weaknesses of the case again. For example, the number and quality of witnesses for the prosecution may be used to justify the estimation of the risk of conviction as 'great'. But if the client wants a clearer statement of what is meant by 'great', problems can arise. This is because the client wishes to know what the risk is, not the lawyer's reasons for thinking that there is a risk of conviction in the first place. On occasion the lawyer may be able to sidestep the issue by using the following: 'by "great" I mean it's more likely than not that you will be convicted'. Although to a law graduate this answer is transparently insufficient and inappropriate, to the lay client it may appear to be an acceptable one. In the worst circumstances it may even be taken as an indication that he or she ought not to question the barrister's advice. Thus there are some shortcomings with this method. However, it also has some advantages. By using everyday language and employing common phrases the level of communication from the lawyer to the client is often high. At a superficial level at least, the client will understand what is being said. Further, this style can be utilised several times in the same conference when dealing with the various issues or options, thus maintaining some consistency, for example by using a series of comparatives: better than, worse than, etc.

Naturally it is important for the lawyer to keep a tally of which item he or she lists as better than the next, and so on. Some review of this list may be necessary as and when changes affect the order of the items on it. In this way the running order can be adjusted in a useful way during the life of the case, for example if fresh evidence is revealed or a witness does not come up to proof. If this happens the lawyer can then say to the client: 'The chances of success have been reduced from a reasonably good chance to a poor chance of the judge finding in favour of our case.' A second advantage is that the lawyer will be protected against criticism from the client. Some clients will not have a disinterested memory and may complain that the court has imposed costs on them for an unsuccessful trial when the lawyer said that there was an excellent chance of success. The client's faulty memory can be checked against your record.

A final warning must be given. As was suggested, explanations of what is meant by good or bad and so on are not easy to give. One reason is that everyone has their own innate understanding of these words but few have the ability to articulate precisely their personalised meaning to others when applied to a particular situation. The inevitable vagueness that follows often leads to misunderstanding.

7.13.4 Metaphors and similes

One can take everyday experiences and adapt them to the particular dilemma faced by the client. The client can, for example, be invited to compare the risks with a financial investment that might provide a series of bonuses. There is a likelihood that the investment may go down as well as up. If the chances of success are particularly low you might compare them with a lottery. These sorts of comparisons can be useful, particularly if talking to a client with little or no experience of the law but the ability to think in an independent fashion. It goes without saying that a simile or comparison must be within the client's personal experience. You cannot expect everyone to have a working knowledge of gambling terms or of the stock market. Whilst this method of communicating risk is entertaining and readily comprehensible, it merely communicates the degree of risk superficially. There is only the hope that the client will be able to pick up intuitively what is not being communicated explicitly. Thus an appeal to the client's real or imagined experiences is made in the hope that there will be a process of convergence. In short, the lawyer hopes that the client will come to share his or her belief of the estimate of the risk without lengthy reasoning.

7.13.5 Numbers, ratios, ranges, fractions, percentages, statistics

Figures carry their own mystique and should be used with caution. Some people will understand that the expressions 'the chances of success are 50:50' and 'the likelihood of us winning is 25 per cent' do not mean that in the first case the chance of success is precisely half or in the second precisely one quarter. However, some people, if asked what these two phrases are saying about the risks involved, may fall into this trap. Therefore, it is necessary to guard against the temptation to believe that what sounds like an accurate statement of the risk is what it appears to be. You therefore have a responsibility to explain to the client clearly and without condescension that you are using the numbers, figures, and ratios adverbially: not as scientific measurements of the risk but as helpful expressions of your estimation of it.

7.13.6 Pounds and pence

If discussing monetary figures there are again several ways of expressing them. The most common way of expressing the outcome will be in pounds and pence. The obvious danger here is that the courts do not award monies in a precise fashion. Note should be made of the difference in civil law between debts and penalties, and damages (see the *Remedies* manual) and in criminal law between fixed and non-fixed fines. Most lawyers favour stating a range within which the final figure can be expected to fall. For example, 'In these sorts of whiplash cases the courts usually award damages from £2,050 to £3,630 (with the 10% uplift recommended in the Review of Civil Litigation Costs Final Report). With the facts as they are in your case I'd expect the final award to be in the £3,000 to £3,500 range.' A similar approach can be taken to fines, and so on. Note should be made of the two ranges given. The first sets the general limits found in cases of the same nature, the second the specific limits that apply to the particular case. In this way the client is informed of the whole picture—it can be of particular use when it comes to advising on appeal. If the court in the whiplash case above only awarded £2,750, the lawyer may wish to point out that whilst it is low, and in his professional opinion appealable, it is not advisable to endure the extra costs and stresses of appeal for only a further £750 at most.

7.14 Non-verbal expressions of your opinion

The lawyer will be closely scrutinised by the client, especially when passing on vital information such as the length of sentence or the chances of successfully defending a civil case. The client will react to the way you give the information that (for him or her at least) is of vital importance. The client will be sensitive to your posture, eye contact, and other indicators of confidence, as well as the pitch of your voice. The client may be able to understand much of your opinion of his or her case and its merits by observing you as well as listening to you. You ought to be aware of these facts throughout the advising stage and remember how it might affect the client's appreciation of the issues and merits of the case.

At different times some deference to the client's emotions ought to be given. Before dismissing an appeal against a custodial sentence, some moments' reflection will tell you that no matter how slim the chance is, the client may be willing to take it. This may be the case even if there are some attendant risks. Even so, there is the danger of being insufficiently forthright if the risk is particularly slim. Clients will often detect your hesitancy, but it is up to you to give the client the benefit of your express and honest opinion.

There may be occasions when you think that the client's chances are rightly low or that he or she richly deserves the sentence that he or she has received. You must not sit in judgement and must keep your opinion on this point to yourself. On these occasions it is particularly important to guard against inappropriate non-verbal communication: practice itself is the best tutor. This is not merely a question of politeness or a counsel for empathy. It is a central consideration when deciding how best to communicate your professional advice clearly and accurately to the client.

7.15   Assisting the client to estimate risk

In some circumstances it is not the barrister who has the necessary knowledge to assess the risk but the client. We have seen in **Chapter 6** various methods to collect such information, and the present chapter has stressed the importance of allowing the client to make the final decision. Just how far the barrister can assist (or interfere) in this process is a matter of degree and context. Clearly, on occasions clients may require a little more time or some extra information, or simply some reassurance that it is their role to make the decision.

As we have already seen, language has its limitations and non-verbal communication can have its own shortcomings. How can you ensure that the client absorbs the information and goes through the process of reflection and assesses the risks involved for himself or herself? There is no easy answer to this problem. However, if you have ensured that you and the client have acted collaboratively and cooperated during the advising process, there ought to be a convergence of estimates. In the best situations there may be perhaps even a shared, mutually understood language in which the different risks can be described and compared freely and clearly.

7.16   Legal counselling

7.16.1   Introduction

In this section we will look at an approach to client advice that takes a different perspective on the client and his or her problems. This approach is known as legal counselling. This form of advice addresses the client's problems broadly and does not particularly isolate the legal options in order to resolve them. As we have already seen, no matter what approach you take to the client's case you should consider the non-legal options as well as the purely legal ones. However, legal counselling gives special prominence to the specifically non-legal options. The philosophy behind this approach is that the law is the refuge of last resort and anything that can help to avoid or cut short the client's involvement with the legal process is preferable to utilisation of purely legal options. However, this is not to say that the law or legal procedures must or can be avoided. Often the client has no option but to accept that they must continue to take part in the legal process, for example if they are a defendant in a criminal case. Nor does this process of client advice seek to avoid exploiting the procedures that are favourable to his or her cause, for example using an interim injunction to settle a neighbour dispute. Nonetheless, the emphasis is on the future beyond the courtroom and the lawyer seeks to help the client to resolve the underlying problems he or she is faced with.

Clearly, legal counselling takes you to the limits of your role as a lawyer and stretches your abilities and resources. It can be a demanding but greatly satisfying process for you and the client. But there are dangers, too. It is important to realise the difference between your professional duties and functions and those of other professionals, for example social workers, marriage guidance counsellors, or financial advisers. You are first and foremost a lawyer and the client instructs you because you can fulfil that specialist function. Given the demands and risks involved you may not feel sufficiently confident to use this form of advising the client in the initial stages of practice. However, it is important that you understand how it functions so that you are prepared to observe it being carried out by senior barristers. Finally, with the ever-rising cost of litigation and the increasing importance of alternative dispute resolution, mediation, and conciliation, you are likely to have to address this type of conference with your clients regularly in the not too distant future.

7.16.2   The legal counselling process

As with any form of advice, before attempting to engage the client in legal counselling you must gather all the necessary information. It is of particular importance when adopting this method of advising to gather sufficient information from the client to reveal all the relevant legal and non-legal options that are available. As in the advising method, you will need to assimilate these new instructions into your existing knowledge of the case. You may need to adjust your preliminary views and opinions of the case if you go ahead with legal counselling.

The next stage is to order the options into logical sets. It may be appropriate to mix legal and non-legal options or to separate contentious from non-contentious options; each case will have to be investigated separately. Then you should analyse and attempt to prioritise the options within each category, or all together, as is sensible and practical. Finally, before you present these to the client, ensure that the options are appropriate and specifically suited to his or her circumstances.

A brief example should help to clarify that the process is more fluid than it might appear at first sight. Imagine that you are instructed by a client to make a Bail Application. The client tells you that he wants bail but knows that he is wanted for charges on other offences at another magistrates' court. You gather as much information as is relevant on the current charges and background personal details of the client as far as they are relevant to the Application for Bail. However, you also go further and invite the client to state why bail is so important to him today. During this process you learn that the client is 27 years old and is planning to marry. However, he also adds that his girlfriend has told him 'to clean up his act', otherwise the engagement will be broken. From your conference and instructions you identify the following factors:

- The client values his freedom.
- He dislikes custody but is realistic about the danger of being picked up on the warrants for his arrest.
- He has a real incentive to put his involvement with the wrong side of the law behind him.

Given the legal and factual circumstances of the case, the options of possible action to take today are limited:

(a) You could advise that the client does not make an Application for Bail, as the chances of it being granted are slim.

(b) You could go ahead and make a Bail Application in the hope that it will be granted and that the client will subsequently leave court before the police inform the prosecutor that there are outstanding warrants for his arrest.

(c) Alternatively, you could counsel the client of the advantages of getting bail today and subsequently surrendering to custody on the outstanding warrants. Once he does that, he could request that all the charges are dealt with together and swiftly. This would enable him to begin to put his past behind him and face the future with his fiancée without the risk of his previous criminal career endangering their marriage.

Options (a) and (b) are both viable, but they ignore the client's background and his non-legal aspirations, which option (c) puts at the centre of the advice. Only by asking the right sorts of questions in the appropriate circumstances can you expect to discover sufficient insight into the client to be able to counsel him or her on the full range of options available.

There are several approaches to counselling that can be utilised, but most follow a similar pattern. It is advisable to follow a suggested pattern if you are unfamiliar with this form of advising; this is because there is often a well-intentioned but misplaced temptation to usurp the client's role of decision maker at the same time as fulfilling one's own as counsellor or adviser. As with any form of advice, this process follows an investigation of the client as a source of further information and instructions. The lawyer establishes and maintains control of the process by setting before the client the list of options that are suitable to the client's requirements. The client is then invited to add any options not included. This list will be broad and general; the object at this stage is to consider as many options as possible. A short discussion of the options may be appropriate here.

However, the lawyer does not pass comment on their suitability; rather, the client is encouraged by the lawyer to lead the discussion of the suitability of the full range of options. The lawyer assists the client to express his or her preferences and to investigate the suitability of the various options. In particular the various strengths and weaknesses of each option are identified and evaluated. An arrangement of options in order of suitability often follows from these investigations.

7.16.3 Key aims of counselling

- To communicate the full range of options to the client in an order that is easy to follow;
- to allow the client sufficient time to consider the options as presented;
- to invite questions or comment from the client to establish clarity;
- to allow the client to make a choice without inappropriate assistance;
- to check that you have correctly understood the client's response;
- if no response is forthcoming, to investigate why and address the reasons for this;
- if more time is required, to give the client a realistic time estimate or deadline for the final decision.

7.16.4 Client-centred counselling

The primary strength and defining feature of this process is the role of the client, who is encouraged to be proactive, cooperative, and collaborative. The client should be working as hard as, if not harder than, the lawyer during the counselling stage. Within the bounds of reason and the constraints of the time available a complete range of options ought to be discussed.

An appropriate style to adopt here is that of the experienced or advising friend. Compare this with the common advice-giving process where the most relevant role will often be that of the expert or specialist. Obviously, with a little subtlety the same lawyer can exploit both roles in one conference. You might consider adopting one strategy for one issue and another for further issues. The key is to maintain control of the conference and to guide the client.

There are some disadvantages to the counselling process. It can be time-consuming and the client is required to have a clear understanding of the whole case for the process to be a successful one. However, there are benefits. Because he or she is fully informed and has participated throughout the procedure, the client is more likely to be satisfied with the decision that is reached. There may be, for example, less uncertainty about the appropriateness and desirability of the next steps in the litigation. Additionally, there may be occasions when the process can be covered in a short time, for example when there are only limited options to consider.

Because the process does demand a lot from the client as well as the lawyer, the client must be informed about what is taking place at each stage. Simple questions such as 'What do you think?' are often inadequate and so careful preparation is required to get the most out of the client and out of the available time. In the final stage of the process the client makes a decision. The client is now on his or her own—the lawyer should only assist when specifically asked to do so or when the client is in clear difficulty, for example when he or she is acting under a misapprehension. The client may need time to consider the options and make the final selection. As this process can be of significant length, the lawyer ought to manage the available time appropriately. Once a preference is expressed, the lawyer may invite or pose questions to the client or invite comment to establish absolute clarity of his or her understanding of the final decision. Further, it may be wise to recap briefly the strengths and weaknesses of the final choice. It is vital that the client makes the choice independently. It is the client who has to live with the consequences of that decision. In this process the lawyer must be vigilant against assuming the client's role. This may even necessitate gently informing the client that you cannot take on the burden of telling the client what to do.

7.16.5 Summary

The advantage of this method of advising is that the client enjoys the freedom to make an informed choice. This is a result of the presentation of the full range of options that are open to him or her. Naturally you will need to encourage the client to think and work independently when you investigate possible options. Thus, you should use questions that are designed to help the client to select and order the options. A cooperative and collaborative approach at these early stages will assist the process and set the right atmosphere for its later stages. However, the time that is necessary to carry out this process effectively can militate against its use when both client and lawyer are under a lot of pressure.

7.16.6 Using legal counselling

There is some debate amongst the commentators about the role of the lawyer in counselling, particularly at the decision stage. Lawyers in the USA are said to be less willing to state their preference to the client, as it is seen to be important to allow the client to choose the options unaided. However, what happens in practice is hard to say. Some

Commonwealth lawyers, for example those from New Zealand, are said to be more will-ing to share, or at least assist, in the process of sifting and selection. The English and Welsh Bar does not appear to have a commonly accepted view; little research has taken place in this jurisdiction in any case. There does not appear to be any professional or ethical objection to the British lawyer effectively mixing joint selection of options with some overt expression of opinions based upon professional experience. (You may wish to experiment with a pure counselling process and one with a mixed constitution.)

7.17 Some specific advising situations

In the final section of this chapter we will look at some conferences that follow a court hearing. These can be particularly difficult to plan for. Most court hearings have an ele-ment of the unknown; indeed, this is why they can be stressful experiences for the client and the source of no little anxiety for the advocate, too.

After a hearing both you and the client will want to discuss its outcome in detail and address the immediate effects of the result. Following your performance in court as an advocate there is often little time for you to do more than come down and collect your thoughts. During your preparation for the court appearance therefore you should always plan for this very important post-hearing conference. You will have little time to pro-duce a plan for this conference as you leave the body of the court and meet the client in the corridor. It is essential, therefore, to have considered the main objectives of this conference in advance.

The following how-to-do-it guides are neither exhaustive nor prescriptive, but they do offer a general format for advising the client that can be applied in most circumstances. However, the post-hearing conference will make similar demands upon your skills as a barrister as that at which you gave your initial advice about the prospects of the case. Therefore, remember to apply all the skills discussed previously so as to enable you to advise the client satisfactorily. Finally, to ensure that you meet the high standards of the profession you must be flexible in your approach to both the unique characteristics of each case and the individual needs of every client. (See generally **Chapter 8.**)

7.17.1 Advising after a successful civil hearing

> **How to do it**
>
> (a) Ensure that the losing party is out of earshot (it may be wise to allow him or her to leave the court building).
>
> (b) Attend to any urgent post-hearing court business first (eg assisting the court to draw up the order).
>
> (c) Explain the judgment or order to the client in plain English, remembering the effect of the costs order and confirming his or her understanding of its effect (note: public funding recoupment if applicable).
>
> (d) Consider the need for preliminary advice on entering or enforcing the judgment.
>
> (e) Check with the solicitor or his or her representative that all necessary docu-mentation is in order and tell the client that you will telephone the solicitor from chambers, if appropriate.

7.17.2 Advising after an unsuccessful civil hearing

How to do it

(a) Ensure that the client understands that the hearing has ended unsuccessfully and explain why his or her case was defeated. Allow time for the client to absorb this.

(b) Explain in plain terms the effect of the judgment or order to the client and confirm that he or she understands this clearly. For example, spell out the danger of being arrested and placed in custody if the client breaches a non-molestation order with a power of arrest attached to it.

(c) Encourage the client to raise any questions about the effect of the judgment.

(d) Offer your preliminary advice on routes of appeal and the chances of success. Remember also to discuss the financial, emotional, and other non-legal implications of an appeal.

(e) Offer the client the opportunity to reconsider alternative legal and non-legal options in the face of the defeat, if there are any.

(f) Discuss and confirm the action that the client must take next (eg return of property, payment of money, observance of injunctions).

(g) Explain to the client the likely methods of enforcement of the judgment or order and any financial effects it will have.

(h) If appropriate, explain to the client the sanctions that the court may apply if he or she disobeys its orders.

(i) Check with the solicitor or representative that all necessary documentation is in order; inform the client that you will telephone the solicitor from chambers, if appropriate.

7.17.3 Advising after a successful criminal trial

How to do it

(a) Ensure that all adverse witnesses and the public are out of earshot, or have left the court building.

(b) Advise the client on the effect of the 'not guilty' verdict, discontinuance, dismissal, etc.

(c) Advise the client of any further procedural matters that are outstanding (eg sentencing of offences pleaded to before the trial).

(d) Advise the client on the retrieval of any property retained by the prosecution, police, or prison authorities.

(e) Counsel on immediate future arrangements if appropriate (eg accommodation, benefits).

7.17.4   Advising after an unsuccessful criminal trial

> **How to do it**
>
> (a)   Ensure that all adverse witnesses, police officers, prosecutors, and so on are out of earshot or have left the court building.
>
> (b)   Explain to the client the effect of the finding of guilt and allow time for this to be absorbed.
>
> (c)   If the sentence has not already been passed, inform the client of the process that will lead to sentence: pre-sentence report interviews, procedure at sentence hearing, the plea in mitigation, etc.
>
> (d)   Give your preliminary advice on the likely form of sentence and its duration.
>
> (e)   If the client has been found guilty after a trial, give your preliminary opinion on the likelihood of success and the attendant risks of an appeal against conviction.
>
> (f)   If bail with conditions attached is granted pending sentence, explain that breach of any condition may result in the client being arrested without warrant and his or her bail being withdrawn.
>
> (g)   If sentence has been passed: see **7.17.5** below.
>
> (h)   Offer to address any immediate non-legal concerns.

7.17.5   Advising after sentence

> **How to do it**
>
> (a)   If appropriate, ensure that all adverse witnesses and prosecution counsel are out of earshot or have left the court.
>
> (b)   Explain to the client in plain terms what he or she is required to do by the sentence. Allow the client time to absorb this.
>
> (c)   Explain to the client any comments passed by the judge when sentencing, including why the court has passed that form of punishment for that period of time.
>
> (d)   Express your preliminary opinion on the likelihood of success of an appeal against sentence and the attendant risks.
>
> (e)   Advise as to any steps that must be taken by the client (eg the payment of a fine by instalments or the requirement to cooperate with the Probation Service).
>
> (f)   If appropriate, inform the client that you will furnish the solicitor with a written advice on appeal against sentence within 21 days.
>
> (g)   Offer to investigate any non-legal concerns the client has (eg by ensuring the solicitor tells his or her family which prison the client has been sent to).

Concluding the conference

8.1 Introduction

As we have seen, first impressions can influence the nature of your relationship with the client from the outset of the conference. The tone which is set when you first meet the client is important both for the conduct of the conference and for your professional involvement with the client throughout the whole of the case. It is equally important to ensure that your client leaves the conference feeling confident and settled with the outcome that has been agreed.

There can be a tendency (especially in early years of practice) for barristers to forget that the realities of the situation in which the client finds himself or herself, and the consequences which can flow from the case, continue long after the conference is concluded. It is all too easy to view the conference in a vacuum and assume that once it is concluded that is an end to the matter. This is, of course, far from being the case.

The reality is that the client has to live with the consequences of any decisions taken at the conference. The results often have far-reaching effects on the client and others who may be in some way dependent upon him or her. It may be that you 'win' the disputed matter there and then, for example by successfully negotiating a settlement of the matter at the door of the court, or persuading the prosecution to offer no evidence against your client. In such circumstances, the outcome for the client will almost certainly be entirely satisfactory. However, it is much more likely that the conference will not be the end of the matter and that the proceedings will continue in some form. Thus, at the conclusion of any conference, whatever the issues, it is essential that the client is both fully aware of what has been decided and confident that the option chosen is the best alternative to adopt in all the circumstances.

In much the same way as with many of the other elements of conducting a professional client conference (meeting the client, case preparation, questioning techniques, advising, and so on), it will be readily apparent that attention to the detail of concluding the conference effectively is equally essential.

The final and lasting impression that the client will take away from the conference is that created at the conclusion of the meeting. The way in which you choose to conclude the conference will clearly be determined by the relevant factors pertinent to each case and the individual requirements of each client, but there are a number of issues that usually arise by the end of any conference. For example, a good rule of thumb is always to try to ensure that you have:

- checked all the details;
- confirmed what has been agreed and decided upon;
- tied up any loose ends;
- reassured the client.

If the client is able to leave the conference feeling confident and reassured about the outcome, then the conference will almost certainly have succeeded in achieving one of its major objectives—client satisfaction. It can be seen, therefore, that a professional, thorough, and competent ending to the conference is just as important as getting it off to a flying start.

8.2   Different locations

Your ability to conclude the conference as satisfactorily as you may wish will, of course, depend on many factors, some of which may not be within your control. If the conference is at chambers with the client accompanied by your instructing solicitor, you will be in the best position to ensure that you draw the conference to an appropriate and full conclusion. However, it is useful to remind yourself that this will not always be so and that conferences can, and do, take place in all kinds of locations and under all sorts of circumstances, for example:

- at the door of the court;
- through the bars of a prison cell;
- in a crowded court corridor; or
- five minutes before you are in front of the tribunal.

The actual location of the conference, and the circumstances in which the conference is conducted, will undoubtedly influence, to some degree, what you can realistically achieve in concluding the conference. However, notwithstanding the location of the conference, or any particular circumstances of the case, many of the factors that contribute to bringing the conference to a satisfactory end are of general application. Consideration should be given to these points wherever the conference is taking place (see **8.4**).

There can, of course, be some real problems with effectively concluding a conference outside chambers. A number of these have been identified and some general guidance to assist you in dealing with any potential difficulties in this respect can be found at **8.5** and **8.6**.

8.3   The stage of the proceedings

As we have seen, it must also be remembered that not every conference that you undertake will necessarily occur immediately before the hearing (or settlement) of the matter. Nor is every conference a straightforward 'one-off' affair—that is, simply gathering information and advising the client accordingly. You may meet your client in conference on several occasions before his or her particular problem is resolved. For example, in a lengthy criminal trial (after the conference(s) at which the merits of the case/advice on evidence/plea, and so on, have been decided), you will usually meet your client at the end of each day's court proceedings to discuss the progress of the case and take further instructions.

In a case involving family breakdown, you may represent your client at several different stages in the proceedings—for example, at the hearing to exclude the other party from the family home; on the subsequent ancillary relief claim; or the application for residence of the children of the family. Many conferences are ongoing and require different considerations at different times. The sequence of events and thus the form of any conference can be variable.

It is important, therefore, when thinking about how best to end each conference (or any one which is a relevant part of ongoing proceedings), to give consideration to the sorts of factors that may influence your decision as to the most appropriate way to conclude that particular meeting. When considering how to conclude the conference most satisfactorily, it is helpful to remind yourself of what stage in the proceedings you have reached. For example, is the conference taking place:

- At the start of the proceedings?
- After advice on merits and recommended further action?
- As part of ongoing proceedings?
- Prior to an attempt to negotiate a solution?
- After the case has been settled?
- After the case has been lost?
- After the case has been won?

Obviously, the actual stage that the proceedings have reached will clearly have some influence on the nature of the way you conclude the conference with your client. If the professional relationship is ongoing, or the matter has still to come to trial, or there are terms of a negotiated settlement to work through, your approach will necessarily need to be tailored to suit those individual requirements.

8.4 General guidance to concluding a conference

It will be apparent that there are many factors that will dictate the way in which you decide to conclude the conference. Whatever stage the case has reached, and whatever the location of the conference, there are some general points that should be applicable to the effective conclusion of every conference.

8.4.1 Ensure that the advice given is fully understood by the client

This may sound rather simplistic. It is remarkable, however, that many clients come away from the conference without having really understood the advice that was given by the barrister. Try to remember that for many clients the conference will cover issues that are of vital importance to that client and invariably his or her future well-being, and more often than not confronting these issues will be an emotionally draining experience. In these circumstances, it is not unusual for clients to appear to agree to almost anything that you tell them. You should always try to ensure that you double-check that what you have said really has been fully understood by the client. For example, if your client accepts your advice that he or she should plead guilty to a charge of burglary which, because of previous convictions, inevitably will attract a custodial sentence, make sure the client really does understand that he or she faces the prospect of going to prison. (See **Chapter 7**.)

8.4.2 Check that the proposed course of action is agreed to by the client

Again, this is often not quite as straightforward as it seems. When you advise the client you are, in effect, evaluating for him or her the strengths and weaknesses of their particular case. In coming to your conclusions about the merits of the case, it is important to ensure the client understands both the nature of the advice given, and the full implications of any potential consequences that may result from adopting your advice. For example, win or lose, the costs implications of a case may be a major factor in the decision that your client will take. It is important that in giving your advice on the merits of the case you also spell out other relevant matters in a clear and comprehensive way. Take an example where the dispute is over a contact order in respect of any child of the family. On the facts it is highly likely that the outcome may well result in a 'victory' for your client in that he or she will probably succeed in obtaining the appropriate order. However, enforcing that order may be an entirely different matter altogether: what if the 'fight' has so soured relations (with the partner or the child) that, for all practical purposes, the contact order is worthless to your client? In agreeing to pursue any course of action, the client must be aware of all the consequences that might flow from taking that course. (See **Chapter 7**.)

8.4.3   Give the client an opportunity to ask any questions or to raise any other worries that he or she may have

It is highly unsatisfactory if the client leaves the conference with some important questions unanswered or real anxieties not addressed. Many clients, through nervousness or fear of appearing foolish, may be reluctant to press you on matters that they believe you might consider irrelevant. It is good practice to make every effort to ensure that your client does have an adequate opportunity to ask questions of you at the appropriate time. In many situations, rather than waiting for the end of the interview, it is preferable to inform the client at the start of the conference that there will be ample opportunity for his or her own questions at the end. By adopting this approach you will have reassured the client that he or she will be given a chance to ask questions before the conference concludes, and in these circumstances he or she will normally be more relaxed and less likely to interrupt the conference as it proceeds. (See **Chapter 4**.)

8.4.4   Understanding further action

Ensure that the client and the solicitor (or solicitor's representative) clearly understand any further action that may have to be taken by either (or both) of them once the conference is over. It is frequently the case that a need for further relevant information, which is not immediately to hand, comes to light during the conference. For example, there may be copies of documents (bank statements, estimates for repairs, bills, correspondence, and so on) that the client has in his or her possession and which will be necessary for the next meeting. Make sure that the client has a comprehensive list of what further documents you need and is fully aware of exactly when you need them. Often the conference reveals a need for further (expert) reports. For example, in claims for personal injury it is often the case that by the time the conference takes place, a further medical examination of your client will be needed. Or there may be a need for a report from another type of expert in the case—for example, a structural surveyor or an expert on chemical compounds—and so on. At the conclusion of the conference, in these circumstances, it should be made quite clear who is expected to be responsible for any appropriate arrangements and by when this should be done.

8.4.5   Reaffirming further action

Following on from this, it is appropriate, at the conclusion of any conference, for you to reaffirm what action(s) you are going to take. The client (and solicitor) need clear and precise information about what you will do and by when you will do it—for example, drafting a statement of claim in a personal injury action, drafting an appeal against conviction or sentence, drafting an advice on evidence, and so on. It is also possible that a question has arisen during the conference that you were not in a position to answer. As we have seen (**2.10**), a golden rule is that if you do not know the answer, you do not guess. Inform the client that this issue is something that you will need to check further. At the conclusion of the conference, remind the client that there is an outstanding issue that you still need to consider, and that you will convey the answer to your solicitor by an appropriate date.

8.4.6 Reassurance about further action

Reassure the client about any further action that may become necessary in proceeding further with the case. If you have come to a decision during the conference that involves embarking on a certain course of action make sure the client understands what taking those next steps actually entails. If, for example, the conference results in a decision to apply under CPR Part 24 for summary judgment, ensure that you inform your client of the procedure(s) and time constraints involved in such an application. (See **5.4.2.**) If your client is awaiting sentence at the Crown Court, ensure that he or she is fully aware of the timescale and the procedures involved and understands exactly what will happen at the next court appearance.

8.4.7 Avoidance of instant decisions

Where possible, try not to elicit an instant decision from the client. It can often be helpful for the client to have an opportunity to weigh up the implications of your advice and the alternative options that may be available before coming to a final conclusion about what course of action to pursue. If the circumstances permit, invite your client to go away and 'sleep on the matter', or to take the opportunity to discuss the available options with any other interested party prior to making the final decision. There is a tendency on the part of many clients to rush into the decision-making process. If an instant decision is not required, it is almost always in the client's best interests to delay coming to a final conclusion until absolutely necessary.

8.4.8 Reassurance about communication

Reassure the client that the lines of communication between you are always open. It is perfectly possible that, after the conference, the client may realise that he or she has forgotten to raise a relevant issue, or something important has occurred to him or her after the conference. In such circumstances, it is essential that the client is aware that information of this kind can, and should, be raised with the instructing solicitor, who will refer the issues to you for consideration.

8.4.9 How to end the conference

A courteous conclusion to the conference is as important as a courteous introduction (see **Chapter 4**). Always make sure you observe normal social decencies when the conference is at an end: shake the client's hand; help the client on with his or her coat; check the client has all his or her personal belongings; and show the client to the door. This may sound obvious, but it is this sort of ordinary, everyday common courtesy that will ensure that the client's memory of both you, and the conference, is a positive one.

8.5 Conference outside chambers

As has been pointed out previously, the type of conference over which you have the most control is the one that is conducted at your chambers in the presence of your instructing solicitor. In these circumstances you are in the best position to ensure that you bring the conference to a comprehensive and satisfactory conclusion—that is, to ensure that all the parties involved are confident and clear about the decisions reached and the course of conduct of future proceedings in the case.

It is clear, however, that because of certain factors that may be beyond your control, your ability to draw some conferences to an entirely satisfactory conclusion could be hampered in some way. The most obvious of these are:

- the location of the conference; and
- limitation on the time available.

Whatever the location, or whatever time you have available to conduct the conference, it is important that you endeavour to comply, as far as possible, with the guidelines set out in **8.4**.

You may have to take a robust view about any unreasonable time constraints that are placed upon you. If you are not satisfied that you have had adequate opportunity to take instructions, you can always inform the court of this fact and seek an adjournment to enable you properly to fulfil your professional obligations to your client. Be warned, however, that while some courts will be sympathetic, others will be less than helpful.

Thus, in these circumstances, time management becomes a critical factor. Despite any difficulties, you should nevertheless attempt to stick to the guidelines for concluding the conference. Clearly, in many cases, some of the points in the checklist will be irrelevant. For example, if you are taking instructions on a Bail Application which is due to be heard in 10 minutes, from a client who is in police custody, many of the niceties for concluding the conference will not be applicable; he or she will not have the luxury of spare time to remember something vital which needs to be conveyed to you after the conference is over or, of course, time in which to consider the advice given. Similarly, a conference at court, prior to an application for a without notice non-molestation injunction, is unlikely to result in the client being dispatched for a list of documents to use at that particular hearing.

It can readily be seen that not every point will need to be addressed when considering how to conclude each conference most effectively. However, many of the points will indeed be relevant and need to be raised with the client. It is your job to ensure, when considering how to end any particular conference appropriately, that you:

- identify the issues which are relevant to the stage you have reached; and
- convey these matters clearly to your client.

8.6 Summary

It will be apparent that every client should leave a conference feeling confident about what has taken place during the meeting, reassured about what will happen next in relation to their case, and satisfied with the outcome. Whatever stage of the proceedings, wherever the conference takes place, and whatever the time constraints, an effective conclusion to a conference should ensure that the client:

- clearly understands the advice given;
- agrees to the course of action proposed;
- is permitted to ask questions and raise anxieties;
- understands any further action he or she (and the solicitor) must take;
- has confidence in any further action you will take;
- understands the future conduct of the case (procedure, timing, etc);
- knows how to contact you.

8.7   Absence of professional client

As we have seen at **3.7**, exceptionally, self-employed barristers may take instructions from a lay client, or settle a potential witness's proof of evidence, in the absence of a professional client.

Invariably these situations arise at the court where the conference with the client is scheduled to take place. It is in these circumstances that you should consider whether it is appropriate to invite your lay client to sign any record—for example, a statement drafted or an endorsement on your brief—of what has been agreed between you at the conclusion of the conference.

Although there is no hard-and-fast rule as to when such a practice is appropriate, the guiding principle is one of 'self-protection'—that is, to ensure that you can establish that at all times you acted within the instructions received from your client. The following two examples show the type of circumstances where such a practice is appropriate:

(a) Your client, in the course of discussions, changes his or her account of what happened on a number of occasions or provides a different account from that included in your instructions or his or her proof of evidence. If this occurs, write down what he or she now says happened and invite him or her to sign and date your note.

(b) Your client wishes to accept an offer of compromise or not to pursue part of his or her claim against your advice. Record your advice, either in a statement or upon your brief, and invite him or her to sign and date this.

8.8   After the conference

When the conference is finished, it is necessary for you to ensure that you have an accurate record of what happened during the conference and what decisions were taken. There are several reasons for this.

(a) It is always dangerous to consign to memory any client-related matters and it is, therefore, essential that you have a detailed written account of the outcome of the conference.

(b) It is not unusual for a considerable amount of time to pass between the dates of the conference itself and the consequent court appearance. Without an accurate and clear account of the instructions received during the conference, your planning for (and conduct of) the trial will be less than effective. (See the *Advocacy* manual.)

(c) It frequently happens, for a variety of reasons, that you will not be the barrister who takes the client's case on to the next stage of the proceedings. A professional colleague who picks up the papers must be able to see, with relative ease, what stage the proceedings are at and what has happened to date.

EXAMPLE

You appear on behalf of a client in an application for a without notice occupation order and non-molestation order. You meet the client at court and successfully obtain the non-molestation injunction. The return date for the full hearing is set for seven days' time. You have another trial on that day and will be unable to represent the client. A suitable endorsement on your brief would be:

CON: Ms Jones St Victor CCt.
        Confirmed details in proof of evidence.
        Severe bruising to l.h. side of face—advised to see doctor after hearing to
        get medical report.

COR: H.H. Judge Bertric
        Without notice App. Non-molestation order granted. Occupation order will
        be heard at full hearing.
        r/t date [. . . . . .]
        LAA Funding

                                                            Signed (. . . . .)
                                                            Date (. . . . .)

8.8.1   Steps to take after the conference

How to do it

After completing any conference (or court appearance for the client) it is essential that you:

- endorse your brief; and

- complete a note of the conclusions reached in the conference, including:

  - the advice given in the conference;

  - instructions received at the conference;

  - further action to be taken by client and/or solicitor;

  - further action to be taken by yourself;

  - further legal research that is required.

Specific ethical problems

9.1 Introduction

This chapter introduces you to the ethical problems that most commonly occur in the conference and during your daily contact with the lay client. There is no substitute for a close study of the Bar Standards Board (BSB) Handbook or familiarising yourself with the ethos of practising barristers. You should also see the **Professional Ethics** manual.

The work of the lawyer can attract a great deal of attention and therefore the standards attached to the work of the barrister are rightly very high. The lay and professional clients invest a great deal of trust in the barrister and the burdens of the work are sometimes heavy. Your professional client has to rely upon you to share the responsibility for the client's case and selects counsel for the lay client having regard to the individual barrister's abilities and experience. The solicitor in effect entrusts his or her client to the barrister. Although the differences between the two professions are diminishing, few solicitors have the time or the relevant qualification to make appearances in the higher courts and, of course, they commonly instruct counsel in other cases. Whatever you say to or do for the client will not only reflect upon your abilities as a barrister but also affect the existing relationship between the solicitor and the client.

The desire to serve both lay and professional clients to the best of one's abilities can, however, lead to any number of ethical dilemmas. This chapter attempts to address some of the more commonly occurring problems that any barrister can face from the earliest days in practice.

9.2 Where to seek help

There are a number of different sources to which you can turn for guidance. The following section makes some suggestions as to the codes and bodies that can assist you, but it also draws your attention to some of the pitfalls that are commonly encountered, even when turning to these obvious agencies.

9.2.1 The Bar Standards Board Handbook

Part 2 of the Handbook contains the Code of Conduct. Although the Handbook is drafted with specific reference to those regulated by the BSB and for use by them, it is also a useful reference tool for consumers of legal services regulated by the BSB. The Handbook's approach is less prescriptive, with more focus and guidance on what the outcome of a rule should be, rather than attempting to define how a barrister should act in every situation. The revised Code includes core duties, rules, outcomes, and guidance. Together they provide the standards of conduct for barristers that are appropriate considering the interests of justice in England and Wales. The old Code had the express desire to preserve and enhance the strength and competitiveness of the independent Bar by setting and enforcing numerous requirements and prohibitions. The new Code contains some but by no means all of these, and the Handbook is of general application to all regulated persons including, of course, self-employed barristers. The new Code of Conduct is not a complete code and other regulations, codes, and rules apply to barristers and their work. For example, see 'rC71 You must give the Legal Ombudsman all reasonable assistance requested of you, in connection with the investigation, consideration, and determination, of complaints made under the Ombudsman scheme.'

It ought to be noted that the new Code applies directly to pupils (see rI7.b).

9.2.2 Annexes to the old Code of Conduct

These appeared as appendices to the old Code and were collections of regulations, guidelines, rules, written standards, terms of work, and other sub-codes that were relevant to the life and work of all manner of barristers. They held different status and one needed to study each one in detail before drawing any conclusions. There is nothing equivalent in the new Code and the old ones are of no application. However, it is suggested that they offer some insight into particular ethical and professional conduct questions and reference to them here and elsewhere in this manual is for that purpose only.

9.2.3 The Bar

The profession is a small one and there are time-honoured traditions of mutual support and help when fellow members experience ethical problems. As both junior and senior members will face similar ethical difficulties you can expect to be asked for your opinion, as well as encouraged to ask questions. The experience of other barristers is a rich source and it is often the quickest route to an agreeable settlement of a problem. However, always take care when discussing a case with a colleague who has not been briefed in the case: client confidentiality must always be respected.

9.2.4 Other qualified lawyers

Apart from fellow barristers, other legally qualified professionals may be willing and able to offer their own advice. However, it should be borne in mind that the Crown Prosecution Service (CPS), solicitors, clerks of court, and other legal functionaries are each governed by their own very different codes of conduct, for example *The Code for Crown Prosecutors*, January 2013 and *The Farquharson Guidelines—The Role and Responsibilities of the Prosecution Advocate*, issued 2002.

9.2.5 The Bar Council of England and Wales

The Bar Council runs a special telephone helpline to assist counsel with urgent ethical problems: the Ethical Queries Helpline. This service can be of great use if you are faced by a problem that demands immediate attention, for example if you are in court. However, it is a helpline and not designed to replace thorough legal research or the guidance that can be gained elsewhere.

9.2.6 The prosecution

The CPS has its own code that covers its work but if the prosecutor is also a barrister he or she is also covered by the Bar Code. The role and responsibilities of a prosecuting barrister were set out in Section 3, Written Standards for the Conduct of Professional Work, para 10 and supplemented by the recommendations of the Farquharson Report on the role of prosecuting counsel and by various Practice Directions issued from time to time by the High Court. Any advice offered should be received with these factors in mind.

9.2.7 Precedents, judgments, and Practice Directions

The Law Reports should be read regularly, with particular attention given to any Practice Directions. These will express the wishes and opinions of senior judges on the duties and working practices of the legal profession. Whilst judges' comments on the professional conduct of barristers appearing before them rarely appear in the headnote, expressions of the judges' views do occur in their judgments. Often terse in nature, these comments clearly express the judiciary's opinion of what is and what is not acceptable conduct for counsel.

9.3 Dealing with ethical problems in conference

In a conference you face real people with real problems and problems that are often in urgent need of your professional attention. If you come across an ethical or professional issue you must always resolve it before you advise the client; otherwise you may mislead the client or act unethically yourself. Whilst in conference there is rarely the opportunity to enlist the help of the previously mentioned documents, agencies, and individuals so some suggestions for avoiding and/or dealing with such situations are made in the following sections. You will, of course, have to adapt them to your own difficulties as best you can. Nonetheless, your constant guides must be honesty and thorough preparation to avoid the problem in the first place, if possible.

9.3.1 Enlisting the assistance of a fellow barrister

In advance of the conference it is acceptable to discuss an issue or problem you perceive in the papers with another barrister. However, confidentiality must be respected and it is often best to pose a hypothetical question to the other counsel. If you have met the client or the client is with you in conference, and you consider it sufficiently urgent to necessitate asking a fellow barrister in chambers for assistance, seek the client's express permission first. Naturally you should only seek this permission following a clear explanation of your reasons. You must explain to the client why you believe it is necessary to enlist the assistance of another counsel and any consequences this will have for the client.

It may even be acceptable to invite the fellow barrister into the conference room. Again, the client's express permission must be sought. One shortcoming of this is that you may endanger the rapport of trust and respect established with the client. The interruption will be disruptive and there is a possibility that you will lose face in the client's eyes. If the problem is an urgent one, a short telephone call may be the quickest and least disruptive solution. In any case it is neither good practice nor polite to leave the client unsupervised and unattended. Therefore, if possible leave the problem to one side and inform the client that you wish to research the point. Most conferences require you to advise on more than one issue, so you can go on to advise on other areas. Nonetheless, you will need to inform the client of your conclusions and so you ought to inform the client that you will contact the solicitor with the answer by a specific date.

9.4 Dealing with ethical problems at court

If you are at court and experience difficulties during the pre-hearing conference, you must inform the court through the usher as soon as possible. You should give an estimate to the court of how much time is required. You cannot expect it to wait for more than a few minutes without a personal explanation to the Bench. However, you should always remember that you have final responsibility for the client's case and that you must protect the client's rights fearlessly (rC15.1, Code of Conduct), but that there is an overriding duty to the court. The kernel of this advice is contained in gC6, Code of Conduct:

> You are obliged by CD2 to promote and to protect your client's interests so far as that is consistent with the law and with your overriding duty to the court under CD1. Your duty to the court does not prevent you from putting forward your client's case simply because you do not believe that the facts are as your client states them to be (or as you, on your client's behalf, state them to be), as long as any positive case you put forward accords with your instructions and you do not mislead the court. Your role when acting as an advocate or conducting litigation is to present your client's case, and it is not for you to decide whether your client's case is to be believed.

9.5 Attendance of professional client at conference

A common problem faced by many junior barristers and pupils is that they meet clients for conference but neither a solicitor nor their representative is present. Because of the relationship between the professions the attendance of the solicitor is normally required. In this section we will investigate the options open to you and the client in these circumstances.

9.5.1 Conference in chambers

The majority of lay clients are brought to chambers by the solicitor or a representative of the firm personally. If no solicitor or representative attends you must make every effort to find out why this has happened. If the client wishes the conference to go ahead without his or her solicitor it is always good practice to have another person present in the conference room. This person will serve some important functions and, as with any professional meeting, you should introduce all the parties to one another and ensure that their roles are clarified. It is a role that often falls to pupils in chambers.

Representatives fulfilling the function of the solicitor have a number of vital roles to fulfil. They will be able to assist you by taking a note of what the client says during the conference. More crucially they will give you some protection should the client accuse you of unprofessional conduct or suggest that you gave advice that conflicts with your record of it. (See **3.3**.)

9.5.2 Prison and hospital conferences

In general, no matter where the conference takes place the same rules of practice and the same provisions of the Code will apply. However, a substitute for an absent solicitor or representative will be difficult to find in these circumstances and it may be necessary to reschedule the conference. If the client is insistent that the conference should continue it will be necessary to ask him or her to sign an endorsement on your brief. This will be to the effect that the client is aware of the circumstances and has been offered but refused an alternative date for a conference.

9.5.3 Court conferences

The general rule used to be that the barrister ought not to conduct the case in court in the absence of his or her professional client or a representative of the solicitor. There were a number of exceptions that applied, which meant that it was rather common for the barrister to be at court without the benefit of the professional client's presence. A revision to the old Code rationalised and widened these exceptions, and the new Code has neatly sidestepped the issue. Looking at the old Code, para 706 made it clear that a barrister who was instructed by a professional client should not conduct the case in court in the absence of his or her professional client or a representative unless the court ruled that it was appropriate or he or she was satisfied that the interests of the lay client and the interests of justice would not be prejudiced. Further, if it was appropriate for barristers to conduct the case in court without a solicitor or a representative present they could, if necessary, interview witnesses and take proofs of evidence (para 707). It is suggested that for those in independent practice, these paragraphs continue to offer sound guidance.

The high costs of litigation and the problems for small solicitors' firms in staffing outdoor work will often result in the barrister meeting the client at court alone. Pupils will often be able to fulfil the role of the solicitor but the client's permission must be sought first and the client should sign your endorsement to the brief.

9.6 Conferences with witnesses

In any case where you are briefed to appear for trial you can expect to meet not only the client but also his or her witnesses. Some time ago, changes to the old Code of Conduct altered the profession's attitude to contact with witnesses and the new Code is, in many ways, consistent with these changes. Consequently, it is especially important that you know and understand the relevant provisions to ensure that you meet the appropriate standard and can justify your actions if called upon to do so.

Core Doctrine 3 states that you must act with honesty and integrity. The rules on honesty, integrity, and independence expand upon this. It is your duty to know the limits placed upon your communications with such witnesses. The most important provisions are now set out. Remember that this is a summary and you must consult the full Code in the *Professional Ethics* manual:

rC9 Your duty to act with honesty and integrity under CD3 includes the following requirements:

.3   you must not encourage a witness to give evidence which is misleading or untruthful;

.4   you must not rehearse, practise with or coach a witness in respect of their evidence;

.5   unless you have the permission of the representative for the opposing side or of the court, you must not communicate with any witness (including your client) about the case while the witness is giving evidence.

Generally, the solicitor will prepare witness statements, but if this has not happened and you arrive at court you can take the necessary written account of the witnesses' version of events, or you may be instructed to draft statements.

rC9 Your duty to act with honesty and integrity under CD3 includes the following requirements:

> .2 you must not draft any statement of case, witness statement, affidavit or other document containing:
>
>> .a any statement of fact or contention which is not supported by your client or by your instructions;
>> .b any contention which you do not consider to be properly arguable;
>> .c any allegation of fraud, unless you have clear instructions to allege fraud and you have reasonably credible material which establishes an arguable case of fraud;
>> .d (in the case of a witness statement or affidavit) any statement of fact other than the evidence which you reasonably believe the witness would give if the witness were giving evidence orally.

See also rC6 Not misleading the court:

> .2 you must not call witnesses to give evidence or put affidavits or witness statements to the court which you know, or are instructed, are untrue or misleading, unless you make clear to the court the true position as known by or instructed to you.

9.6.1 Conclusion

It is generally preferable that the solicitor interviews the witnesses and takes proofs of evidence and drafts the witnesses' statements. However, if this is not practicable you may assume these tasks. Nonetheless, before taking this step you are required to think whether or not an adjournment is the correct course of action.

9.6.2 Witness coaching and discussing the evidence with witnesses

If you do have contact with a potential witness other than in court itself the Code sets out strict rules at rC9, quoted at **9.6**. You should note that these provisions apply when you wish to call any witnesses including your lay client. In this section we will discuss the acceptable limits of your contact with witnesses in both these circumstances. Note carefully that there is an important distinction between criminal cases in the Crown Court and all other cases.

Paragraph 6.3.1 of the Written Standards for the Conduct of Professional Work in Section 3 of the old Code of Conduct set out the general principle for cases in the Crown Court:

> . . . with the exception of the lay client, character and expert witnesses, it is wholly inappropriate for a barrister in such a case to interview any potential witness. Interviewing includes discussing with any such witness the substance of his evidence or the evidence of other such witnesses.

Note the three important exceptions. You may interview your lay client, his or her character witnesses, and any expert witnesses who appear for him or her. A close study of the rest of para 6.3 shows that it made special provisions for the rare occasions when it was advisable to depart from the general principle.

Paragraph 6.2 of the Written Standards for the Conduct of Professional Work offered some detailed guidance when interviewing or discussing a witness's evidence in all other circumstances. Paragraph 6.2.2 reminded the Bar that this was generally the role of the solicitor, not the barrister. Paragraph 6.2.4 also warned that such discussions between counsel and witness could lead to the suspicion of coaching, and thus tended to diminish the value of the witness's evidence. This remains particularly true when such discussions take place before you have been supplied with a proof of the witness's evidence or if they take place in the absence of the solicitor or the solicitor's representative. This paragraph also reminded the profession that barristers may unwittingly contaminate the witness's evidence.

9.6.3   Permissible contact with witnesses

As we have seen, there is no longer any rule that prevents you from having contact with witnesses in cases outside criminal cases in the Crown Court for the purpose of discussing the case. There is also no longer any rule in any case to prevent you having what might be termed social contact with witnesses you intend to call and examine in chief. Indeed, there has been a welcome sea change in the profession's attitude to witnesses and one that ought to benefit members of the public who come to court as witnesses. You can introduce yourself to the witness and explain your role. You might also want to help settle the witness in for what can be quite a long wait. More importantly, you will want to explain the court's procedures and especially those surrounding the giving of evidence. You ought also to allow the witness an opportunity to ask you questions about these procedures. On the other hand, some witnesses will require some human or emotional support too.

It is the responsibility of a barrister, especially when the witness is nervous, vulnerable, or apparently the victim of criminal or similar conduct, to ensure that those facing unfamiliar court procedures are put as much at ease as possible.

9.6.4   Advising witnesses to tell the truth

All adult testimony is given under one of the different forms of the oath or affirmation. The degrees of seriousness with which individuals make these solemn declarations vary greatly. You may need to remind the potential witness of the gravity of the proceedings. It ought also to be noted that the Perjury Act 1911, s 1, creates a specific offence of giving falsehoods in court whilst under oath or affirmation—that is, perjury. After the completion of a trial, any witness who has blatantly given false testimony may have to face charges of perjury. Even if the case is not pursued by the CPS, considerable embarrassment and inconvenience can be caused by the investigation.

A lesser but not uncommon threat is that judges and magistrates sometimes see fit to pass comment on the apparent untruthfulness of a witness after the case has concluded. Whilst little directly flows from this, it can be the cause of considerable embarrassment for the parties involved. In any case, witnesses who are obviously lying or who appear untrustworthy in court will not assist the client's case. It is therefore advisable politely to inform such a witness that their presence is not required. You should avoid any judgemental language, but you should use your professional experience to exert control and maintain the conduct of the client's case.

9.7   Calling the client as a witness

During the conference before a trial you will have to advise the client whether or not to give evidence in his or her own case, but the decision must be taken by the client.

Thus, it is permissible and even desirable for the barrister to express his or her opinion about the necessity and wisdom of the client giving evidence. However, this decision, like any decision that affects the client directly, remains with the client personally. This guidance is of equal application to civil cases as it is to criminal ones. If a client wants to give evidence, you cannot prevent him or her from doing so, but you owe the client a duty to express your opinion on the matter clearly.

9.8   Criminal cases: pleas

One of the most common instructions to counsel engaged in criminal work is to advise on plea. The consequences for your client of a guilty plea can be enormous. Your client will undoubtedly feel under a great deal of pressure and look to you for advice and re-assurance. The client who faces criminal proceedings will not always be honest with you. Your client may attempt to test the water before committing himself or herself to a course of action, by posing hypothetical questions hinting that they are guilty, but only in order to learn the consequences of telling you the truth. Other clients may explicitly inform you that they committed the crime but insist upon maintaining a not guilty plea. Further, some clients may want to plead guilty, even though they deny to you that they were the perpetrator, to protect the real culprit. The new Code does not make special provision to assist the profession when faced by such dilemmas. Guidance gC9 states:

C3.5 makes it clear that your duty to act in the best interests of your client is subject to your duty to the court. For example, if your client were to tell you that he had committed the crime with which he was charged, in order to be able to ensure compliance with Rule C4 on the one hand and Rule C3 and Rule C6 on the other:

.1   you would not be entitled to disclose that information to the court without your client's consent; and

.2   you would not be misleading the court if, after your client had entered a plea of 'not guilty', you were to test in cross-examination the reliability of the evidence of the prosecution witnesses and then address the jury to the effect that the prosecution had not succeeded in making them sure of your client's guilt.

Guidance gC10 goes on to state:

However, you would be misleading the court and would therefore be in breach of Rules C3 and C6 if you were to set up a positive case inconsistent with the confession, as for example by:

.1   suggesting to prosecution witnesses, calling your client or your witnesses to show; or submitting to the jury, that your client did not commit the crime; or

.2   suggesting that someone else had done so; or

.3   putting forward an alibi.

Section 3 of the former Written Standards for the Conduct of Professional Work offered more specific guidance in more complex situations, which, it is suggested, remains of assistance even though it is necessary to read this guidance in the light of the new Code.

9.8.1   The innocent client who wishes to plead guilty

This section deals with the circumstances in which a client insists on pleading guilty although he or she has expressly informed the barrister that he or she did not commit the offence. The former Written Standards for the Conduct of Professional Work stated:

11.5.1 Where a defendant tells his counsel that he did not commit the offence with which he is charged but nevertheless insists on pleading guilty to it for reasons of his own, counsel should:

(a) advise the defendant that, if he is not guilty, he should plead not guilty but that the decision is one for the defendant; counsel must continue to represent him but only after he has advised what the consequences will be and that what can be submitted in mitigation can only be on the basis that the client is guilty;

(b) explore with the defendant why he wishes to plead guilty to a charge which he says he did not commit and whether any steps could be taken which would enable him to enter a plea of not guilty in accordance with his profession of innocence.

11.5.2 If the client maintains his wish to plead guilty, he should be further advised:

    (a) what the consequences will be, in particular in gaining or adding to a criminal record and that it is unlikely that a conviction based on such a plea would be overturned on appeal;

    (b) that what can be submitted on his behalf in mitigation can only be on the basis that he is guilty and will otherwise be strictly limited so that, for instance, counsel will not be able to assert that the defendant has shown remorse through his guilty plea.

11.5.3 If, following all of the above advice, the defendant persists in his decision to plead guilty:

    (a) counsel may continue to represent him if he is satisfied that it is proper to do so;

    (b) before a plea of guilty is entered counsel or a representative of his professional client who is present should record in writing the reasons for the plea;

    (c) the defendant should be invited to endorse a declaration that he has given unequivocal instructions of his own free will that he intends to plead guilty even though he maintains that he did not commit the offence(s) and that he understands the advice given by counsel and in particular the restrictions placed on counsel in mitigating and the consequences to himself; the defendant should also be advised that he is under no obligation to sign; and

    (d) if no such declaration is signed, counsel should make a contemporaneous note of his advice.

9.8.1.1 Comments

You should note the following points:

(a) The Written Standards are not part of the new Code.

(b) Apparently barristers do not have a discretion to withdraw: it appears that they must continue to represent the defendant. However, note para 11.5.3(a).

(c) The advice that you must give and records to be made were prescribed by the Standards, but there is nothing equivalent in the new Code.

(d) The usual provisions of the new Code on the confidentiality of a client's disclosures apply.

9.8.2 The client admits guilt but wishes to plead not guilty

See **9.8**. In these circumstances, the barrister's role was limited by the former Written Standards for the Conduct of Professional Work, para 12, Confessions of Guilt:

12.1 In considering the duty of counsel retained to defend a person charged with an offence who confesses to his counsel that he did commit the offence charged, it is essential to bear the following points clearly in mind:

    (a) that every punishable crime is a breach of common or statute law committed by a person of sound mind and understanding;

    (b) that the issue in a criminal trial is always whether the defendant is guilty of the offence charged, never whether he is innocent;

    (c) that the burden of proof rests on the prosecution.

12.2 It follows that the mere fact that a person charged with a crime has confessed to his counsel that he did commit the offence charged is no bar to that barrister appearing or continuing to appear in his defence, nor indeed does such a confession release the barrister from his imperative duty to do all that he honourably can for his client.

12.3 Such a confession, however, imposes very strict limitations on the conduct of the defence. A barrister must not assert as true that which he knows to be false. He must not connive at, much less attempt to substantiate, a fraud.

12.4 While, therefore, it would be right to take any objections to the competency of the Court, to the form of the indictment, to the admissibility of any evidence or to the evidence admitted, it would be wrong to suggest that some other person had committed the offence charged, or to call any evidence which the barrister must know to be false having regard to the confession, such, for instance, as evidence in support of an alibi. In other words, a barrister must not (whether by calling the defendant or otherwise) set up an affirmative case inconsistent with the confession made to him.

12.5 A more difficult question is within what limits may counsel attack the evidence for the prosecution either by cross-examination or in his speech to the tribunal charged with the decision of the facts. No clearer rule can be laid down than this, that he is entitled to test the evidence given by each individual witness and to argue that the evidence taken as a whole is insufficient to amount to proof that the defendant is guilty of the offence charged. Further than this he ought not to go.

12.6 The foregoing is based on the assumption that the defendant has made a clear confession that he did commit the offence charged, and does not profess to deal with the very difficult questions which may present themselves to a barrister when a series of inconsistent statements are made to him by the defendant before or during the proceedings; nor does it deal with the questions which may arise where statements are made by the defendant which point almost irresistibly to the conclusion that the defendant is guilty but do not amount to a clear confession. Statements of this kind may inhibit the defence, but questions arising on them can only be answered after careful consideration of the actual circumstances of the particular case.

9.8.2.1   Comments

(a) The Written Standards are not part of the new Code.

(b) As is made clear in para 12.6, the guidance was offered for the situation where a defendant made a clear *confession* to counsel that he did commit the offence charged. Two other difficult situations were apparently excluded:

    (i)   where a defendant gave or has given a series of inconsistent statements; and

    (ii)   where the defendant all but damned himself or herself out of his or her own mouth but stopped just short of a full confession.

No specific assistance was offered by the Written Standards for the Conduct of Professional Work or the old or new Code for these and similarly difficult scenarios.

(c) Whilst para 12 did not contain an explicit direction to the barrister to continue to represent the client, it would appear that it was preferable that they do so. Indeed, para 12.2 stated that a confession was not in itself 'a bar to that barrister appearing or continuing to appear in his defence'. Nor is the barrister 'released from his imperative duty to do all that he honourably can for his client'.

(d) If the barrister continues to represent that client all the usual provisions of the Code, of course, continue to apply.

(e) The paragraph placed no overt duty upon the barrister to explain the effect of this type of plea. However, it would affect the conduct of the client's defence. Therefore it is essential to explain this in plain terms to the client. Thereafter the conference will concentrate on the limitations placed upon the conduct of the defence and the likelihood of an acquittal.

9.8.3   Advising on pleas in general

A barrister acting for a defendant should advise his lay client generally about his plea. In doing so you may, if necessary, have to express your advice in strong terms. You must, however, make it clear that the client has complete freedom of choice and that the responsibility for the plea is the client's.

Common sense and the spirit of the Code suggest that you express your advice firmly but within the limits of reasonableness. Barristers must not compromise their professional standards in order to please their clients, the Court or third parties, but must be courteous in all their professional activities. The Foreword to the new Code says of barristers that, 'In their practice they must provide a competent and professional service, keep their knowledge fully up to date, give sound advice and deal frankly and courteously with clients, colleagues and others.' The barrister's duty is to offer the advice that he or she is briefed to give and it is the client who makes the final decision. He or she is the person who will have to answer the arraignment and face the consequences of the tribunal of fact's declaration of guilty or not guilty.

9.9 Withdrawal from a case: professional embarrassment

Guidance gC12, gC73, and gC87 of the new Code cover some circumstances where it is permissible and necessary to withdraw from a case. The new Code does not offer such clear injunctions and guidance on withdrawal and professional embarrassment as the old one did. You should therefore read these paragraphs with care, and consider the core duties and outcomes as a whole. If, following a thorough questioning of the client and a studious consideration of the ethical and professional situation, you conclude that you can no longer represent the client, you must withdraw from the case. However, of course, you will have to advise the client of your decision. A great deal of tact will be necessary and so too a very clear explanation for your decision.

9.10 Physical contact with the client

Although your contact with the client is often only brief, there can be moments when a natural reaction or a social nicety can be the cause of embarrassment, or even professional concern. In this section we will look at some of the more common problems and scenarios that you can expect to encounter in practice as a barrister.

9.10.1 Greetings

The tradition amongst barristers that they do not shake hands does not extend beyond members of the profession. Therefore, it is quite acceptable and polite to greet both lay and professional clients with a handshake.

9.10.2 Comforting clients

As a result of the pressures that litigation brings with it, you can expect to face clients who cannot control their emotions during a conference. This is not surprising, as you will be questioning your client on the very heart of the matter upon which they have come to seek your help. Distressed or weeping clients ought to be allowed time to settle themselves; a box of tissues is often a useful commodity in the conference room. However, there are limits to the comfort that you might wish to offer. Any physical contact, for example, should be avoided. It is all too easy for the client, who is after all a stranger, to misread kind intentions of this nature. Therefore confine your consolation to some kind words and a tissue or glass of water if necessary.

9.10.3 Expressions of gratitude by the client

Some clients will attempt to express their gratitude to you after the successful resolution of their case. Again, physical contact is best avoided with an appropriate degree of tact. A professional distance between you and the client must be maintained and the dignity of the court respected, even in its corridors. In any case, you will often have much business to conclude immediately following the case, not least the post-hearing conference itself. To be able to offer the appropriate advice in a professional atmosphere you will need to maintain the correct rapport between yourself and the client.

9.11 Money laundering: the Proceeds of Crime Act 2002 and the Terrorism Act 2000

Part 7 of the Proceeds of Crime Act 2002 (POCA) consolidates primary legislation on money laundering and extends the force of law in this area by creating a set of offences and duties relating to 'criminal property'—that is, property which is, or which represents, a person's benefit from criminal conduct. As a legal adviser, you need to understand the full extent and impact of POCA to ensure that you and your clients do not commit any of the offences. In many cases your solicitor will be at greater risk of committing offences and breaching duties than you. However, in your role as a legal adviser and representative you will share some of the risk. Under POCA it is immaterial who carried out the criminal conduct or who benefited from it and it is immaterial whether the conduct took place before or after 24 February 2003, when Part 7 came into force. It is knowledge or suspicion of the illegitimacy of the property, not the criminal activities per se, that triggers the offences.

POCA materially affects the duty of confidentiality that you owe your client under Core Duty 6 of the Code of Conduct, and in January 2016 the Bar Council's Ethics Committee issued revised guidance in *Money Laundering and Terrorist Financing*. It is a criminal offence in the UK to finance or facilitate the financing of terrorism. The Terrorism Act 2000 creates offences, disclosure limitations, and statutory defences similar to those under POCA, and there are similar 'tipping off' offences within the regulated sector. The Bar Council's guidance is not 'guidance' for the purposes of the BSB Handbook I6.4, and it has not been approved by HM Treasury. Nor is it a definitive statement of the law or of the effect of the law, and therefore you are strongly advised to read relevant judgments, such as *Bowman v Fels* [2005] 4 All ER 609 on POCA in full, and to familiarise yourself with the relevant sections of POCA and the Terrorism Act 2000. What follows should be treated merely as an introduction to the most common dilemmas you may face when advising a client in conference, with reference only to POCA.

9.11.1 The offences

Among others, the Proceeds of Crime Act 2002 created three new offences that apply to any type of criminal conduct where a benefit is gained, no matter its value, whenever the criminal conduct occurs. The offences are:

- s 327 concealing criminal property;
- s 328 with knowledge or suspicion being concerned in an arrangement which facilitates (by whatever means) the acquisition, retention, use, or control of criminal property by or on behalf of another person; and
- s 329 the acquisition, use, or possession of criminal property.

These offences carry a penalty of 14 years' imprisonment. Clearly, POCA, and in particular s 328, has far-reaching consequences for the legal profession, which can have dealings with suspicious property. Indeed, after its introduction there was a great deal of confusion about the effect of POCA, particularly in family financial applications. Former High Court guidance was comprehensively revised by the Court of Appeal in *Bowman v Fels*, and it remains current.

9.11.2   Consent as a defence to the s 328 arrangement offence

Section 328(2)(a) creates a defence to the arrangement offence. The offence is not committed by a person who makes an authorised disclosure under s 338 and, if the disclosure is made before the act is done, who has the appropriate consent (usually through the National Crime Agency—Economic Crime Command (NCA)). A disclosure report must be made in writing and the report form may be downloaded from <http://www.nationalcrimeagency.gov.uk/>. Consent may be express or deemed. NCA has seven working days (the notice period) within which to notify the person making the disclosure of its consent or refusal, starting with the first working day after the person makes disclosure. If a notice of refusal is served on the person making the disclosure there is then a moratorium period (31 days starting with the day on which the person receives notice of refusal). At the expiry of that period, the person is deemed to have consent. NCA has published revised advice on seeking consent in February 2015: *Obtaining consent from the NCA under Part 7 of the Proceeds of Crime Act (POCA) 2002 or under Part 3 of the Terrorism Act (TACT) 2000* <http://nationalcrimeagency.gov.uk/publications/515-obtaining-consent-from-the-nca-1/file>.

9.11.3   Section 328 and legal professional privilege

If you, as a client's legal representative, were under a duty to disclose to NCA matters of the nature covered by s 328, this would bring about a clash of duties: that owed to your lay client and that owed under the Proceeds of Crime Act 2002. The appeal in *Bowman v Fels* raised important issues relating to this aspect of POCA and its application to the legal profession. Indeed, because of its importance, the Bar Council, the Law Society, and one of NCA's former manifestations, the National Criminal Intelligence Service (NCIS), were all granted permission to intervene in the appeal. The issue at the heart of the appeal was one of public law, which until that point had caused very great difficulties in solicitors' offices and barristers' chambers and in the orderly conduct of contested litigation throughout the country.

The Court of Appeal carefully analysed Parliament's intention (the figures in square brackets below refer to specific paragraphs in the judgment) and, in particular, how two European Union directives, Council Directive of 10 June 1991 (91/308/EEC) ('the 1991 Directive') and Council Directive of 4 December 2001 (2001/97/EEC) ('the 2001 Directive'), had been translated into English law. It concluded that the language of s 328 had caused great uncertainty within the legal profession, particularly because Parliament had given a much wider meaning to the phrases 'criminal conduct' and 'criminal property' than was required by one of the relevant EU directives [7]. Since POCA had come into force lawyers had become concerned that this section might mean that they themselves were exposed to the threat of criminal sanctions if they did not make 'an authorised disclosure' of any information which led them to know or suspect that their client—or some other person, often the opposing party in family proceedings—was involved in the acquisition, retention, use, or control of property derived from criminal conduct. Until the judgment in *Bowman v Fels* lawyers felt obliged to wait for appropriate consent before they took any further steps for their client. They believed that they were protected from breaching lawyer–client confidentiality by the terms of s 338(4), which provides quite simply that '(4) An authorised disclosure is not to be taken to breach any restriction on the disclosure however imposed' [8]. In some cases, these disclosures were being made to NCA and the result was long delays before lawyers could feel free to take steps on their clients' behalf again. (In practice, however, the requisite consent is issued within a day or so in the greater majority of the cases in which lawyers make a disclosure to NCA.)

The Court of Appeal posed the question whether lawyers outside what is described as the regulated sector (see **9.11.4**) are obliged to make any disclosures to NCA at all in breach of lawyer–client confidentiality, and if so in what circumstances [9]. The question was whether s 328 meant that as soon as lawyers acting for a client in legal proceedings discover or suspect anything in the proceedings that may facilitate the acquisition, retention, use, or control (usually by their own clients or their clients' opponents) of 'criminal property', they must immediately notify NCA of their belief if they are to avoid being guilty of the criminal offence of being concerned in an arrangement which they know or suspect facilitates such activity (by whatever means) [20]. More fundamentally, the issue at the very centre of the appeal was whether s 328 applies to the ordinary conduct of legal proceedings at all. There was also a narrower issue: if s 328 does apply to the ordinary conduct of legal proceedings, whether Parliament can be taken, without using clear words to that effect, to have intended to override the important principles underlying legal professional privilege (LPP) and the strict terms on which lawyers are permitted to have access to documents disclosed in the litigation process [24].

The Court of Appeal thoroughly analysed the 1991 Directive, the 2001 Directive, POCA, and the linguistic and policy considerations, before it concluded that the proper interpretation of s 328 is that it is not intended to cover or affect the ordinary conduct of litigation by legal professionals. That includes any step taken by them in litigation from the issue of proceedings and the securing of injunctive relief or a freezing order up to its final disposal by judgment. The Court of Appeal did not consider that either the European or the UK legislator can have envisaged that any of these ordinary activities could fall within the concept of 'becoming concerned in an arrangement which. . . facilitates the acquisition, retention, use or control of criminal property' [83]. It went on to state that legal proceedings are a State-provided mechanism for the resolution of issues according to law. Everyone has the right to a fair and public trial in the determination of his or her civil rights and duties, a right which is secured by Article 6 of the European Convention on Human Rights. Parliament cannot have intended that proceedings or steps taken by lawyers in order to determine or secure legal rights and remedies for their clients should involve them in 'becoming concerned in an arrangement which . . . facilitates the acquisition, retention, use or control of criminal property', even if they suspected that the outcome of such proceedings might have such an effect [84].

This very significant judgment forms the core of the guidance from the Bar Council mentioned previously. In summary, the guidance is that:

(a) Section 328 does not affect the ordinary conduct of litigation by legal professionals. That includes any step taken by them in litigation from the issue of proceedings and the securing of injunctive relief or a freezing order up to its final disposal by judgment. Such steps do not come within the meaning of 'becoming concerned in an arrangement which . . . facilitates the acquisition, retention, use or control of criminal property'.

(b) Proceedings or steps taken by lawyers in order to determine or secure legal rights and remedies for their clients would not involve them in 'becoming concerned in an arrangement which . . . facilitates the acquisition, retention, use or control of criminal property', even if they suspected that the outcome of such proceedings might have such an effect.

(c) Section 328 does not override LPP. (But note the Bar Council's guidance on disclosure and LPP carefully.)

(d) Section 328 does not affect the terms upon which lawyers are permitted to have access to documents disclosed in the litigation process.

(e) Settling litigation does not amount to 'becoming concerned in an arrangement which . . . facilitates the acquisition, retention, use or control of criminal property'.

The exclusion of litigation and proposed litigation from the ambit of s 328, together with the express retention of LPP in respect of s 328, means that most barristers do not need to seek consent to act from NCA or to make disclosures about their clients or their opponents' clients. Along with the Court of Appeal, the Bar Council expressed the hope that this approach to the construction of POCA will remove the difficulties that have impeded the orderly conduct of litigation since s 328 became law.

9.11.4 The regulated sector: disclosure of knowledge or suspicion of money laundering

Section 330 of POCA creates an offence of failure, by a person in the regulated sector, to disclose knowledge or suspicion of money laundering where the information came to the person in the course of business in the regulated sector. The definition of the regulated sector under POCA has been revised to be consistent with that given in the Money Laundering Regulations 2007. Barristers undertaking non-contentious advisory or transactional work that consists of the provision of advice about the tax affairs of their clients or certain financial or real property transactions are likely to be affected. However, following the reasoning in *Bowman v Fels*, a barrister involved in the ordinary conduct of litigation or its consensual resolution is unlikely to fall within the regulated sector. A barrister within the regulated sector must comply with ss 330 and 333A and with the Money Laundering Regulations 2007. In short, there are four conditions to be met before a person in the regulated sector commits an offence. First, that they know or suspect, or have reasonable grounds for knowing or suspecting, that another person is engaged in money laundering. Second, that the information or other matter on which their knowledge or suspicion is based or which gives reasonable grounds for such knowledge or suspicion came to them in the course of a business in the regulated sector. Third, that they can identify that other person or the whereabouts of any laundered property or they believe, or it is reasonable to expect them to believe, that the information they hold will or may assist in identifying the launderer or the whereabouts of any laundered property. Finally, that they do not make the required disclosure as soon as is practicable after the information or other matter came to them. Note that there is express statutory saving for LPP, s 330(6). The extent to which LLP is saved is unclear, and given the serious penal consequence of the statute for you if you do not make a relevant disclosure, the Bar Council's advice is expressed cautiously;

However, if you are aware of prima facie evidence that you are being used in the furtherance of a crime, you should make a formal disclosure. This position accords with the guidance offered to solicitors by the Law Society. Whether such prima facie evidence exists will need to be determined by you based on all of the facts known to you.

9.11.5 The tipping-off offence and a defence for professional legal advisers

The tipping off offence, ss 333A–333D, only affects the regulated sector. Section 333A aims to prevent those about whom disclosures have been made from frustrating any investigation. It would be lawful for a barrister in the regulated sector to tell his or her client of a disclosure made about another party in so far as this was not likely to prejudice any subsequent investigation. However, a barrister in the regulated sector must not inform his or her own client of a disclosure or an investigation unless he or she does so in order to dissuade him or her from engaging in conduct amounting to an offence (see s 333D).

9.11.6 Prejudicing investigations offence and a defence for professional legal advisers

By s 342 an offence (punishable with up to five years' imprisonment) is committed by a person who knows or suspects that a confiscation investigation, a civil recovery investigation, or a money laundering investigation is being or is about to be conducted and who makes a disclosure which is likely to prejudice the investigation. This section applies whether or not there has been a disclosure to NCA. There is a defence, ie where the disclosure is made by a professional legal adviser in connection with the giving of legal advice to the client etc, unless the disclosure is made with the intention of furthering a criminal purpose. However, in relation to these activities, knowledge or suspicion must be disclosed only if it came to the person on or after 1 March 2004 (Proceeds of Crime Act 2002 (Business in the Regulated Sector and Supervisory Authorities) Order 2003, SI 2003/3074, art 4).

9.11.7 Conclusion and cautions

When you work within the regulated sector you will have to remain vigilant to the possibility that your actions may leave you vulnerable to a conviction under s 330. Although this is of greater concern to tax and chancery specialists, all lawyers should exercise caution, as it is the subject matter of the transaction, not the specialism of the lawyer, which is relevant.

Another area for caution is where you have a concern that the litigation is in fact a sham in order to pursue money laundering. It is not unknown for criminals to use legitimate legal processes to launder criminal proceeds. This can happen in proceedings as diverse as divorce settlements to multi-million-pound company transactions. If you are in any doubt or under any suspicion, seek advice from the Bar Council.

Finally, you should note the case of *R v Griffiths (Philip)* [2007] 1 Cr App R (S) 95, concerning the appropriate custodial sentence for a solicitor convicted of failing to disclose to the authorities that he knew or suspected that a money laundering offence was taking place. At the end of the judgment reducing his sentence, Mr Justice Leveson stated that:

> We do not leave the case without underlining to all professional people involved in the handling of money and with an involvement in financial transactions the absolute obligation to observe scrupulously the terms of the legislation and the inevitable penalty that will follow failure so to do.

Specific client needs

10.1 Introduction

Meeting the wide-ranging needs of individual clients in a variety of circumstances has been referred to in general terms throughout the previous chapters in this manual. More specifically, **Chapter 3** considers the needs of a range of clients whom you are likely to meet in practice and provides, by way of illustration, examples of some typical scenarios which you should expect to encounter during your career as a barrister. This chapter will develop this theme and examine, in greater detail, a range of specific client needs (and potential client difficulties) about which you should have awareness.

You should also be aware, however, of the dangers that exist when trying to work out exactly how any individual may or may not react in any given circumstances. Thus, it is important to remember that any attempt to identify and analyse the needs of individual clients, with any certainty, necessarily runs the risk of being inaccurate and, at best, unscientific.

It is perfectly proper—and indeed part of your professional duty—for you to consider the likelihood of certain clients having particular or special needs when you are instructed to represent them, and when you are preparing the case for the conference. However, you should be aware of the dangers which can exist in this area, especially in forming preconceived ideas about the client's particular requirements or attitudes and possibly getting the wrong end of the stick. The best advice is:

- always consider what potential problems might exist; and
- ensure that when you are planning how best to approach these, you proceed with care and caution.

This chapter cannot and does not purport to predict, with any degree of accuracy, what any individual client's needs will be, or the way in which an individual client will react in any given situation. By the same token, it would, of course, be equally impossible to identify the complete range of specific individual needs that every client may have.

What follows seeks to identify certain categories (or groups) of clients to whom special consideration should be given when meeting them in conference. Some of the categories of clients referred to will be obvious, others less so. It also seeks to identify certain specific situations with a client in which you may be likely to find yourself, and which are known to have the potential to cause some difficulties, especially for those new to practice.

The illustrations which follow are intended to provide examples of the sort of client needs (and client difficulties) to which you should be giving some consideration. You will also appreciate, when dealing on a professional level with a variety of different clients from wide-ranging and diverse backgrounds, the importance of attempting to ensure that you make a conscious effort to consider how best you can meet the individual needs of each and every client.

In addressing such matters as these, it is useful to remember that you should always:

- remain open-minded;
- expect anything;
- be flexible;
- stay non-judgemental.

10.2 The client who is reluctant to reveal critical information

When meeting any client in conference, you necessarily become intimately involved, in a very short space of time, with that individual's personal life. Many people find it difficult to reveal potentially sensitive details about themselves or their life, especially to a person whom they regard as a total stranger. It is important that you remember this and show consideration for the client's emotional reactions when dealing with possible sensitive areas. Your ability to elicit the necessary information is obviously central to your ability to represent the client properly.

Embarrassment or painful memories are likely to result from the introduction of topics as diverse as family life, physical and mental health, money and wages, sex and lifestyles, religion, and political allegiance. If these or similar topics are pertinent to the case, they must be dealt with. You would not be doing a professional job if these subjects were simply glossed over, swept under the carpet, or ignored altogether. There may, of course, be unwillingness on the part of the client to discuss these topics, and it is certainly not unusual to encounter this sort of difficulty in practice. The following are some examples of the sorts of issues about which clients may find difficulty expressing themselves, and a range of possible solutions which may assist you in considering how best to deal with this sort of problem:

(a) It can often be difficult for a client to provide information that may be prejudicial to another party with whom he or she is intimately involved. There are many reasons for this, for example fear of damaging the relationship or of being perceived as being disloyal, or quite simply fear of the consequences of speaking the truth.

(b) Your client may find it difficult (or embarrassing) to admit to an illicit sexual relationship between him or her and a third party. This difficulty could be caused by a number of things, for example, a desire not to be seen as 'a guilty party', a wish to protect others from genuine hurt, or anxiety about the practical or financial consequences which could flow from such an admission.

(c) It can be distressing to admit to a condition which may be perceived as a weakness or to reveal matters which your client thinks may make outsiders think less of him or her and damage the chances of success in the case, for example having suffered a nervous breakdown, having been the victim of sexual abuse, having a history of violent behaviour, or being an alcoholic or a compulsive gambler.

(d) It is not unusual to find reluctance on the part of a client to admit to supporting an extreme political party, or to being a member of an unusual religious sect. In such circumstances, there can often be a tendency for clients to resist being seen as a member of any sort of minority group because of the (albeit erroneous) impression they perceive such an interest may give to the outside world.

If your client demonstrates a reluctance to discuss any issues that are clearly relevant to the case, you must take the lead. Some gentle encouragement to accompany the question may be required. It is important to remember to guard against the temptation to help the client answer the question by using an inappropriate leading style. People under stress are highly suggestible. It is also important to recognise that most human beings have an enormous capacity for denial—that is, effectively being able to block out information about which they feel ashamed and/or embarrassed. In your capacity as the client's legal adviser, you must try to ensure that you are able to break down these sorts of barriers. You need to persuade your client that it is essential that you are in full possession of all relevant information if you are to represent his or her best interests. You must obviously retain your professional detachment, but this does not prevent you from expressing sympathy or empathy with the client.

10.2.1   Dealing with reluctance to cooperate

> ### How to do it
>
> If you find yourself in the position where you suspect that your client is failing to be as forthcoming as you would like, or feel necessary for the conduct of the case, you may find the following of assistance:
>
> - Decide what personal or sensitive material is required because of its relevance to the case.
> - Acknowledge to the client that you recognise these questions are potentially intrusive.
> - Explicitly state to the client your justification for having to ask potentially intrusive questions.
> - Remind the client of the confidentiality of the conference.
> - Remind the client of your need to be armed with all the relevant information if you are to represent him or her to the best of your ability.
> - Attempt to maintain a neutral manner when approaching a potentially sensitive topic.
> - If the client tentatively volunteers the relevant information, permit them to complete what they have to say.
> - Attempt to be economical with your questions in order to gather the relevant material in the shortest time and cause the least upset.
> - Do not pass any judgement or express any personal opinion on what has been said.
> - Secure the client's express permission before using the information even if it is for the benefit of the case.

10.3   The client under stress

There will be occasions in practice where your client will demonstrate signs of extreme stress at the conference. As we have seen in **Chapters 2** and **3**, when confronted with a frightening predicament, or an alarming situation that seems out of their control, some clients may take this badly and react accordingly.

Stress can manifest itself in many forms and you should not be surprised to encounter a wide range of emotions from clients, ranging from extreme anger to severe (and visible) distress.

10.3.1 Anger—'don't shoot the messenger'

Sometimes, you will be able to predict anger with a fair degree of accuracy, for example the client who is sentenced to a lengthy custodial sentence, or fails to gain a residence order in respect of his or her children, or has a large award for payment of damages entered against him or her. In these circumstances, a reasonable human reaction would be one of anger. The problem is that it is often you who has to deliver the 'bad news' and take the brunt of any angry reaction on the part of the client. In other situations, predicting any (or some) degree of anger is not quite so straightforward. It is useful to remember, however, that disappointment, shock, or sometimes even relief, can often result in a person becoming angry and agitated.

10.3.1.1 Dealing with anger

> **How to do it**
>
> Whatever circumstances give rise to the client becoming angry, and whether it is predictable or not, you should be aware of the possibility that this can happen, and give some thought to the best way of handling such a situation should it arise. Some assistance may be derived from the following:
>
> - Whatever the client says, you must remain completely passive and not overreact yourself.
>
> - Remind yourself that this is not a personal attack and that it is (more than likely) the system that is causing the anger in the client.
>
> - Permit the client time to vent his or her emotions.
>
> - Demonstrate a suitable degree of empathy with the situation.
>
> - Remain completely non-judgemental.
>
> - Do not permit yourself to be swept up in any recriminations.
>
> - When the client has calmed down, try to revisit the realities of the situation and focus upon any positive points.
>
> - Where possible, avoid taking any instructions until the client is suitably calmed down.

10.3.2 Severe distress

The reverse emotion to that of anger is one of distress. It is frequently the case that in conference your client will demonstrate signs of severe distress at the circumstances in which he or she finds himself or herself, or at the unpalatable news you have had to deliver. The most obvious manifestation of this will be tears—uncontrollable sobbing for lengthy periods is not unusual—but other signs are the client physically shaking or visibly paling. If this happens at court and immediately prior to a hearing, you should obviously seek a short adjournment until your client has recovered sufficiently to continue with the proceedings. Most courts will be sympathetic to such an application

10.3.2.1   Dealing with distress

How to do it

In conference at chambers, or at a different stage in the proceedings, where your client becomes severely distressed, it may be useful to consider the following:

- Some acknowledgement of the difficult situation in which the client is placed and a suitable degree of sympathy is usually appropriate.

- Ensure that you appear entirely non-critical of the client's behaviour.

- Remain completely objective and non-judgemental.

- Give the client time to get the distress out of his or her system.

- Where possible, take a break in the proceedings.

- When the client has calmed down, attempt to reassure him or her about any positive aspects of their case.

- Try to ensure that the client does not have to make any important decisions until he or she has sufficiently recovered.

Much of what is outlined previously can be seen as common sense. And, of course, there is a whole gamut of other emotions that clients may exhibit in conference. What is important to emphasise is that you should expect to encounter many different kinds of emotional responses from your clients. It is often said that 'being forewarned is being forearmed', a piece of advice which, when considering a client's emotional reaction, you should keep uppermost in your mind.

Perhaps the best advice is that at all times you attempt to anticipate any likely difficulties, and to ensure you are adequately equipped to handle the variety of emotions which you will undoubtedly encounter in meeting the many clients who will instruct you.

10.4   The juvenile client

Children and young adults will need to consult lawyers for a variety of reasons in both civil and criminal proceedings. It is important to remember that if your lay client is a child, you owe him or her the same professional duties and courtesies as you would do to an adult client, and the usual rules for good practice will also apply.

That having been said, there are clearly some additional, and special, considerations that should properly be given to the conduct of any conference in which your client is a child. You should be aware of the rules of criminal procedure and evidence as they relate to juveniles. (See further the *Evidence* manual, the *Criminal Litigation and Sentencing* manual and the Judicial College's guidelines on dealing with young witnesses <https://www.judiciary.gov.uk/publications/jc-bench-checklist-young-wit-cases/>.) You should also remember the Code oC14 that 'Care is given to ensure that the interests of vulnerable clients are taken into account and their needs are met.' Guidance is offered at gC41 in the following terms:

You should remember that your client may not be familiar with legal proceedings and may find them difficult and stressful. You should do what you reasonably can to ensure that the client understands the process and what to expect from it and from you. You should also try to avoid any unnecessary distress for your client. This is particularly important where you are dealing with a vulnerable client.

Under rC21, you must not accept instructions to act in a particular matter if:

.8   you are not competent to handle the particular matter or otherwise do not have enough experience to handle the matter.

Guidance at gC71 states: 'Competency and experience under Rule C21.8 includes your ability to work with vulnerable clients.'

10.4.1   The role of the adult

It is advisable, whenever possible, to ensure that there is another adult in attendance at the conference. It is usual for the adult to be a parent or near relation (uncle/cousin/grandmother/elder brother, and so on). However, depending on the circumstances, it may be the case that a social worker or similar professional will have immediate care of the child in loco parentis.

If the adult in attendance is a parent, you should be aware of some difficulties that can frequently arise. Many different factors can contribute to these difficulties. Sometimes the relationship between parent and child is already damaged and lines of communication between them poor. More often than not, however, the difficulties caused are usually the result of genuine concern on the part of a caring parent about the well-being of his or her child. However, unless you take positive steps to avoid it, such concern can and does interfere with the conference process. Often a concerned parent will attempt to dominate the child. This may manifest itself by the parent attempting to answer the questions on behalf of the child. Whether this is motivated by misplaced concern, or by other selfish considerations, this behaviour is unacceptable.

It is frequently the case that the child may be fearful of angering, hurting, or disappointing the parent, in some way, by giving answers which may be unpalatable. Often a child will look to the parent in an attempt to receive some guidance before answering your question. Where possible, this must be avoided.

The golden and immutable rule is that your instructions must come from the child personally and from no one else.

It is often useful to identify, at an early stage, the roles of all the people in attendance at the conference, so that everyone present is aware of each person's function. In addition, it is often useful to remind all parties, at the outset of the questioning, that it is only the child's answers that are relevant.

10.4.2   Creating and maintaining good relations with the child client

Children are often suspicious of strangers, so do not be surprised if at first you are treated with caution, doubt, and even hostility, by the child. It will normally take some time before you manage to establish a position of trust between you. If you can allocate a bit of time to establish a rapport with the child before moving into the conference proper, this will often assist.

A golden rule is not to talk down to the child. Even very young children are usually aware when they are being patronised or condescended to by an adult. Such behaviour is counterproductive to establishing good relations with a child client. Obviously, some adjustments to your language and use of vocabulary will often have to be made to suit the circumstances and in order to ensure that the child understands what you are saying. In this respect, try to speak plainly and clearly and convey to the child that you are confident that he or she understands what is being said.

Children do tend to have a shorter attention span than adults and you should expect to provide a greater explanation of the whys and wherefores of the questions that you address to them. Children are often more inquisitive (less polite) than adults and you will often have to provide answers to a range of questions on issues which you may consider irrelevant. In this respect, you will require a great deal of patience and a recognition that often less progress than you had hoped for will be achieved in the available time.

In many cases, you can expect displays of emotion such as anger, fear, boredom, and tears. You can also expect that, unlike adults, children are capable of running through the whole gamut of these emotions only, after a short recovery time, to behave as if nothing untoward had occurred.

10.4.2.1   Establishing rapport with a child client

How to do it

As with all clients, it is important that the child client has the opportunity to have his or her say and that the atmosphere you create in the conference is both cooperative and collaborative. When considering ways in which best to achieve this, the following checklist may be of assistance.

- Establish the roles of all people present in the conference room.
- Provide a clear explanation of the purpose(s) of the conference.
- Spend as much time as appropriate to establish a relationship of trust between you and the child.
- Do not patronise the child.
- Choose your language with care.
- Ask questions in a way that assists the child in providing the relevant answer.
- Be prepared to spend more time on explanation and repetition of the questions that you ask.
- Ensure that the child answers your questions with the minimum of outside intervention or coaching by other people present.
- Be prepared for displays of emotion.
- Remember to extend to the child all the normal courtesies that you would pay to an adult.
- Remember that the child is the client and the child is the person who is instructing you.
- If the child is to give evidence, consider whether to seek the services of a court intermediary.

10.5   The client who is under the influence of drink or drugs

There will be occasions in conference when you realise that your client is under the influence of drink or drugs (or both). In many cases, you will clearly be able to detect the presence of alcohol or an illegal substance, as the effects will be quite apparent. In other cases, however, the effects might not be so obvious and you should be alert to some of the telltale signs of drug or drink abuse; for example, slurring of words, drowsiness, dilated pupils, red-rimmed eyes, lack of concentration, shaking hands, very short temper, and so on.

If at any stage of the proceedings you are certain or you suspect that your client is, or may be, under the influence of drink or drugs, it is advisable to take some action to protect your client (and, of course, yourself). In such circumstances, it is usually proper to ensure that:

- your client is not unduly disadvantaged by his or her condition; and
- where possible (if it is appropriate), there is a suitable adjournment in proceeding with the case.

The dilemma for you, as a barrister, is not easy. You are obliged to comply with the rules of professional conduct set out in the Bar Standards Board's Handbook which, inter alia, bind you to the 'cab-rank rule'. A strict interpretation of this could be that it is simply not your role to determine whether or not your client is fit to instruct you: once instructed, you are basically obliged to get on with it.

However, it is strongly recommended that, if you find yourself in this type of situation, the best course of action is to use your common sense. While there is nothing in the Code of Conduct that specifically addresses the point, Core Duty 2 provides the injunction: 'You must act in the best interests of each client.'

It may be taken, therefore, that at all times it is your duty to protect your client and his or her best interests. If your client is 'the worse for wear', it is clearly not in his or her best interests to make any potentially irrational decisions, or to be obliged to provide you with any ill-conceived or hasty instructions. By the same token, if you are acting towards your client in good faith, it would be improper for you to permit any such decisions to be taken in circumstances in which it is obvious to you that your client is incapable of exercising sound or reasoned judgment.

In practice, therefore, what should you do if you suspect that your client is under the influence of drink or drugs?

10.5.1   At court

If you turn up at court and discover that your client is not in any fit state either to instruct you properly, or to make an appearance, it is perfectly proper to make an application for an adjournment. In such circumstances, it would be highly unusual for the court not to be accommodating. The next step is to discover the precise extent of your client's debilitation. If it is merely a question of waiting until the effects of drink/drugs have worn off, the case can proceed when your client has sobered up. If not, and in your opinion your client is in need of additional help and support, it would be appropriate to consider referring the problem on. Your instructing solicitor (or the Duty Solicitor at court) would normally be the first contact in this respect. Whatever you decide, however, you must remember that the court appearance still has to take place, and your primary duty is to represent your client. It is also essential to remember in circumstances such as these that you still owe your client a duty of confidentiality. Any steps that may involve you in straying outside the ambit of your instructions, should only be taken with the full knowledge, consent, and agreement of your client.

10.5.2   In chambers

The matter becomes slightly less pressing (for you at least) if the conference is in chambers. In these circumstances, where the prospect of a court appearance is not imminent, and the client is invariably accompanied by your instructing solicitor (or the solicitor's representative), you will have much more room to manoeuvre. You are still faced with the same difficulty, however, in that it would (almost certainly) be improper to take instructions from a client who is visibly under the influence of drink or drugs. Under these conditions, it is advisable to invite the client to cancel the conference and rearrange the appointment for a more suitable time. Make sure that the solicitor (or solicitor's representative) is aware of precisely what you are doing, and why you are taking this course of action. In these circumstances, it is more appropriate for the solicitor to confront the problem(s) with the client. In this way, your professional responsibility to the client will not be compromised.

10.6 The client who is suffering from mental health problems

As with children, when dealing with clients with mental health problems, you should remember the Code oC14 that 'Care is given to ensure that the interests of vulnerable clients are taken into account and their needs are met.' According to some estimates, as many as one person in four will suffer from some form of mental health problem, and one person in 50 will have serious mental health problems. The better mental health charity Mind's 'Types of mental health problems' web pages offer pithy overviews of most common mental health conditions: <http://www.mind.org.uk/>.

10.6.1 Introduction

On the basis of those statistics, the chances of your being instructed to represent a client with some of these difficulties is reasonably to be expected. As a trained lawyer, you are obviously not expected to be an expert in the field of mental health. You should be aware, however, of the possible difficulties which clients may find themselves in and what potential problems this could cause you in your professional involvement with the client. There are many forms of mental disorder, ranging from serious mental impairment, which renders a person incapable of managing his or her own affairs, through to the other end of the spectrum where, for a variety of reasons, a person is temporarily in a state of mental distress which renders him or her particularly vulnerable at a given time and limits his or her ability to cope with day-to-day living.

10.6.2 Serious mental impairment

It appears that serious mental impairment falls into four general categories: those born with serious mental impairment; those who suffer accidental brain damage (at birth or in an accident); those who suffer from a nervous breakdown; and those people who suffer from senile dementia (an ever-increasing elderly population makes this last category the largest group).

Part 2 of the Mental Capacity Act 2005 gives the Court of Protection authority to make orders and give directions in relation to the estates of persons who, by reason of mental disorder, are incapable of managing their property and affairs. In these circumstances, the position is usually reasonably straightforward as far as your involvement is concerned. A power of attorney is granted which appoints a receiver to handle that person's affairs. This can be a temporary appointment (until the person has recovered sufficiently) or enduring (see Sch 4 to the Mental Capacity Act 2005). If you are instructed by a client who is represented by a deputy (or some other person officially designated to handle the client's affairs), you will obviously take your instructions from that person.

10.6.3   **State of mental distress**

The circumstances outlined in 16.6.2 are very unusual. It is much more likely that in practice you will encounter clients from the other end of the spectrum—that is, a client who is suffering from some form of mental distress which, although falling short of the categories outlined in the previous section, is nevertheless potentially disruptive to the conference and your ability to represent that client as effectively as you would wish. We have seen that being in trouble, especially with the law, often causes people to react emotionally, to overreact, or to act in a way that is totally out of character. In fact, it is not unusual, or surprising, for a client to display a whole gamut of emotions. In some circumstances, however, such behaviour may indicate that your client is actually suffering from a form of mental distress.

Some indicators that your client may be in some kind of difficulty may include such signs as:

- hearing or seeing things that others do not;
- extremes of mood;
- rapid changes of mood;
- eating problems;
- lack of sleep;
- reduced desire to communicate with others;
- lethargy;
- very high energy levels.

Although the list is far from exhaustive, these are the sorts of signs that may give you a clue that your client is mentally distressed. If you suspect this to be the case, what is the most appropriate way to handle the situation?

10.6.3.1   Protecting the client

As we have seen in **10.5**, it is your duty at all times to protect your client and his or her best interests. You will have to make a judgement as to whether it is in your client's best interests to proceed with the conference and whether he or she is in a fit condition to exercise sound and reasoned judgement. If you are in any doubt that it is proper to continue the proceedings, you should consult your solicitor and decide what further action to take. In these circumstances, it would be usual for your instructing solicitor to take the lead with the client, make any necessary decisions, and instruct you accordingly. Again, perhaps the best advice in this situation is that you exercise your common sense in the matter to ensure that your client is not unnecessarily disadvantaged. Clearly, if despite your concerns, you are instructed to proceed with the conference, you will have to do just that.

10.6.3.2   Immediate action

When your client behaves in a manner that suggests he or she may be suffering from mental distress, it is important for you to try to:

- be sensitive;
- attempt to allay any fears;
- be non-judgemental;
- remind him or her of the confidential nature of the conference.

10.7 Language barriers

There will be occasions on which you are instructed to represent a client who does not have sufficient command of the English language to enable him or her to instruct you fully in conference. In such circumstances it would be usual for the client to be accompanied by an interpreter for the purposes of the conference.

When the conference is at your chambers, it is normal practice for the solicitor to arrange for a suitable interpreter to attend with the client. It should be the same for a conference that is scheduled to take place at court. Occasionally, for a variety of reasons, you will discover that a suitable interpreter has not been instructed. One of the major reasons for this is frequently that the client himself or herself has felt unable (or unwilling) to admit to being less than fluent in English. It is essential, in these circumstances, that where you consider that proceeding with the conference would be to the disadvantage of your client, you suspend the proceedings until an interpreter has been found. The most important factor is obviously to ensure that there is a level of communication between you and your client which facilitates a full, two-way flow and exchange of relevant information to enable the client both to understand what advice is being given and also to give instructions.

When you find yourself in the situation where it is necessary for an interpreter to attend the conference with your client, and who is clearly going to be the person with whom you conduct the relevant dialogue, there are some points which you should bear in mind:

(a) Recognise that in these circumstances, the client is likely to feel even more disadvantaged than an English-speaking client who is in some kind of trouble.

(b) Make sure that your introduction(s) and any initial formalities of the conference are clearly understood by your client.

(c) Check that you pronounce (and spell) the client's name correctly and address the client in the proper form. (See **Chapter 11**.)

(d) Ensure that the client is fully informed as to why there is a need for an interpreter to be present and understands that it is on the information that he or she provides to the interpreter that you will provide your advice.

(e) Make sure the interpreter is fully aware of the need for complete accuracy in the translation of your client's instructions. A gentle reminder that the interpreter should remain entirely objective is usually a sound policy.

(f) Be prepared for the fact that any conference conducted via an interpreter will normally take much longer than one conducted by participants solely in English.

(g) Be aware of the fact that such conferences require you to exercise a high degree of patience.

(h) On completion of the conference, ensure that your client really does understand the full implications and impact of any conclusions that have been decided.

(i) If the case is one that is to continue to a court hearing, ensure that the solicitor, the other side, and the court are aware of the need for interpreting facilities.

(*Note*: if the conference is followed by a court hearing at which you are instructed to act as the client's advocate, you should be aware that conducting a contested case in court with an interpreter can create some additional difficulties—see the *Advocacy* manual.)

10.8 Conclusion

It will be apparent that in practice you will encounter a wide range of people from a variety of backgrounds who will become your clients. Each client whom you are instructed to represent will come to the conference with his or her own needs, expectations, emotional responses, and problems. It is part of your professional duty to ensure that, in every case, you give adequate consideration to how best to deal with all the requirements of your client.

It would be impossible, of course, for this text to address every single permutation in this respect. The intention is rather to illustrate the types of issues which you might encounter in practice and to raise your awareness of the sorts of steps which you could consider taking when dealing with individual clients.

In the same way, it would be equally impossible for you to anticipate with any certainty how each client will present in the conference, or to predict with any accuracy what specific needs any client may have. The best advice for good practice in dealing with your client is to try to ensure that when considering his or her likely needs you remain flexible, open-minded, objective, and non-judgemental.

Finally, in considering the needs of individual clients, it is essential for every intending practitioner to be fully in touch with the fact that we live and work in a multicultural, multi-ethnic society. This means, of course, that your clients are likely to come from every walk of life, encompassing a diverse range of cultures, backgrounds, and religions, and from a wide variety of socio-economic and educational backgrounds. The following chapter, **Chapter 11**, addresses these issues more specifically.

Cross-cultural communication

11.1 Introduction

Lord Justice Brooke CMG, the author of the first part of this chapter, was chairman of the Race Relations Committee of the Bar Council between January 1989 and December 1991, and the first chairman of the Ethnic Minorities Advisory Committee of the Judicial Studies Board between March 1991 and September 1994. In 1993, he delivered the eighth Kapila Fellowship Lecture at the Inns of Court School of Law on 'The Administration of Justice in a Multi-Cultural Society'.

The second part of this chapter offers brief at-a-glance guidance for effective cross-cultural communication.

11.2 Cross-cultural communication by Lord Justice Brooke CMG

Britain is now a multicultural society. [Since the 1990s, net immigration has become an increasingly important factor in population growth in the UK. Net international migration from abroad (the difference between long-term migration into and out of the UK) remains the largest factor in population growth. This is a trend that is predicted to continue.] (Editor's note: The text in square brackets updates Lord Justice Brooke's contributions which were first written in the mid-1990s. Further details on UK population trends are available from <http://www.statistics.gov.uk/>.) Britain also attracts many visitors, for business, tourism, or study, for example, whose homes are elsewhere. In the normal course of things most barristers will conduct conferences from time to time with people of different cultures from their own.

Culture is a very potent force in all our lives. It affects the way we think, the way we talk, the way our families are structured, the way we use the spoken word, and the way we use different parts of our bodies—our eyes, our shoulders, our hands, and so on—to communicate our thoughts. If you are not alert to the possibility, sometimes, of the likelihood of a communications breakdown when you act for a client from a different culture, there will be all the makings of a potential miscarriage of justice, for which nobody will be to blame but yourself.

The *Judicial Studies Board Handbook on Ethnic Minority Issues* contains this important piece of advice:

Most of the time in our daily lives we experience no difficulty in communicating with others. We speak the same language, and feel we understand one another—at home and at work—pretty well. If something seems unclear or we want more information, all we have to do is ask. If no one does this, we assume we have been understood.

This assumption does not necessarily hold up where the two people communicating with one another come from different cultural backgrounds. It may, of course, be obvious to one or both parties that they have not understood. Quite often, however, this is not the case; they may *think* they have understood correctly, but in fact they have not done so. The message may have been read quite differently from how it was intended. People are likely to 'read' behaviour from the point of view of their own cultural groups, without being aware of the possibly different meaning attributed to it in the culture of the other party. It is when this quite natural tendency towards 'ethnocentrism' creeps in—ie where parties interpret the behaviour in terms of their own cultural frameworks, and do so unconsciously—that the greatest danger of cross-cultural misunderstanding arises.

In cross-cultural situations, culture—normally the means to successful communication—paradoxically can become the barrier to such success. [For the most up-to-date version of equal treatment advice to judges, see Equal Treatment Bench Book, 2013 with 2015 amendments <https://www.judiciary.gov.uk/wp-content/uploads/2013/11/equal-treatment-bench-book-2013-with-2015-amendment.pdf>.]

An important conference skill is the ability to communicate to your client that you really understand their problem. In this way, they are much more likely to have confidence in entrusting their affairs—and sometimes their hopes of happiness or liberty—to you.

A bad start to a conference is to get the client's name wrong. Names are very personal to people, and they may feel, 'If my barrister can't even get my name right, what hope has he or she of getting anything else right?' You must do your best to avoid pronouncing their name wrong, or committing other avoidable mistakes, such as asking a Hindu client what her Christian name is. By way of example only, an unmarried Chinese woman called Cheung Lan-Ying should be addressed as Miss Cheung, and a devout Muslim called Mohammed Rahman Khan should never be addressed by the holy name Mohammed alone: this would cause grave offence. If in any doubt, ask your client how he or she would like to be addressed. That way you can't make mistakes.

It is always wise to be on the lookout for misunderstandings when your clients may have been using common English words in a different sense from the way in which you are accustomed to use them, words like 'afternoon' or 'dinner' or 'family' or 'uncle' or 'cousins', for instance. Sometimes people in court are accused of being liars when they use a word in a way that is familiar to them, but not to the opposing advocate or, often, to the judge. It is your job to spot any possibility for misunderstanding when you read the conference papers beforehand, and then to be on top of your client's explanation of what the word means to them when you appear in court.

And you should always be on the lookout for problems with body language. Don't necessarily think your client is shifty and not fit to be believed if he or she does not look you in the eye. It may be very natural for them not to look straight in the eye at somebody they may treat as having authority over them. In some cultures, too, using a loud voice does not necessarily indicate loss of control, nor need it indicate hostility or an aggressive disposition, a matter that often leads to misunderstandings in the street between citizens and the police. In the same way, an expansive use of the hands and arms may be some people's way of expressing themselves comfortably. It is impossible to lay down hard-and-fast rules about body language, particularly at a time of so much cultural diversity. All one can hope to do is to be on one's guard not to pick up signals that are quite wrong.

It may also sometimes be necessary to obtain a very clear understanding of some matter that is very important to a client in relation to his or her religion. For instance, it may be extremely important for a young Muslim, remanded on bail, to attend the mosque with his family on a weekday evening, and the barrister needs to be aware of this when questions of a curfew come up. Or a Hindu may need his case adjourned so that he may attend his father's funeral: the barrister needs to know that if the oldest son does not light the funeral pyre, his father's soul will not be released from his body to ensure its smooth passage to the afterworld. If you act for a Rastafarian, it is wise to learn about their beliefs and their style of living beforehand: clients really appreciate it if you take this sort of trouble, before meeting them in conference, to understand things that are important to them.

Very often, too, a barrister needs to understand a client's family system when they meet in conference. Again, it is very dangerous to generalise, but a few basic ground rules may help. Family patterns in Britain are characterised by diversity and change generally. Ethnic minority families merely add an additional dimension. You must beware of stereotyping ethnic minority families. There are no typical forms of Indian or Afro-Caribbean family, any more than there are typical forms of French or Italian or English family.

Extended families in African and Asian cultures, however, traditionally reflect a corporate approach to family affairs, and family ties tend to be very much stronger. Such families may be misunderstood as being simply 'extensions' or 'nuclear' families. When the Ethnic Minorities Advisory Committee of the Judicial Studies Board [now the Judicial College] was first formed, I remember being very struck by some evidence we received from a group of Asian interpreters in the West Midlands. They said that they often witnessed family cases being decided by English judges, with the help of English advocates and English social workers, as if the only alternatives for the child were the father, the mother, or foster parents or a children's home. There was a great wall of ignorance about the fact that in the extended Asian family there are plenty of relatives who would welcome the child into their own homes as if he or she was their own child: the existence of this wall of ignorance was causing a great deal of heartache in the families concerned.

In minority ethnic communities, greater emphasis tends to be placed on discipline in bringing up children, and there is often bemusement and concern at the 'liberal' approach of many British parents. In some parts of West Africa, moreover, it is usual for children to be brought up not in the parents' household but that of relatives (as it used to be in parts of Europe) so that among West Africans, in particular, 'fostering' may be seen as normal and indeed beneficial for a child. Grandparents, too, may play more significant roles in many ethnic communities, both with regard to children and the management of family property and affairs generally.

The corporate style of family organisation is reflected in the system of arranged marriages in many Asian cultures. Traditionally these were an opportunity to create alliances between family groups. On the other hand, arranged marriages in the British context focus more on selecting a suitable partner for the individual family member. Increasingly they are now allowing the latter an element of choice. The important thing is to do your best to understand the social and family dynamics at work, and not to condemn practices simply because they are unfamiliar and inconsistent with your own culture.

Divorce is a case in point. In all South Asian communities, divorce is strongly disapproved of socially, and divorce arrangements are particularly liable to disadvantage women. Although the English courts are bound to administer English family law, this does not mean that there may not be plenty of problems being stored up within an extended family if divorce is used by a member of that family as a means of bringing a marriage to an end.

It is not only in a family law practice that a barrister will run into great difficulties if he or she doesn't understand these things, and a lot more besides. Often, in criminal trials or civil litigation, issues crop up which require the advocate to see the world as his or her client sees it. The conference is likely to be the last chance you will get of acquiring the knowledge you need. The golden rule must always be: if you don't know, ask. In a multicultural society the ignorance of a barrister about important features of a client's culture certainly doesn't signify bliss for the client—very much the reverse.

11.3   At-a-glance guidance for effective cross-cultural communication

One of the most effective ways to create conditions for excellent communication between you and clients is to learn more about them and understand their cultural context. With this knowledge, there is a good chance that the messages that flow between you will be made and received effectively. To achieve the appropriate level of understanding of others, you need to have good self-knowledge and be willing to recognise and curb any prejudices you hold about other people and to correct any assumptions or misconceptions that you may hold about the groups to which they belong.

11.3.1   Types of diversity

Society is made up of a myriad of individuals, each of whom has characteristics that are personal to them. It goes without saying that, as a barrister, you can expect to encounter a wide diversity of people. Some of the differences between you and other people are clear as soon as you make contact with them, but others will only emerge over time as and when revelations about lifestyles or beliefs are shared. Here is a list of some indicators of diversity; consider how your profile fits within each indicator as well as your clients'. Note which are inherent to an individual and which become a characteristic because of upbringing or personal choice. Ask yourself how your own personal characteristics influence your view of the world; how they affect how other people interact with you and how they influence your interpretation of other people's behaviour:

- gender;
- age;
- ethnicity;
- language;
- physical and mental abilities;
- sexual orientation;
- religious, philosophical, and political affiliation;
- socio-economic background; and
- educational experience.

11.3.2   Stereotyping and discrimination

Discrimination may be direct or indirect, and you need to guard against both when dealing with clients and people.

- Direct discrimination is where a person is treated less favourably on the grounds of an inherent or avowed personal characteristic.

- Indirect discrimination is where a requirement is applied equally to all groups, but has a disproportionate effect on the members of one group because fewer of its members can comply with it.

We all use predications as a way of coping with the uncertainties of everyday life, and stereotypes can sometimes help us to predict how the people around us will react. However, they have very limited use on their own and can be extremely dangerous in the context of criminal and civil justice, leading to direct or indirect discrimination. The following list suggests ways to overcome or, at least, contain stereotyping when you hold a conference with a client:

- Patience and politeness are good bridges to cross-cultural divides.
    - Ask the client how they wish to be addressed—using correct titles and accurate pronunciation of names shows clients respect.
    - Observe your own cultural norms about personal space and contact, but be prepared to adjust them where possible.
- If you know or suspect that the client has a disability, in advance of the conference make appropriate arrangements (eg special seating, an interpreter, large-print copies of documents).
- Observe your client throughout the conference to check for comprehension.
    - Be prepared to explain anything you say in plain English.
    - Slow down or offer a break if necessary.
- Be open to learning more about the culture your client is part of—this information will almost always assist you to advise and represent them better.
- Watch your language—avoid terms that could be construed by your client as offensive, disrespectful, or demeaning; for example:
    - Don't confuse mere adjectives—such as black, disabled—with qualified nouns—for example, black people, a disabled person.
    - Don't confine the term 'British' only to English, white people, who are Christian.
    - Don't apply the term 'immigrant' to people from non-white ethnic groups—unless you are referring to someone who has recently moved to the UK from abroad.
- Avoid causing the client embarrassment by inappropriate humour or ridicule.
- Be up to date—every culture changes and what was acceptable or even good practice in the past may not be so today.

11.3.3 Diversity and justice

The effect that gender, race, and other characteristics have on individuals' involvement in the justice system is beyond the scope of this manual. What follows are therefore no more than signposts for you as a guide for before and during a conference.

- Fair treatment involves taking into account (not ignoring) difference—in the light of what has or will happen to your client, have their differences been taken into account?
- Treating everyone the same is not fair treatment—were institutions and their staff prepared to adjust or be flexible in their dealings with your client?

- Different communities may have different experiences as claimants, victims, defendants, witnesses, representatives, or suspects—what was your client's experience?
- Courts and tribunals have a duty to conduct fair proceedings—what do you need to inform the court to ensure justice for your client?

You can learn more about the different impact that the systems of justice have on ethnic minority and other groups by searching relevant government, professional, and interest group websites for statistics and reports. The Judicial College website <https://www.judiciary.gov.uk/about-the-judiciary/training-support/judicial-college/> is a key source for information about the measures members of the judiciary should take to address the existence, appearance, or risk of discrimination in the courtroom.

How to judge an effective conference

12.1 Introduction

From the previous chapters in this manual it will be apparent that:

- there is a need for intending practitioners to acquire sound client conference skills; and
- the acquisition of these skills is far more complex than might, at first sight, appear.

Having established these two basic principles, it is clearly necessary to consider whether it is possible accurately to:

- judge a performance of a client conference;
- assess how well the skill has been acquired; and
- determine where improvements/adjustments can be made.

In answering these questions in the affirmative, this chapter seeks to demonstrate that it is possible to:

- judge whether a client conference is effective; and
- assess to what level of competence the skills have been acquired.

12.2 Background

We have already seen that the acquisition and development of effective and professional conference skills are dependent on three main factors: practice; criteria-based performance feedback; objectively-stated performance and assessment criteria. (See **Chapter 1.**)

12.2.1 Performance criteria—practice and role play

During the course you will be asked to conduct a conference in a number of different situations in order to practise your conference skills. Every teaching session will emphasise one or more aspects of holding a conference. It will be clear from the papers, which you receive in advance of each class, what particular aspect of the skill that session will address. You may be asked to prepare a conference plan, to consider questioning in detail, to concentrate on creating a good relationship with the client, to advise on legal issues and procedure, or to consider whether there are any alternative non-legal solutions, and so on. In this way, different aspects of the skill, the component parts as it were, will be considered in detail throughout the course. By the end of the course, you will be expected to conduct a full client conference that addresses all the aspects of the client conference.

Practice is essential to developing your conference skills and the benefits of practice cannot be emphasised too strongly. In this respect it is recommended that you take full advantage of the video recording facilities provided by your course provider.

As well as practising conference skills as the barrister, you will be required to role-play the client for your colleagues. Being on the 'receiving end', and gaining some experience of what it is like to be the client, will also give you an invaluable insight into what does or does not make a conference effective. You should recognise that participating fully in the role play on the course is a central part of your own learning process and that of your colleagues, who will be dependent on you to act as a realistic client.

This chapter examines in more detail the performance and assessment criteria that have been developed by The City Law School to (a) facilitate the acquisition and development of conference skills techniques and (b) demonstrate on what basis a performance will be judged.

12.3 Performance and assessment criteria

Many years of experience at The City Law School of both teaching the acquisition of and assessing the competence of conference skills have led to the development of performance and assessment criteria that are identical. Thus, in both your performance in class and your assessment at the end of the course, the criteria by which your skills in conducting a client conference are judged are the same. The purpose of this is to ensure that you are fully aware of the criteria on which your in-course performances are evaluated, and that the criteria-related feedback which you receive on your performance(s) during the course accurately reflect the criteria by which you are assessed in conducting a client conference at the end of the course.

The criteria have been designed to test and judge whether, in conducting a client conference, you can demonstrate an ability to:

- prepare effectively for the conference by understanding the facts, procedure, law, and evidence relevant to the case;
- ask questions that are appropriate in the context and that elicit the relevant information;
- advise appropriately on the basis of instructions received;
- structure the conference in a time-efficient way;
- communicate effectively with the client and respond appropriately to the client's concerns and questions;
- observe the rules of professional conduct.

It is recommended that you should become entirely familiar with these criteria and clearly understand what is meant by each one. In this respect, it would be useful to consider each criterion separately. What follows is not intended to be a fully comprehensive list of all the factors that contribute to satisfying each criterion, but rather an overview of the sorts of elements to which you should give consideration when thinking about ways of performing (and improving) the skill.

12.3.1 Criterion 1: preparation

You will already be aware that adequate preparation and planning for any conference is a job that has to be undertaken thoroughly and with precision if the conference is to be efficient. Effective preparation and planning can be broken down into two distinct parts: the preparation for the content of the conference, and the plan for the conduct of the conference itself. It is essential that your preparation includes adequate legal and factual analysis of the client's problem. Competent preparation will demonstrate that you:

- identify the objectives of the conference;
- identify the facts, procedure, law, and evidence relevant to the case.

Effective preparation means that you are more likely to ensure that the whole conference runs smoothly and addresses the relevant issues involved in the case. Sound planning means that you can put your preparation into practice—that is, to ensure that the structure of the conference, the sequence of questioning, and your advice to the client is as a result of careful and detailed analysis. (For further detail, see **Chapter 5**.)

12.3.2 Criterion 2: questioning

Central to your ability to conduct an effective client conference is your ability to decide what questions you need to ask the client and in what order and style you should ask them. The skill of efficient questioning is reflected in your ability, as the questioner, to draw out of the client the necessary information—that is, the necessary information which you require in order to be in a position to advise your client. In questioning your client competently, you should demonstrate that you can:

- deal with all relevant issues;
- use appropriate questioning techniques;
- clarify gaps and ambiguities;
- elicit the necessary information to be able to advise;
- show a clear understanding of the client's version of events;
- obtain full instructions.

Effective questioning has two further important qualities. When eliciting information from a client in conference you must ensure that you:

- do not inappropriately use leading questions or suggest the answers; and
- do not fire questions at the client as if you were conducting a cross-examination in the witness box. (See **Chapter 6**.)

12.3.3 Criterion 3: advising

The advice that you give to your client can really be seen as the heart of the whole conference. To be provided with a resolution to the legal predicament in which the client finds himself or herself is why the client has instructed you and it is usually his or her ultimate objective. Giving effective advice encompasses many separate issues, which will necessarily vary with each conference, depending on the situation. In almost all client conferences, however, in providing competent and effective advice, you should ensure that you:

- explain the issues to the client clearly and unambiguously;
- ensure that the client understands what has been discussed;
- explain procedural, legal, and evidential issues to the client;
- advise on the strengths and weaknesses of the case;
- explain (in the light of the above) what further action should be taken.

To advise appropriately really does mean that: a client expects you to provide full and clear advice on his or her problem. You are the expert and you are being paid to exercise your professional judgement on behalf of the client. The final decision on what to do is always up to the client, but remember that the client cannot make any such decision(s) without you providing a clear and full evaluation of the merits of his or her case, and a summary of the available options. In this respect, you should have the confidence to be robust in the advice that you provide for your client. (See **Chapter 7**.)

12.3.4   Criterion 4: structure and time management

It should be apparent that an effective conference is one that is structured in a logical and sensible sequence, which your client (and instructing solicitor) can readily follow. This is essential not only for clarity, but also because most conferences, especially those conducted in the early years of practice, are limited by time constraints (eg the conference which takes place 15 minutes before a court appearance, and so on). In almost every conference which you conduct, the client will be much more reassured (and, therefore, cooperative) if he or she is fully aware at the outset of what the aims of the conference are, in what order you intend to deal with the relevant issues, and when you are going to answer the critical question of how the matter could be best resolved. A competent structure to the conference should ensure that you:

- follow an agenda as far as practicable;
- are time-efficient;
- control the conference effectively;
- achieve the conference objectives, as far as is possible.

Conducting the conference in a structured manner also means that you should demonstrate that you are in control of the conference and, accordingly, ensure that the client's attention is focused on the relevant matters in hand. (For further detail, see **Chapters 4** and **8**.)

12.3.5   Criterion 5: communication

There are many aspects of behaviour that contribute towards creating an effective interchange between you and your client. Much of what is required is born of basic common sense and an application of plain ordinary courtesy. It is useful to remind yourself that your client is, after all, a human being, just like you. To work well, and to ensure that the client responds in the most appropriate and cooperative way during the conference, you need to be sensitive to your clients' fears, anxieties, and likely needs, as well as being aware of the legal predicament in which they find themselves. In seeking to communicate effectively with your client, try to ensure that you:

- put the client at ease, using appropriate language;
- ensure that the client understands the objectives of the conference;

- listen to the client;
- allow the client to raise concerns;
- reassure and sympathise with the client in a non-judgemental manner;
- deal with non-legal concerns.

Where possible, and/or appropriate, attempting to satisfy these aims will, in large measure, reassure the client and consequently ensure that you communicate effectively. However, perhaps the best overall reassurance which you can give a client (in addition to the above) is to remember that at all times you must appear to be completely non-judgemental in your manner and entirely objective about the case. (See **Chapters 2, 3,** and **4.**)

12.3.6 Professional conduct

You are required at all times to act within the provisions (and the spirit) relating to professional conduct set out in the Bar Standards Board's (BSB's) Handbook, which sets out the standards that the BSB requires barristers to comply with in order for it to be able to meet its regulatory objectives. So for example, you must act within your instructions at all times and not:

- invent facts;
- agree to mislead the court in any way;
- mislead your client;
- provide answers or invent defences for your client;
- in any way coach your client.

It follows that a student shall fail a Bar Professional Training Course skills assessment if either:

(a) his/her legal or other analysis is so clearly incorrect that it would:

  (i) put the client's interests at risk; and/or

  (ii) put the potential barrister at risk of liability for negligence or a disciplinary finding;

or

(b) his/her written or oral presentation is so poor that it would:

  (i) render no valuable service to the client; and/or

  (ii) put the client's interests at risk; and/or

  (iii) put the potential barrister at risk of liability for negligence or a disciplinary finding.

12.3.7 Conclusion

The performance and assessment criteria set out in **12.3.1–12.3.6** form the basis of the feedback you will receive in order to improve your performance and are the measure which is used in order to assess the standard of your performance at the end of the year.

Proper application of these criteria can ensure that a judgement of the effectiveness of any performance can be both objective and accurate. The following illustrations are intended to provide examples of this.

EXAMPLE 1

The performance being appraised is that of Criterion 5: Communication. The feedback/assessment could be something like this:

> The way you introduced yourself to the client was effective, as was the manner in which you gave a clear indication of the order in which you intended to deal with the matters in hand. This clearly put the client at ease and reassured him that you were in command of the case. However, the main problem was that you permitted the client rather to dominate the conference. The result was that the conference turned out to be the client questioning you rather than the other way round. In consequence, you were unable to complete the conference in time. You have got to learn how to manage your time more efficiently. You should aim to be client-centred rather than allow yourself to become client-dominated. Next time try to ensure that you politely remind the client that there is a lot to get through in a short space of time and that, if you do not get through the relevant matters, you will not be in a position to advise him properly.

EXAMPLE 2

The performance being appraised is that of Criterion 3: Advising. The feedback/assessment of the performance could be something along these lines:

> You had clearly prepared for this conference in a thorough and detailed way. It was particularly impressive that you had recognised the importance of the ss 76 and 78 PACE points, and how they could affect the admissibility of your client's confession and the whole of the prosecution case. Your major difficulty, however, was in explaining this point to your client in language that he could fully understand. In order for the client to be in a position to instruct you, he has first to have a clear evaluation, from you, of the strengths and weaknesses of the case against him. You obviously knew the legal position, but you failed to convey this clearly enough to your client. Try to ensure that next time you give particular consideration to your use of language and how to explain legal terms in plain English, which the client can readily understand.

It should be apparent from these examples that feedback and/or judgement of a client conference performance can be objective and accurate, provided the performer is clearly informed and able to understand:

- what worked;
- what did not work;
- most importantly why; and
- in what way improvements can be made.

12.4 Summary

Developing the skills necessary to conduct an effective client conference and accurate assessment of the performance of the skills is clearly possible. To succeed in acquiring the necessary level of competence to pass the assessment in conference skills, it is recommended that you:

- practise as much as possible; and
- are completely familiar with the assessment/performance criteria.

Practitioners' perspective

13.1 Introduction

In the previous chapters, this manual has attempted to provide some insight into the problems that can often arise when conducting a client conference. In the course of identifying some of the difficulties that you may encounter, the manual offers a range of possible solutions, and some suggestions of methods of good practice that you may wish to adopt.

The main objectives of the manual are to ensure, as far as possible, that when you are in practice as a barrister, and specifically when you meet any client in conference, you are able to perform your role effectively and efficiently and, above all, provide a service to the public which is of the appropriate professional standard.

How does the theory translate into practice? Obviously you will not be in a position to judge this for yourself until you are in practice. However, it may be useful to consider how practitioners actually do regard conducting a client conference and to see what insight can be gained from those who perform this role in their practice, virtually on a daily basis.

The essays that follow have been written by two practitioners and reflect their experience in practice. Both these practitioners are very experienced in their specialist areas, and both have worked closely with staff and students at The City Law School for many years as practitioner instructors.

13.2 The criminal practitioner, by Carl Teper

The usual mental image created by the word 'conference' conjures up the idea of a room in chambers at 5 o'clock in the afternoon, a solicitor in attendance with the lay client, a brief, and cups of tea being passed around. Forget it for now!

The first conference I ever had (and most of the Bar has) was through the wicket of a cell door at a local magistrates' court. In my case the client did not know why he was there, or so he said, but was prepared to plead guilty to anything as long as he got bail. I had been told by my clerk, 30 minutes earlier when I was sent to court with the back sheet, that the most important thing was to get the Legal Aid application signed, which was also the view shared by my instructing solicitor—whom I had never met and in fact never even spoken to.

Most of us will conduct, for at least the first few years, conferences in this manner and it will continue into the Crown Court, where the conference will often be a hurried affair before the trial is called on or the mitigation delivered. You will often not have had the brief for very long, and probably on at least a couple of occasions will only just be at court meeting the client whose trial is on in an hour's time with the solicitor on his way with the brief! On occasions you will be sitting—or perhaps making tea—in chambers when your clerk will come in and tell you to get to court as a bench warrant, which was issued on the last occasion your client failed to appear, is to be executed. This may mean not just a Bail Application, but also the resolution of the case if your client is going to plead guilty when the warrant is executed. There may not even be time to speak to your solicitor.

You will soon begin to appreciate what is meant by that old saying, 'All you need to succeed at the Bar is high spirits, a little law and relatively clean fingernails.' High spirits so as to remain calm, unflappable, and in command of the situation, a little law to get whatever necessary adjournments are needed, and clean fingernails to pass the Legal Aid application through the wicket in the cell door. Because if you can cope with this type of situation you can cope and succeed at the Bar, and indeed with anything that may come your way.

In all these conference situations, quick thinking and appropriate action will be required. You must assure your client that you are in control and that their destiny is safe in your hands. (Make sure you have professional indemnity insurance when you utter such words.) Your client may never have been arrested before and he may be frightened out of his life at being in custody. Often due to the shortness of the time, your questioning of the client will have to be straight to the point, gathering all the information you need to deal with his situation. Your client must feel reassured because you are there dealing with his case and giving it special attention.

You cannot prepare for every eventuality. Early on in my practice I was asked to represent a client who had been summonsed to the magistrates' court for grievous bodily harm. This was a private prosecution and the victim was conducting the prosecution side of the case. I met my client, who was late for court, and quickly filled in the Legal Aid form. We had decided to elect Crown Court trial, as this would probably put an end to the case, as the victim would not have the organisation to prepare the case for committal. The Metropolitan Police solicitors (as they then were), for good reasons, were not interested in prosecuting this case which had arisen out of unsupported cross-allegations. The case was called on, the client, victim/prosecutor, and I entered Court 2. I had told my client how to deal with the question of election and that a date would then be fixed for the committal; all he had to do was step into the dock. I reassured him; he had nothing to worry about, I insisted. However, at this point the victim/prosecutor removed a gun from a Kentucky Fried Chicken box and shot my client in the head. I had not prepared for this unfortunate turn of events—although I did have my Legal Aid form signed.

The moral of this very true story is to be prepared for anything. Preparation for conferences through cell doors and court corridors will play a large part of the first years of your practice at the Bar. To deal with these situations and advise your client correctly will require a fine understanding of how the court system works. This is learnt by observation in pupillage and by putting into use the conference skills you will have learnt on the Bar Professional Training Course. One without the other is of no use. It is the successful combination of both that will achieve results that will please your solicitors, achieve the best result for your client, and bring some immense satisfaction to yourself.

Do not expect things to be put on a plate for you. If you are instructed in a case at short notice and a conference is required at court or in the cells, prepare as best you can. You will have your own mental checklist, depending on the situation you are in. In the cells it will be to calm and reassure the client, establish why he is there, deal with any instructions you receive, find out which court your case is in, who is sitting, complete Legal Aid forms or check that Legal Aid is in existence, endorse your brief, etc. Every situation will require a different assessment and different action—your learnt knowledge and learnt skills will and should give you the confidence to deal with these situations.

There will be conferences in chambers when the brief has arrived in good time and you must have read it thoroughly. Gone are the days when you can pick the papers up and look at your client and solicitor and say, 'Well what's all this about then?' There will also be times when the papers have only just arrived or when your clerk may have forgotten to tell you that the brief came in yesterday, has only just been put in your tray, and the conference is arranged that day and the trial is first on tomorrow morning. Do your very best. If you have not read the brief because it has just arrived, delay for as long as is reasonable for you to get to grips with the case. It is unlikely to be a complex mortgage fraud, and if it is you cannot and will not be expected to know it inside out, and the conference may just be a public relations exercise with the client. On the other hand, it may be a shoplifting case, which you can deal with very adequately, in the conference, whenever the papers arrived. Often the best way into a case is to read the instructions—if there are any—and then the client's interview, in which the allegations would or should have been put to your client by the police officer investigating the alleged offence. The solicitor or his representative may only just have been instructed in the case and the client may know that you could not possibly have read the papers, and will not expect it either. In that sort of situation you can be quite open. Every case, every conference will be different and require different mental checklists and preparation.

Do not depend too greatly on the person in attendance from your solicitors' office. It may be the senior partner who prepared the brief and knows it inside out; on the other hand, it may be an outdoor clerk who will have no knowledge of the case, and even less interest. I remember once an outdoor clerk from a solicitors' firm arriving in chambers wearing an expensive designer black suit and tie and shiny black shoes, but sadly he had no shirt or socks on, the tie just hung round his neck like a noose and he was also wearing bright pink-framed glasses. The conference went perfectly well. I was polite to the client, dealt with his needs, and gave him the necessary advice to give him confidence for his trial, which was the following day. I was careful not to discuss the case with the outdoor clerk, as the client might have been concerned if he had discovered the solicitors' representative knew absolutely nothing about his case. It is not a bad idea to have the solicitor or his representative come into your room first of all to check and see what he knows, if anything, about the case and to find out a little about the client.

The next day I arrived at court, as did the client, in good time and the case started. No one from the firm of solicitors had arrived. Suddenly the court door opened and the outdoor clerk arrived dressed just as he was the day before. The judge was very annoyed and it was I who was told off for allowing the outdoor clerk to come to court dressed as he was. So be prepared.

13.3 The civil practitioner, by Bartholomew O'Toole

13.3.1 Introduction

'Your conference is ready Sir, it's Miss Scott, the senior litigation partner from [a large City firm] and her client X plc's company secretary, the head of their legal department and their assistants, six of them altogether, I'll bring in the extra chairs . . . '

'Your conference is ready Sir, Miss West, the new outdoor clerk with [a small high street firm] and her client Mr Lewis, who wants contact with his daughter. It's brief in conference I'm afraid, Sir!'

These are just two contrasting extremes of a clerk's introduction to a conference in which you may one day be instructed. In one case you will be fully instructed ahead of time, there will be less need for questioning, more for your urgent expert advice, probably on a well-defined but vital issue. In another, you will know nothing of the case before the conference begins but, drawing on your experience in practice, you will identify the issues, seek detailed clarification on relevant facts, perhaps offer little advice in conference, but undertake to provide a written advice within seven days.

The variety of subject matter, clients, and even solicitors is enormous. The venues for conferences range from chambers, solicitors' offices, sites, to court prior to virtually any hearing attended by the lay client. Conferences may take place by telephone and even by television link yet, from family law, through personal injuries to multi-million pound commercial litigation, whether you are instructed privately or under a Legal Aid order, common principles are to be observed.

13.3.2   Guidelines

Before conducting conferences you will have read the invaluable guidelines set out in the earlier chapters of this manual, perhaps have gone further and consulted some of the further reading recommended at the end, and had the benefit of pupillage during which, being familiar with the papers, you will have observed practitioners in conference, perhaps with a complete mastery of many complex issues, or struggling to identify one simple issue concealed within inadequate instructions. You will have had opportunities to recognise effective preparation and to distinguish different styles and listening and questioning techniques, adopted almost unconsciously by the practitioner, with a view to eliciting clear instructions and giving sound advice. This will have provided a substratum of understanding of the skills demanded in conference, which will crystallise rapidly as you experience the process when in practice in your own right.

13.3.3   Barrister–client relationship: the provision of a professional service

Fundamental to the conference is the recognition of the relationship between the barrister and client or, more accurately, between barrister, professional client, and lay client. It is professional, to be distinguished from educational, personal, social, or family relationships and relationships between colleagues or 'equals'. Never confuse these. You have been instructed by reason of your expertise to provide a service, at a fee, for the lay client, to whom you owe your first duty. The important concomitant duties to your professional client and, in Legal Aid cases, to the Legal Aid Agency are secondary: the lay client comes first. If your professional service is effective, your client's needs will be served; if not, he is better going elsewhere.

13.3.4   Preparation

This must be diligent, including reading and digesting the papers thoroughly and researching the law. Ideally you will be adequately instructed to be able to give some advice in conference, but if important new instructions are received so that there has been no preparation beyond your previous experience in that field, you will quite possibly have to withhold final advice until you have been able to research the law, and follow up the conference with a telephone advice or, more likely, an advice in writing. The better solicitors will have included in your instructions a carefully selected series of documents consisting of most, if not all, of what you need to comprehend the facts and identify the issues. The most illustrious, such as the Treasury Solicitor or the leading City firms, may have gone even further and referred you to the relevant legislation and even case law upon which the case is likely to turn. At the other extreme it is not unknown for solicitors to send their complete original file to chambers and instruct counsel to read, sift, and advise generally in conference! This may be little more than a solicitor's cry for help, but the client's needs must be served with equal diligence, even though you will have been shouldered with unwieldy extra work in perusing much irrelevant material.

13.3.5   Purpose of the conference

Maintain a broad view of the purpose of the conference, namely to take instructions, to assess the client as a witness, and to advise on evidence, merits, quantum, remedies, timing, and costs. Use time efficiently. Adopt a sense of perspective; for example, if the client in a personal injury case has suffered paraplegia it would be unusual to have to discuss small items of special damage: advise the solicitors to deal with it if they have not already done so. Be economical in the use of words: the client will understand and remember this far better than a lengthy discourse.

Be yourself, but never think about yourself, nor disclose matters that are personal to you. If you harbour doubts about the rectitude of your client or the morality of his stance in the litigation, do not reveal them, nor allow them to cloud your judgement of the merits of his case: he is seeking first your professional opinion on the merits and advice on evidence, quantum, remedies, etc, not your opinion about his character. On the other hand, bring a critical eye to bear on the instructions you receive: they will be partial and may be less than truthful or reliable; if you accept them without question and advise on a false premise, the client will be at risk when, in due course, the court brings its own eye to bear on the case.

Your client is best served by direct, sometimes hard advice, given tactfully, with sensitivity and discretion. Think laterally: rather than confine your questions to the bare background set out in your written instructions, consider what other points could arise. Bring your experience of the world and of human character into play: if the client maintains an implausible set of facts it should probably be discreetly and appropriately pointed out.

13.3.6   Undivided attention: effective listening and questioning

In conference the client needs and deserves your undivided attention. Give him an early opportunity to speak. Listen acutely. Your use of appropriate words will follow if the listening is incisive and provided the preparation is adequate. Attend fully to him or her and pursue relevant points thoroughly by asking supplementary questions: if the listening is acute these arise naturally and will clarify ambiguities left in the original answers. They may fortify your client's account or expose important weaknesses in his case. All this will improve the quality of your advice, which will follow. Pause momentarily where necessary to allow the client to answer the question. He may have been withholding some vital information which he is prepared to reveal if allowed time and space. Apart from the general duty to tell the truth, information which your client might think he should withhold may not necessarily be damaging to his case, and may even assist him: his own judgement on this should not be relied upon. On the other hand, it may seriously damage his credibility if something new emerges at trial that should have been included in his witness statement, or worse still, if his testimony flatly contradicts the witness statement. At worst an entire cause of action or head of damage could be overlooked because of the failure to pursue proper enquiries. Effective questioning is more akin to a game of chess than a quiz: the next question should be determined by the answer to the last; a pre-prepared list can only point to the general areas for investigation. Ask all relevant questions to establish or clarify the facts; do not lightly assume that the solicitor has exhausted all relevant areas of enquiry, or that your instructions are fully up to date.

When questioning, show alertness and sensitivity to your client and his needs. Be familiar with and use freely but appropriately the well-documented different types of questions: open—broadly identifying the subject matter and inviting the client to express his general concerns; closed—confining and narrowing the subject matter, seeking to elicit specific information; probe—seeking detailed clarification on a specific matter (eg 'Exactly where did that occur?'); mirror question—reformulating the client's last instructions, to put them into question form; reflective—summarising the client's instructions and seeking further clarification on his feelings; summary—summarising the client's instructions and seeking further clarification on the facts; comparative—asking for a comparison between the state of affairs before and after a given event; hypothetical—establishing the client's views on hypothetical courses of action; leading (with great caution)—suggesting the answer. Each of these, used at different times, may be precisely what is needed to elicit information or instructions. Cultivate variety in your approach. Let your choice of questions arise naturally from moment to moment: it cannot be planned out fully in advance. Some flexibility and spontaneity will be needed.

13.3.7 Observation

In a case that may turn on the oral evidence of a few witnesses, the assessment of your client as a witness is often an integral purpose of the conference, vital to concluding on the prospect of success in the litigation. Watch closely his response to questions on matters of detail: is he reasonably firm and clear in his recollection? Is it consistent and does it tally with what he said and did on previous occasions? If not, is his explanation for the difference satisfactory? Is his account plausible? How does it compare with accounts given by other witnesses, including the other party? Is it supported by the documentation? Is it verifiable through independent sources? This is just a selection of the tests that may be applied. Remembering that the client may be fiercely cross-examined if the case goes to trial, you might imagine yourself instructed by the other side. How would you cross-examine? You may ask your client hard, cross-examination-type questions, put him under pressure and note his responses (remember the illustrative scene in Sir Terence Rattigan's play, *The Winslow Boy*). This will enable you to take a view on his credibility; however, if you take this course of action, first warn your client.

13.3.8 Advice

If able to give an opinion without further instructions, express yourself unequivocally, albeit that you may have to confine your assessment of the prospect of success to 'reasonable', or 'better than evens'. Give the client your clear view of the merits, quantum, remedies, etc, and any risks in the litigation; explain that the risks in proceeding are his, so that he understands that he may take or not take the risk in the light of your advice, not in a vacuum. Give your advice, however cautiously, wherever possible. Do not let any doubts conceal your balanced opinion. Take matters as far forward in your advice as possible, but if you are clear that it is impossible to advise prior to establishing further facts which are not clear in conference, say so, perhaps suggesting a further conference later, or undertaking to provide a written advice once the outstanding matters have been resolved. If you need further specific instructions, identify them to the solicitor in conference and ensure that he has noted what further steps are needed.

13.3.9   Public relations

It soon becomes apparent during pupillage that most clients are referred to barristers by solicitors on the basis of their or their chambers' goodwill. The importance of this is never to be underestimated. Without it, you have no instructions, and cannot practise. Of more immediate significance to you than the erosion of the monopoly of the Bar is the professional and lay clients' right to seek advice elsewhere. You are not entitled to goodwill: it must be cultivated, earned, and maintained. A conference should not be treated primarily as an opportunity to create goodwill, but it should be recognised that goodwill is at stake whenever you meet a client. Good manners, courtesy, tidiness, appropriate dress, language and tone of voice, sensitivity, and confidence are fundamental supplements to the issues referred to in the previous paragraphs. Both professional and lay clients will have expectations of you in this regard which, if not met in conference, could lead to your being de-instructed. If you lose sight of this you will do so at your peril! Solicitors and their representatives deserve equal courtesy to the client. If you are concerned to raise a query about their performance or their judgement in handling the case, do it in the absence of the lay client. Address solicitors as fellow professionals. If you are attended by an unqualified clerk, be friendly, perhaps consult him for his views on the case, but rarely on the law, upon which he will not expect to be asked to assist. Avoid asking questions that suggest that you do not trust the solicitor to have dealt with a matter competently.

13.3.10   Ethical and professional obligations

A good deal of what has been written previously derives from the BSB Handbook. This should be studied at the beginning of your career and consulted at regular intervals thereafter, especially if doubts arise as to the appropriateness of any course of professional conduct.

14

Sample exercise

IN THE EAST LONDON CROWN COURT   Indictment No.

THE QUEEN

v

SHIRLEY JENKINS

INSTRUCTIONS TO COUNSEL
TO ADVISE IN CONFERENCE

Criminal Legal Aid

Kemball & Co
10 Eastcheap
London E2
020–7272 1144
Ref: K Johnson

<u>IN THE EAST LONDON CROWN COURT</u>

THE QUEEN

v

SHIRLEY JENKINS

INSTRUCTIONS TO COUNSEL
TO ADVISE IN CONFERENCE

Counsel has herewith:

1. The indictment.
2. The prosecution statements.
3. Ms Jenkins' proof of evidence.
4. List of Ms Jenkins' previous convictions.

Counsel is instructed on behalf of this publicly funded defendant who is charged with theft (shoplifting). Instructing Solicitors advised her to elect trial by jury as, in their experience, she is likely to get a fairer hearing there than she would receive in the magistrates' court.

Instructing Solicitors are very concerned about Ms Jenkins, who is a young single mother with a lot of domestic problems.

Before Ms Jenkins gives her final instructions on the allegation of theft she wants counsel's advice as to whether she would be guilty of theft if her child picked up the goods and, having realised outside the shop what had happened, she decided not to take them back. Perhaps this could be dealt with in conference.

We have not been able to take full instructions on the contents of the witness statements. Counsel is asked to advise in conference as to Ms Jenkins' plea (in order that the Defence Statement can be drafted if appropriate) and the likely outcome of the case.

INDICTMENT

THE QUEEN

v

SHIRLEY JENKINS

who is charged as follows:

<u>STATEMENT OF OFFENCE</u>

Theft, contrary to section 1(1) of the Theft Act 1968

<u>PARTICULARS OF OFFENCE</u>

SHIRLEY JENKINS on 10th September 2016 stole two multi-pack jars of baby food, a bottle of perfume, and a deodorant stick belonging to Supa-Save plc.

Officer of the Court

Statement of Witness

STATEMENT OF	Christine Morgan
Age of Witness (date of birth)	Over 21
Occupation of Witness	Store Detective

This statement (consisting of one page signed by me) is true to the best of my knowledge and belief and I make it knowing that, if it is tendered in evidence, I shall be liable to prosecution if I have wilfully stated in it anything which I know to be false or do not believe to be true.

Dated the 10th day of September 2016

Signed C Morgan   Signature witnessed by A J Lightly

I am a store detective employed by Supa-Save plc.

On 10th September 2016 I was working at the Whitechapel Road branch. I was dressed as a normal shopper, so as not to draw attention to myself.

At about midday I noticed a young woman, whom I now know to be Shirley Jenkins, acting suspiciously. I have seen her in the store before and I have been suspicious of her before. She was dressed in jeans and a sweatshirt and was pushing a small child in a pushchair. There was a basket hanging off one of the handles of the pushchair. She first went to the tobacco kiosk near the doors. She bought a packet of 20 Silk Cut cigarettes and put it in her bag. She then came towards the middle part of the shop.

That section of the store was not crowded at that time and I concealed myself behind a display of ecological washing products. The layout of the display was such that I could see through it and I had a good view of the defendant.

I saw her look all about herself and then furtively select two multi-pack jars of our own-brand baby food and put them in her basket.

She then moved down the store to the toiletries section. I followed her. Again she looked all round herself and then selected a bottle of perfume and a roll-on deodorant stick. These, too, were placed in the basket.

She then left the store without paying for the goods hidden in her basket. I followed her out of the store and arrested her.

The value of goods taken was as follows: two multi-pack jars of baby food (£14.50); one bottle of 'Delight' perfume (£10.99) and one roll-on deodorant (£1.20). No one had permission to take these goods without paying for them. I produce the goods as Exhibits CM/1–4.

I am willing to attend court and give evidence.

Signed C Morgan   Signature witnessed by A J Lightly

Statement of Witness

STATEMENT OF   Alan Lightly

Age of Witness (date of birth)   Over 21

Occupation of Witness   Police Constable

This statement (consisting of one page signed by me) is true to the best of my knowledge and belief and I make it knowing that, if it is tendered in evidence, I shall be liable to prosecution if I have wilfully stated in it anything which I know to be false or do not believe to be true.

Dated the 10th day of September 2016

Signed A J Lightly   Signature witnessed by S Blood

On 10th September 2016 at about midday I was on duty in full uniform in Whitechapel Road. A member of the public told me something was happening outside the supermarket called Supa-Save.

I ran to the entrance of the store and saw a young woman, whom I now know to be Shirley Jenkins, being restrained by another older woman, whom I now know to be Christine Morgan. Both women were shouting and screaming. There was a young child in a pushchair. The scene was very confused. Miss Morgan explained that she was a store detective from Supa-Save and alleged that Miss Jenkins had stolen certain items. I asked Miss Jenkins to show me the contents of her shopping basket. On top of a pullover, at the top of the basket, were two multi-pack jars of baby food, a small bottle of perfume, and a roll-on deodorant stick. I cautioned Miss Jenkins and said: 'You have heard what this lady alleges? Do you wish to say anything?' Miss Jenkins replied: 'I don't know nothing about them. Kylie (pointing to the child) must have put them in.'

Miss Morgan then said 'Rubbish. The child never touched anything. I followed her out and she screamed at me. I want her locked up.'

I said to Miss Jenkins that I was not satisfied with her account and at 12.21 I told her I was arresting her for theft. I further cautioned her and she replied, 'Fucking typical. I'm already on a conditional.'

Because of the child, the Custody Officer was keen to process Miss Jenkins as quickly as possible and so she was not interviewed.

In the charge room Miss Jenkins said to me, 'Look, I'm really hard up and I can't face any more aggro. If I admit it can't I just have a caution or something?' I replied: 'I'm sorry, love, but it's not up to me. It's up to the Crown Prosecution Service to decide whether to prosecute or not.'

At 2 pm I was present when the defendant was charged. The charge was read over to her and she was further cautioned to which she made no reply.

Signed A J Lightly   Signature witnessed by S Blood

PROOF OF EVIDENCE

Shirley Jenkins will say:

I am 22 years old. I live at Flat 309 (8th floor), Dream Heights, Cheapside Road, Tower Hamlets.

I have one child (Kylie) aged two. I am not married and I have not seen Kylie's father since she was born. I am unemployed and I am claiming benefit.

I have been in trouble with the police before. I have a conviction for shoplifting and one for assault. In July 2015 I was fined £100 for stealing some goods from another supermarket. I'm still trying to pay that off. And in June this year I was charged with actual bodily harm and got a conditional discharge for six months. I'm in breach of that order if I get convicted of this offence.

On 10th September 2016 I went into Supa-Save to buy some cigarettes. I didn't have much to do and so I wandered round the store looking at all the things I couldn't afford. I didn't put anything into my bag, but Kylie could easily have done as she does pick things up and the bag was hanging down beside her on the pushchair. Before I give my final instructions about this, I want my barrister to advise me whether it amounts to stealing if I realised when I was outside the shop that Kylie had taken something and I didn't take it back.

I was just leaving the supermarket when this official-looking woman grabbed me and said, 'You're both coming with me. I'm going to do you for shoplifting.' Then I was arrested.

ANTECEDENTS

NAME:	Shirley Jenkins
AGE:	22 (d.o.b. 21.7.94)
ADDRESS:	Flat 309 (8th Floor), Dream Heights, Cheapside Road, Tower Hamlets.

DATE	COURT	CONVICTION	SENTENCE
15.7.15	East London Magistrates	Theft x 4	Fined £25 on each.
27.6.16	East London Magistrates	ABH	Conditional Discharge six months.

FURTHER READING

Bedingfield, D, *Advocacy in Family Proceedings*, 2nd edn, Family Law, 2013.

Binder, DA, Bergman, P, Tremblay, PR, and Weinstein, IS, *Lawyers as Counselors: A Client-Centered Approach*, 3rd edn, West Publishing Co, 2011.

Chapman, J, *Interviewing and Counselling*, Cavendish—Essential Legal Skills Series, 2000.

Clements, P, *The Diversity Training Handbook: A Practical Guide to Understanding and Changing Attitudes*, 3rd edn, Kogan Page, 2008.

McConnell, P and Talbot, J, *Mental Health and Learning Disabilities in The Criminal Courts: Information for Magistrates, District Judges and Court Staff*, <http://www.mhldcc.org.uk/>, 2013.

Morison, J and Leith, P, *The Barrister's World and the Nature of Law*, Open University Press, 1992.

Payne, SL, *The Art of Asking Questions*, Princeton University Press, 1992.

Pilgrim, D, *Key Concepts in Mental Health*, 3rd edn, SAGE Key Concepts Series, 2014.

Schubert, K, *The Law Firm Interview: A Guide for Law Students*, Steinberger Editions, 2002.

Shaffer, T and Elkins, J, *Legal Interviewing and Counselling*, West Group, 2004.

Sherr, A, *Client Interviewing for Lawyers*, Sweet & Maxwell, 1996.

Susskind, R, *Tomorrow's Lawyers: An Introduction to Your Future*, Oxford University Press, 2013.

Susskind, R, and Susskind, D, *The Future of the Professions: How Technology Will Transform the Work of Human Experts*, Oxford University Press, 2015.

Thompson, N, *Promoting Equality: Working with Diversity and Difference*, 3rd edn, Palgrave Macmillan, 2012.

INDEX